INDIAN AIR FORCE
in its
Centennial Decade

INDIAN AIR FORCE
in its
Centennial Decade

Edited by

Air Vice Marshal **Anil Golani** MPhil psc+

Wg Cdr **Swaim Prakash Singh** MPhil psc+

Foreword by

Air Chief Marshal **VR Chaudhari** PVSM AVSM VM ADC
Chief of the Air Staff

Centre for Air Power Studies
New Delhi

in association with

KNOWLEDGE WORLD

KW Publishers Pvt Ltd
New Delhi

The Centre for Air Power Studies is an independent, non-profit, academic research institution established in 2002 under a registered Trust to undertake and promote policy-related research, study and discussion on the trends and developments in defence and military issues, especially air power and the aerospace arena, for civil and military purposes. Its publications seek to expand and deepen the understanding of defence, military power, air power and aerospace issues without necessarily reflecting the views of any institution or individuals except those of the authors.

Centre for Air Power Studies
P-284, Arjan Path
Subroto Park
New Delhi 110010

Tele: (91-11) 25699131

E-mail: capsnetdroff@gmail.com
website: www.capsindia.org

ISBN 978-93-94915-59-6 Hardback
ISBN 978-93-94915-60-2 ebook

Published in India by Kalpana Shukla

KW Publishers Pvt Ltd
4676/21, First Floor, Ansari Road
Daryaganj, New Delhi 110002
Phone: +91 11 43528107
Marketing: kw@kwpub.in
Editorial: production@kwpub.in
Website: www.kwpub.in

Printed and bound in India

Contents

वायु सेनाध्यक्ष
CHIEF OF THE AIR STAFF
★★★★

एयर चीफ मार्शल वी आर चौधरी
प वि से मे अ वि से मे वा से मे ए डी सी
Air Chief Marshal VR Chaudhari
PVSM AVSM VM ADC

Tel : (011) Off : 23012517
Res : 23017300
Fax : 23018853

वायु सेना मुख्यालय
नई दिल्ली - 110011
Air Headquarters
New Delhi - 110011

FOREWORD

1. Over the last nine decades, IAF has come a long way in transforming into a leaner, meaner and stronger force with highly focussed and multi-skilled personnel to fight tomorrow's wars. IAF has demonstrated unrivalled adaptability, innovation and resilience to become a technology-intensive fighting force that operates modern aircraft, weapon systems, radars, and communication systems. Our glorious history is replete with sagas of professional fortitude and commitment displayed by men and women in blue in the face of insurmountable odds. IAF is built on this edifice, brick by brick with valuable contributions from all quarters.

2. The year 2022 had been a significant year for India as it celebrated its platinum year of independence, with the next 25 years predicted to be the 'Amrit Kaal' or "Golden Era" for the country. The Indian Air Force too, shall strive for strategic autonomy and transform into a self-reliant, modern air and space force.

3. The book "IAF in its Centennial Decade" makes for a good read with articles covering the full swath of operations. I congratulate Air Vice Marshal Anil Golani (Retd) and Wing Commander Swaim Prakash Singh for editing this book. I am confident that this book will be an interesting read for practitioners of air power as well as the academia.

Jai Hind!

Air Chief Marshal
Chief of the Air Staff

15 **Jun 23**

Editor's Note

While the past may not always offer a peek into the future there do come seminal moments in the journey of nations and organisations that offer an opportunity to pause, reflect, contemplate and crystal gaze into the future. The Indian Air Force (IAF) came into being as an auxiliary arm of the Royal Air Force on October 8, 1932, just about two decades after the first manned flight. The first squadron of the Air Force, No. 1 Sqn, was raised on April 1, 1933, with four Westland Wapiti aircraft and five Indian pilots. From a fledgling air force with just one flight of Westland Wapiti biplanes, the IAF has traversed to become one of the leading Air Forces of the world, globally acknowledged as a professional force having earned its spurs through many conflicts and challenges. As the IAF entered its Centennial Decade, a book project was conceived with the aim to cover its glorious past and offer a sneak preview into its future trajectory. With the help of an avid historian whose interest in IAF history is unparalleled, serving IAF officers, veteran luminaries who have served the IAF with pride, this project has come to fruition with the hope of adding to the literary discourse on the IAF.

Divided in two sections, Section I covers the glorious past of the IAF since its inception. The first chapter, "A Sneak Preview of the IAF" covers the genesis of the IAF and its transformation through the two world wars and India's independence in August 1947 to the IAF shedding the 'Royal' prefix subsequently. The chapter gives the reader an insight into the organisational structure of the IAF as it was conceived, its reorganisation post-World War II, the formation of various branches of the IAF and some interesting anecdotes that invariably get lost in the annals of history over a period of time. The next chapter "IAF Through

Wars: A Story Telling" covers pre-independence operations in the North West Frontier Province, the two Burma Campaigns during the Second World War and the post-independence conflicts from the Kashmir War in 1947-48 to the Kargil War in 1999. The next chapter in the first section, "Helicopter Saga of the Indian Air Force" covers the induction of the rotary wing fleet into the IAF to its baptism in the conflict in the 1962 Indo-China war, 1965 and 1971 wars with Pakistan, Op Meghdoot in the highest battlefield of the world, the Siachen Glacier and Op Pawan in Sri Lanka. The last chapter in the first section, "IAF's Airlift Capability: Face of the Nation" covers the yeoman service by the transport fleet of the IAF from tactical and strategic airlift, HADR, non-combatant evacuation and nation-building.

Section II covers the future trajectory of the IAF starts with, "Air Power as a Tool of Comprehensive National Power". The chapter covers the contribution made by the IAF towards national security through military, diplomacy, political and economic instruments of national power. The next chapter, "Future of Combat Aircraft" explains the fifth and sixth-generation fighter aircraft technologies, the aircraft currently deployed and those under planning and the future requirements of the IAF. The chapter on "Exploiting Air Power Beyond the Continent: Challenges and Opportunities" covers the advantages that would accrue to India utilising its geographical location to exert influence in the Indo-Pacific region, using the IAF to deter threats and build bridges and partnerships with friendly foreign countries in the region to mutual benefit, peace and prosperity. "Future Integrated Air Battle Management" talks about the effects of technology that have driven doctrines hitherto and the need for the doctrine to drive technology in prosecuting warfare in the present scenario. The synergistic effects of employing land, maritime, air, space and cyber assets of the nation are an inescapable necessity that can be fulfilled by incorporating an integrated battle management concept. The chapter, "Air Defence is not Defensive" shatters the widespread and popular myth of air power being a defensive arm in protecting and securing national airspace. The AD umbrella that needs to respond to every threat 24x7x365 whether peace or war and its salience in operations needs to be understood to realise that AD is only a conjoint twin of offensive air operations, which is an essential requirement for national security.

The chapter on "Helicopter Operations in Contested Battlespace" explores the employment of helicopters in warfare from a historical perspective to understand the dynamics of future wars. The employment of helicopters in urban and contested battlespace against ground-based threats poses unique challenges and how this needs to be navigated in the Indian scenario has been discussed in the chapter. The last chapter, "From an Air Force to An Aerospace Force" speaks about the increasing ubiquity of the space domain in everyday life and its importance in military operations, the rising threats to space assets and the role of armed forces in the space domain. The continuum of the air and space domain and the desired capabilities of an aerospace force are discussed in this chapter.

I am indeed indebted and grateful to all the contributors whose painstaking and laborious effort has culminated into this book project. I would also like to thank Wg Cdr Swaim Prakash Singh, Senior Fellow CAPS and my co-editor without whose help this would not have been possible. I am sanguine that the literary effort would find acceptance with military aviation enthusiasts, professionals and academia in the field, students and everyone else who has an interest in the IAF and national security, and the latest developments in technology and aviation.

Happy reading!

Anil Golani

About the Editors and Contributors

EDITORS

Air Vice Marshal **Anil Golani** MPhil, psc+ (Retd), Additional Director General, CAPS

A Qualified Flying Instructor and an Instrument Rating Instructor and Examiner, commissioned into the Fighter stream of the IAF in December 1982. He raised and commanded the first Harpy squadron of the Indian Air Force and also commanded an Air Defence Direction Centre and an operational base. One of the few to have served in senior ranks in both the Joint Services Commands of the country, Andaman & Nicobar Command as the Air Force Component Commander and Strategic Forces Command as the Chief Staff Officer (Air Vector). The other joint services appointments include Air Officer Commanding Maritime Air Operations in Mumbai and Chief Instructor, Air Force, at Defence Services Staff College, Wellington. He has done the Staff Course, Higher Air Command Course and a year's course in International Security & Strategy at the Royal College of Defence Studies, London. He superannuated from service in November 2019.

He has published articles and book chapters on air power and national security in newspapers, books and accredited journals. He has edited a book *Air Power and Emerging Technologies* in 2022. He likes to play Golf, read and write on issues concerning the nation.

Wing Commander **Swaim Prakash Singh** MPhil, psc+ Senior Fellow, CAPS

A Master Fighter Controller and AWACS Mission Commander with over 1,000 hours of flying has also been Directing Staff at DSSC, Wellington.

He commanded two Mobile Observation Flights which were awarded with CAS Unit Citation in 2006. He raised and commanded a Transportable Radar Unit and resurrected a Signal Unit. Has been Director Operations at the Integrated Air Command and Control Centre. The officer was part of the three member tri-Services Indian Expert team to review the course curriculum of the Command and Staff College of Tanzania in 2016 which led to the opening of Indian Armed Forces Training Team there in 2017.

He has been writing on various issues related to defence, aerospace power, and international relations. His articles have found a place in peer-reviewed prominent journals of MP-IDSA, CAPS and Indian Institute of Public Administration (IIPA). He has been a speaker and panellist in seminars of national and international repute.

Presently, the officer is working on a book project on "Air Power and the Integration of the Indian Armed Forces". He is employed as a Senior Fellow at the Centre for Air Power Studies, New Delhi.

CONTRIBUTORS

Anchit Gupta is Managing Director at a Private Equity fund called Samara Capital, where his role is to acquire Companies, help them grow (as a board member) and sell them a few years later. Some of the Companies they currently own include the iconic Paradise Biryani out of Hyderabad, Sapphire Foods (which runs about 600 stores of Pizza Hut and KFC in the country), Marengo Hospital Chain, More Retail (3rd largest Food and Grocery retailer in the country) amongst many others.

Anchit completed his schooling at various KVs across the country. He holds a B.Sc (Computer Science) from Delhi University, an MBA and MS (Finance) from ICFAI University, an MBA from Kellogg School of Management at Chicago, USA and the CFA Charter and started his career with the global consulting firm Mckinsey & Co, about two decades ago before moving to the Private Equity industry.

Born to an Air Force officer and a family with multiple members in the armed forces, he is passionate about the Indian Air Force. He frequently writes about Indian Air Force History across multiple forums.

Air Marshal **Bharat Kumar**, PVSM, AVSM (Retd) is an alumnus of the National Defence Academy, Defence Services Staff College and Voroshilov General Staff Academy. He commanded a MiG-21 Squadron and Air Force Stations at Jaisalmer and Gwalior. He also served as AOC HQ MAO. He has held many staff appointments both at Command and Air Headquarters with distinction. He retired in 1997 as the AOC-in-C Southern Air Command.

After hanging up his uniform, he wrote for various professional military journals. His book, *An Illustrated Dictionary of Aviation*, was published in the USA and has been translated into Chinese and has an Indian edition as well. He has authored ten books related to various aspects of the history of the Indian Air Force and has contributed chapters to numerous other books on the same subject.

He is a Fellow of the Aeronautical Society of India, All India Management Association and a Distinguished Fellow at the Centre for Air Power Studies.

Through his 36-year career in the Indian Air Force, veteran Air Commodore **Nitin Sathe** (Retd) has flown every helicopter in the IAF inventory of his time—from the Chetak to the Mi-35.

He volunteered to be a member of the team rebuilding the IAF base at Car Nicobar after it was devastated in the 2004 tsunami and stayed on the island for a year to fulfil this important mission. Thereafter, he was deployed to the United Nations Peacekeeping Mission in the Democratic Republic of Congo as CO of the Attack Helicopter Unit. He was also the first commander of the 'Anti Naxal' Operations and has headed a premier selection board of the IAF.

He has written four books so far: *A Few Good Men and the Angry Sea* on the IAF mission in Car Nicobar; *Born to Fly* on the incredible life of Flying Officer MP Anil Kumar, the fighter pilot who became an inspiration to millions after an accident left him a quadraplegic; *Up in the Sky*, a collection of stories on his life experiences as a helicopter pilot; *War Stories*, a collection of spoken history features on the 1971 War and the Kargil War. Settled in Pune, the veteran writes for the print and digital media and follows his passion of travel and adventure and also motivates youth to join the armed forces.

Air Marshal (Dr) **Rajeev Sachdeva** AVSM (PhD) (Retd) is an alumnus of the Flying Instructional School (FIS), College of Defence Management (CDM) and National Defence College (NDC). Cat 'A' Qualified Flying Instructor with over 7,200 hours, his last appointment was as Deputy Chief of Integrated Defence Staff and officiating Additional Secretary (Air) at DMA. Holds a Doctorate in Management, Certified 'A' Project Manager by IPMA, Switzerland, a Distinguished Fellow, & Member Council at USI, Executive Committee Member of USI & CAPS and Fellow at the academic council of i2p2M. Important Appointments held includes Command of An-32 Sqn, AOC Chandigarh, CI at Fixed Wing Training Faculty, Centre Director (Aviation) NTRO and SASO, HQ SAC. A truly Purple Officer, having served in all four verticals of HQ IDS and Commandant of College of Defence Management. He is a recipient of Ati Vishist Seva Medal.

Air Marshal **Anil Chopra** PVSM AVSM VM VSM (Retd) is a QFI, test pilot, and a pioneer of Mirage-2000 fleet, who has commanded a Mirage Squadron and the Aircraft and Systems Testing Establishment (ASTE) of the Indian Air Force. He was the team leader of MiG-21 Upgrade (Bison) project in Russia for four years. He commanded operational airbases in both Western and Eastern sector. He was AOC J&K, ACAS (Inspections) and retired as Air Officer-in-charge Personnel (AOP). He was a member of the Armed Forces Tribunal, and member of the Executive Council of Jawaharlal Nehru University (JNU) for two years. An avid writer and author, he has published over 700 articles on strategy, defence and Aerospace, and authored three books. Air Marshal runs a website "Air Power Asia" that is primarily focused on educating on air power and strategic issues. He took over as Director General of the Centre for Air Power Studies on February 12, 2021.

Air Marshal **Amit Dev** PVSM AVSM VSM (Retd) was commissioned in the IAF, in the Flying Branch on December 29, 1982. He is an alumnus of Tactics and Air Combat Development Establishment, Defence Service Staff College, College of Air Warfare and National Defence College.

In his 39 years of distinguished service, he held many important command and staff appointments. His command appointments include a fighter squadron, an Air Defence Direction Centre and a fighter airbase. His key staff appointments at Air Headquarters were Director of Air Staff (Inspection), Principal Director of Air Staff (Inspection), Assistant Chief of Air Staff (Inspection), Director General Air (Operations) and Air Officer-in-Charge Personnel. He also headed the air arm at the Strategic Forces Command. He is the former Air Officer Commanding-in-Chief of Eastern Air Command and Western Air Command.

His educational qualification includes a bachelor's degree from Jawaharlal Nehru University, MSc from Madras University and MPhil from Osmania and Madras University.

Air Marshal **Diptendu Choudhury** PVSM AVSM VM VSM (Retd) is a former Commandant of the National Defence College with over 5,000 operational sorties on fighters, and extensive experience in air and joint operations at strategic, operational and tactical levels. Experienced in policy formulation, doctrine and strategy development, he has led three international exercises and been a member of two defence talks. An alumnus of the Royal College of Defence Studies UK, a MA in Strategy and International Security from King's College, London, an MPhil in Defence and Strategic Studies, and a PhD in air power. He is a distinguished fellow of VIF and CAPS, and an avid scholar, writer and speaker on strategy, air power and national security.

Air Commodore **R Varma** VM was commissioned in December 1994 and has over 4,500 hours of accident incident free flying on various helicopters and fixed-wing trainer aircraft. He is a Qualified Flying Instructor, Helicopter Combat Leader and graduate of Defence Services Staff College and College of Air Warfare. He has commanded an Attack

Helicopter Squadron and a Helicopter base. His staff appointments include tenures at Air HQ (VB), HQ EAC and Directing Staff at DSSC and CAW. He is presently tenanting the appointment of Air Cmde Training (Flying) at Air HQ (VB).

Group Captain **T H Anand Rao** is a Senior Fellow at the Centre for Air Power Studies. His research area is "Space Security" and "Space Domain Awareness". He has published articles on issues concerning "space security" and has authored a book titled *India's Space Security Dilemma.* He has been a panellist in seminars of national and international repute.

He was commissioned in 1991. He has flown the Jaguar and MiG-21 aircraft and is qualified in all operational roles. He is also a Qualified Flying Instructor. A graduate of the Defence Services Staff College, he has served in many operational and staff appointments, including as Flight Commander of a flying sqn, SAS&IO and Chief Operations Officer at two forward air bases, and Joint Director Flying Training at Air HQ. He was a member of the project management group for the induction of Pilatus PC-7Mk-II.

List of Table and Figures

TABLE

FIGURES

Introduction

As the Indian Air Force enters its centennial decade, it is indeed a great milestone considering that the first controlled, heavier-than-air powered flight took place only in the early 20th century, just 120 years ago. Indian pioneer aviators and designers had jumped on the aviation bandwagon very early.

Sriram Venkatasubba Setty (1879-1918) was an Indian aviator and professor from Mysore, Karnataka, India. He was known as the first Indian aviation expert, who assisted with the design of the Avro 504 in England in 1911.

The initial history of Indian aviation in India can be traced back to February 18, 1911, when the first functional Civil Aviation flight to Allahabad took off for Naini covering around 10 km. Henri Pequet, a French pilot, flew 6,500 mails to Allahabad using a Humber aircraft.

Lieutenant Indra Lal Roy (1898-1918) was the first and only Indian flying ace, who in WW I had shot down 10 aircraft in July 1918, while serving in the Royal Flying Corps and its successor, the Royal Air Force.

Air Marshal Aspy Merwan Engineer DFC (1912-2002) was the first Indian, in 1930, to fly solo from London to Karachi in less than one month and thus became the first to win the Aga Khan contest. He later became the second Air Chief of IAF. Manmohan Singh (1906-1942), competed with Aspy Engineer but reached one day later. Singh later also became the first Indian to fly solo to South Africa from England. He subsequently joined the Royal Indian Air Force. The other contestant JRD Tata, later founded Tata Motors and Air India. JRD dispatched a postal package from Karachi to Juhu airport on October 15, 1932.

It became the country's first official airmail service. His airline later became Air India.

Wg Cdr KK 'Jumbo' Majumdar DFC was the first IAF officer to be awarded the Distinguished Flying Cross (DFC). Later he was awarded a bar to DFC for operations in Europe. Finally, 22 IAF personnel were awarded DFC in WW II. Among them was Sqn Ldr Arjan Singh, who later rose to become the Marshal of the Indian Air Force, the only five-star officer of IAF.

IAF was established on October 8, 1932, with just one squadron. Significant expansion took place in the early years of World War II. It finally began to come on its own after India's independence in 1947. IAF became the first Asian Air Force to induct a jet fighter, the Vampire F Mk 3 in 1948. Ever since the Service has been "Touching the Sky with Glory".

IAF is credited with a stellar performance in 1947-48 and was directly responsible for saving Poonch, Srinagar, Leh and Ladakh by landing and sustaining Indian troops against Pakistani intruders. IAF's great operational acumen was visible in all the major operations and wars ever since. These included 'Op Vijay' for Goa liberation; transport and recce operations in the 1962 India-China war; and the 1965 India-Pakistan war. In 1971 during the war for the Liberation of Bangladesh, IAF achieved total air supremacy within the first three days of the war in the east, allowing a blitzkrieg-like ground force movement. The Tangail air-drop and Meghna Heli-crossing were classic operations that are studied in major military colleges around the world.

IAF went through its first transformation in the 1970-80s with the induction of Jaguar, Miarge-2000 and MiG-29 modern fighters. It also saw inductions of An-32 and IL-76, and a huge fleet of Mi-8 class helicopters. In 1984, Sqn Ldr Rakesh Sharma became the first and only cosmonaut from India when he flew aboard Soyuz T-11 as part of the Soviet Interkosmos program.

In 1995, IAF released its first Doctrine. IAF played a game-changing role in the 1999 Kargil conflict, and the precision bombing not only hastened the end but saved many lives. The transport and helicopter fleets made round-the-clock flights to sustain Indian troops. After Kargil, IAF went through yet another transformational change. It saw inductions of air superiority fighters of the Su-30 class. It got its first UAVs, Flight Refuelling Aircraft (FRA), and the Airborne Early Warning and Control (AEW&C) aircraft among others. IAF quickly became a network-centric force that acquired medium-range precision weapons and regional reach. India started driving indigenous aircraft production with Light Combat Aircraft (LCA) and Advanced Light Helicopter (ALH) programs coming of age.

Another round of transformation began around 2010 when India got access to the American aerial platforms. Starting with Boeing P-8I for the Indian Navy, IAF inducted the large transport aircraft, Boeing C-17 Globemaster III, and Special Operations aircraft Lockheed C-130-J. Subsequently were inducted the heavy-lift Boeing CH-47 Chinook and the Boeing AH-64E Apache attack helicopters. And then joined the 36 Rafale aircraft with the inventory of modern weapons and electronic warfare suite. Over the years, IAF's inventory has been diverse and it has executed its tasks and roles with professionalism and élan.

IAF today is the fourth largest Air Force, and released "Doctrine of the IAF—Roadmap Beyond 2022", last year. The document clearly reflects the change of IAF from just an air power to aerospace power, and looks much more forward compared to the last variant of 2012. The doctrine revisits the evolving and changing nature of aerospace power and the influence and impact on principles of war. How the aerospace power is a very critical component of national security has been elucidated. In keeping with the evolutionary nature of aerospace power and the need to stay relevant across the spectrum of conflict in an inter-connected environment, IAF is fast transforming from a continental Air Force to one with global reach. It now has trans-domain operations capability, and prides itself for its reach, flexibility, versatility, responsiveness and offensive lethality. It works towards favourable asymmetry. IAF's all top-end fighters refuel in the air. IAF repeatedly flies long 8-10 hour missions. It is in a position to dominate from Malacca strait to the Gulf of Aden. IAF's capability for Anti-Access and Area Denial (AA/AD) is increasing. It will go up further when India further strengthens the airbase infrastructure and assets at the Andaman and Nicobar Islands.

IAF is totally networked and its automated Integrated Air Command and Control System (IACCS) allows combat engagements and control across the sub-continent. The IAF is conscious that technologies such as cyber, electronic warfare, artificial intelligence (AI) and robotics, hypersonic flight and weapons, directed energy, and manned-unmanned teaming are already changing the way militaries engage. Operations will be executed simultaneously in multi-domains.

IAF has to get the number of fighter squadrons to the requisite strength commensurate to the threat on India's border. Numbers will be required also to meet India's rising global stature and responsibilities, and the fastest-growing economy. Similarly, for a continental-sized country like India, the number of AEW&C and FRA would have to go up.

Space is already the enabler for most Intelligence, Surveillance and Reconnaissance (ISR), communications, and navigation and targeting capabilities on Earth. The domains of air and space have already begun to merge and need to be exploited together. For the success of any surface or sub-surface campaign, aerospace superiority would be the starting point.

IAF is working closely with other Services for joint operations. In fact, aerospace has become so critical to all surface and sub-surface operations. The joint doctrines are continuously being updated. IAF has repeatedly demonstrated its huge role in HADR missions, being the first responder.

Clearly, the future is technology driven. Technologies are impacting the way one will fight. Aerospace is the domain that has led with cutting-edge technologies. The need for self-reliance has been well underscored. The benefits of indigenisation are the highest in aerospace technologies which are not only the front end but also face early obsolescence. IAF is supporting and driving the indigenous development of aviation-related technologies, platforms and weapon systems.

Combat engagements of the future will be at farther distances. The speed of engagement will be at electronic or hypersonic velocities. Air defence of the homeland and military assets will be crucial. Air and space will give flexibility at both strategic and tactical levels. Getting timely target information will be a high priority. Unmanned systems will proliferate. Manned, unmanned mix will be more common. AI will be embedded in most systems. Defence of networks from cyber and kinetic threats would be crucial. Information flow and information warfare will have to be managed. Greater emphasis would be on simultaneous Multi-Domain Operations (MDO). Warfare will thus be hybrid. Jointness will remain key for better and more coordinated effects. In all this, the human would continue to be an important and over-riding link in the chain.

This Centre for Air Power Studies book, *Indian Air Force in its Centennial Decade*, very holistically looks at IAF's glorious past and future trajectory. The contributors are not only domain experts but also have years of hands-on operational experience. The book should make a great read for both practitioners and scholars of air power.

Happy Reading!

Anil Chopra
Air Marshal (Retd)
Director-General Centre for Air Power Studies

Figure 1.5: ORBAT of Air Command. ACSEA in early 1945 to the extent relevant to Indian Sub-Continent (*see p. 11*)

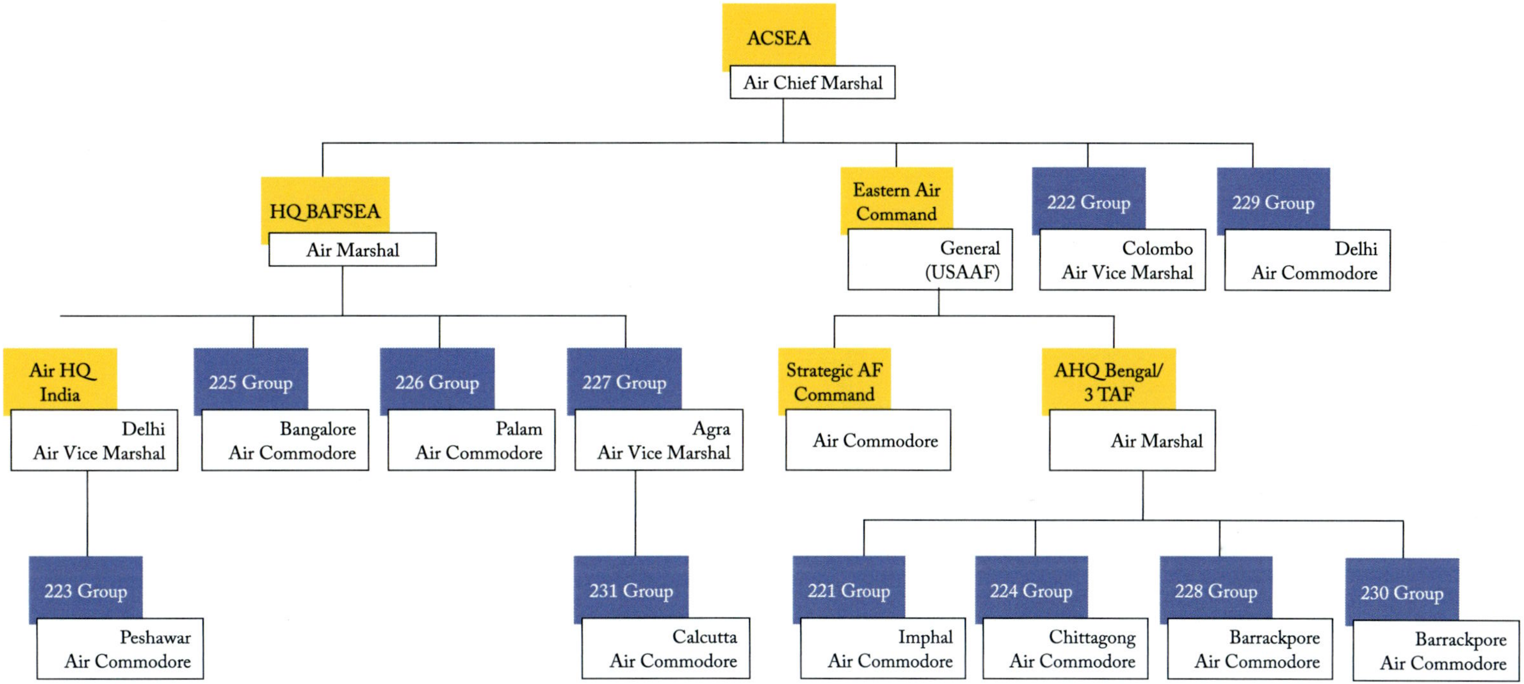

Source: Authors Creation.

Figure 3.2: Bangladesh Political Map (*see p. 49*)

Source: Istock Photo, at https://www.istockphoto.com/vector/bangladesh-political-map-gm544475614-97866077.

Figure 3.3: Phases of Operations (*see p. 51*)

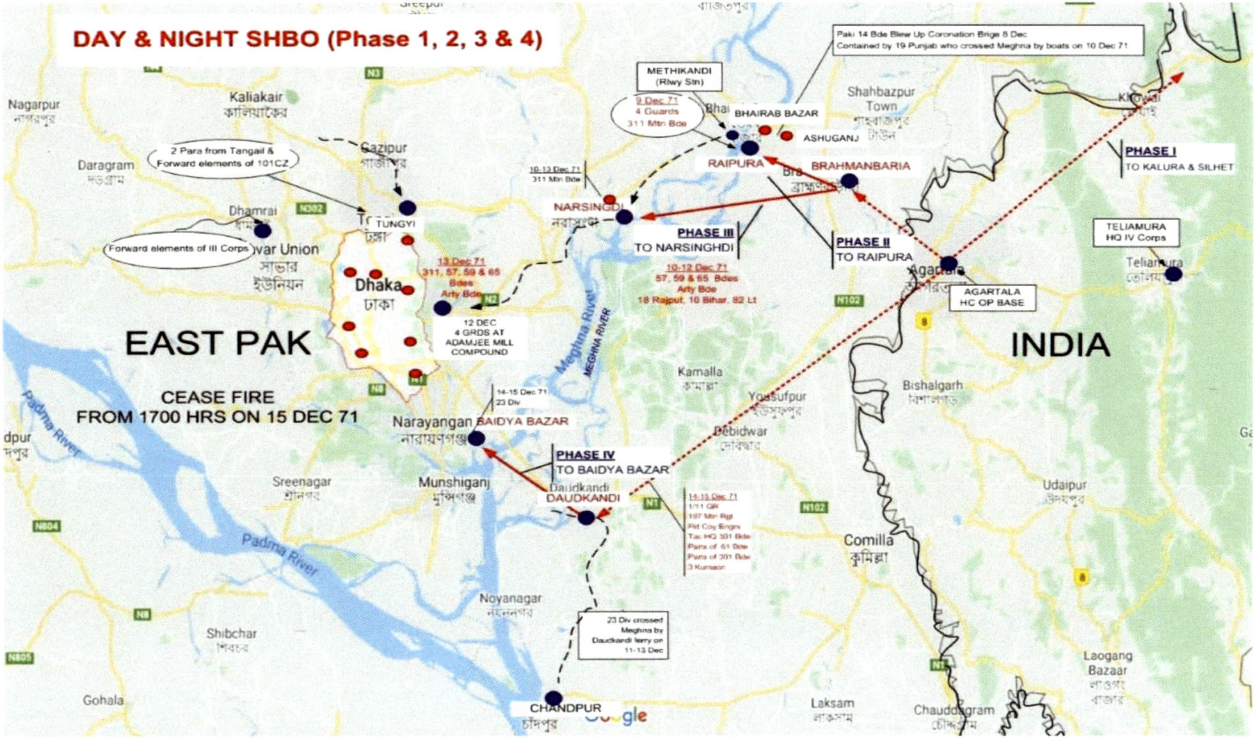

Source: Air Commodore Ram Mohan Sridharan (Retd).

Figure 3.4: The Chetak and Cheetah Operations in the Siachen Glacier (*see p. 53*)

Source: CO 114 HU, Air Force.

Figure 3.5: Siachen Glacier and NJ9842 (*see p. 55*)

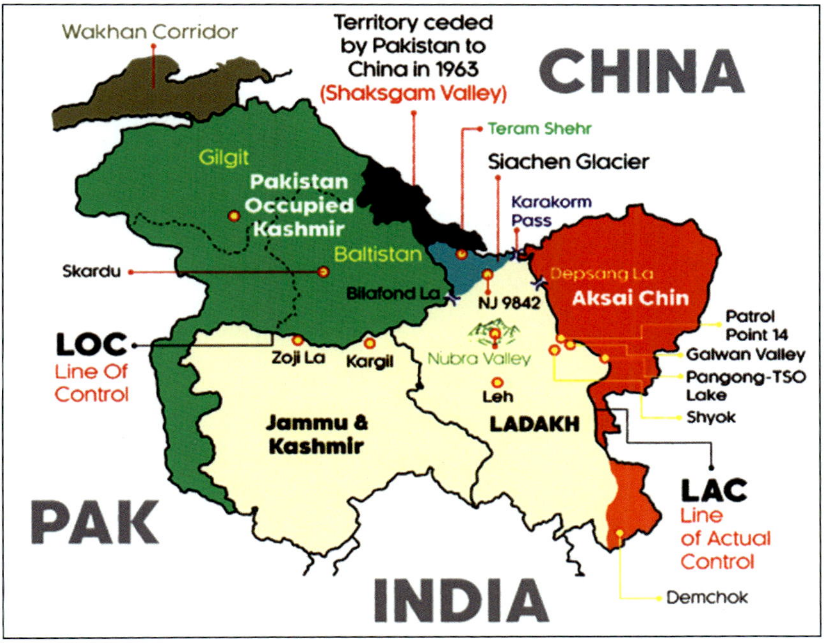

Source: Organiser.org https://organiser.org/wp-content/uploads/2023/02/50a49f38-ce64-45d2-b1ba-5331f421e0ac.jpeg

Figure 3.6: Entry to Siachen Glacier (*see p. 59*)

Source: CO 114 HU.

Figure 3.7: Helicopter Operations in Op Pawan, Sri Lanka (*see p. 59*)

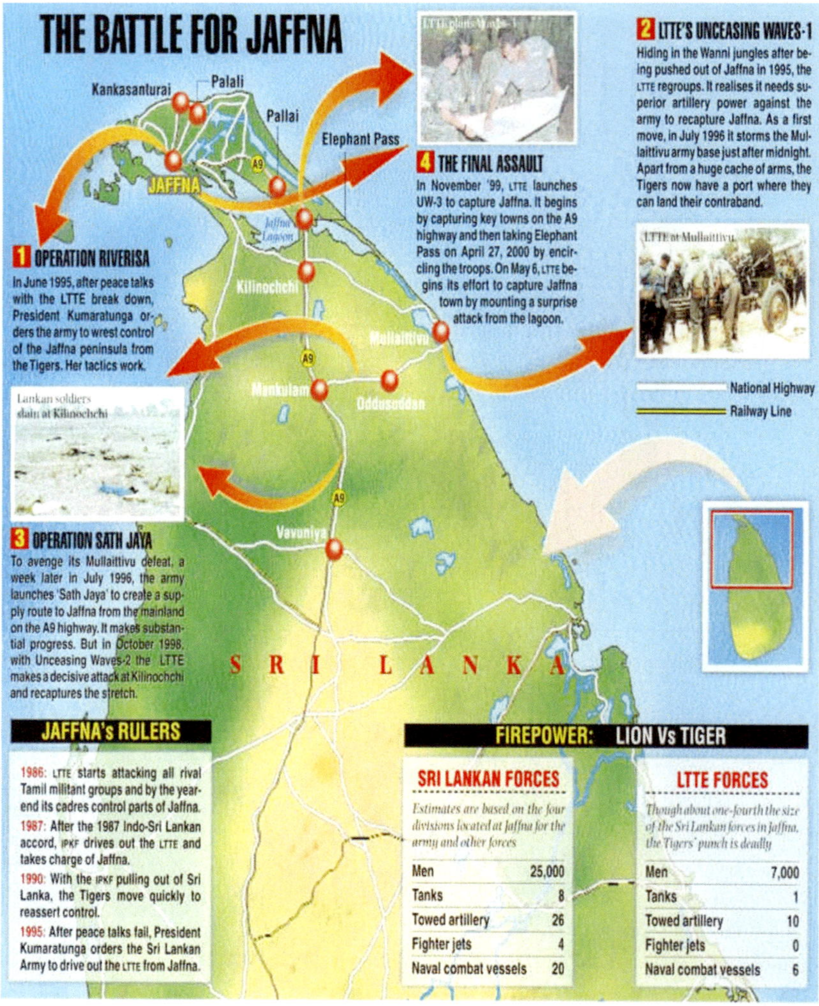

Source: *India Today*, at https://www.indiatoday.in/.

Fig 4.1: Ways Means and Ends (*see p. 75*)

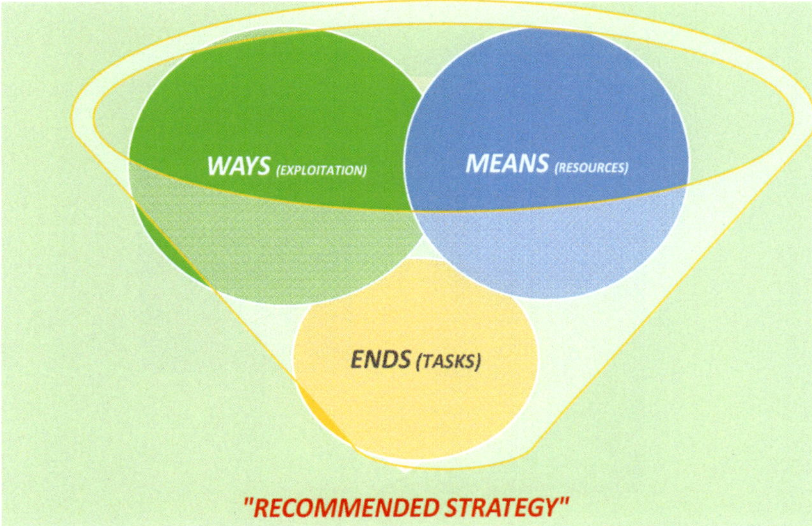

Source: Author's creation.

Figure 7.1: Current IAF Inventory (as of August 18, 2022) (*see p. 121*)

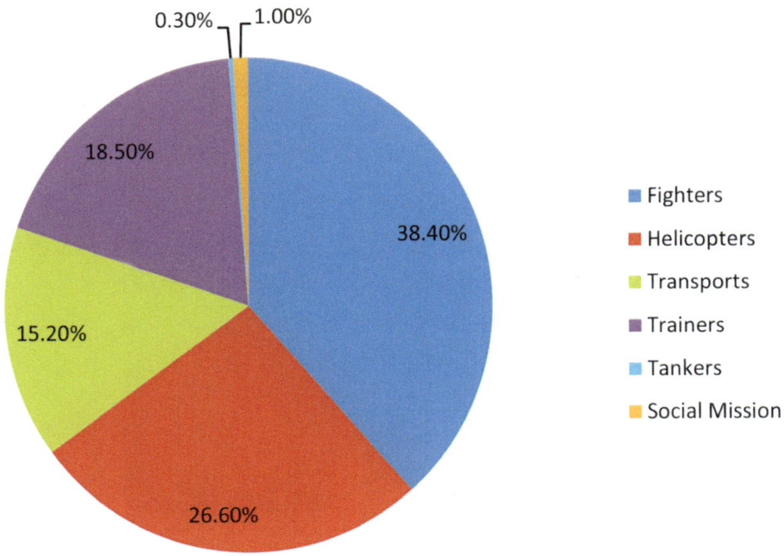

Source: WDMMA.org https://www.wdmma.org/indian-air-force.php.

Figure 11.3: Aerospace Force at a Glance (*see p. 192*)

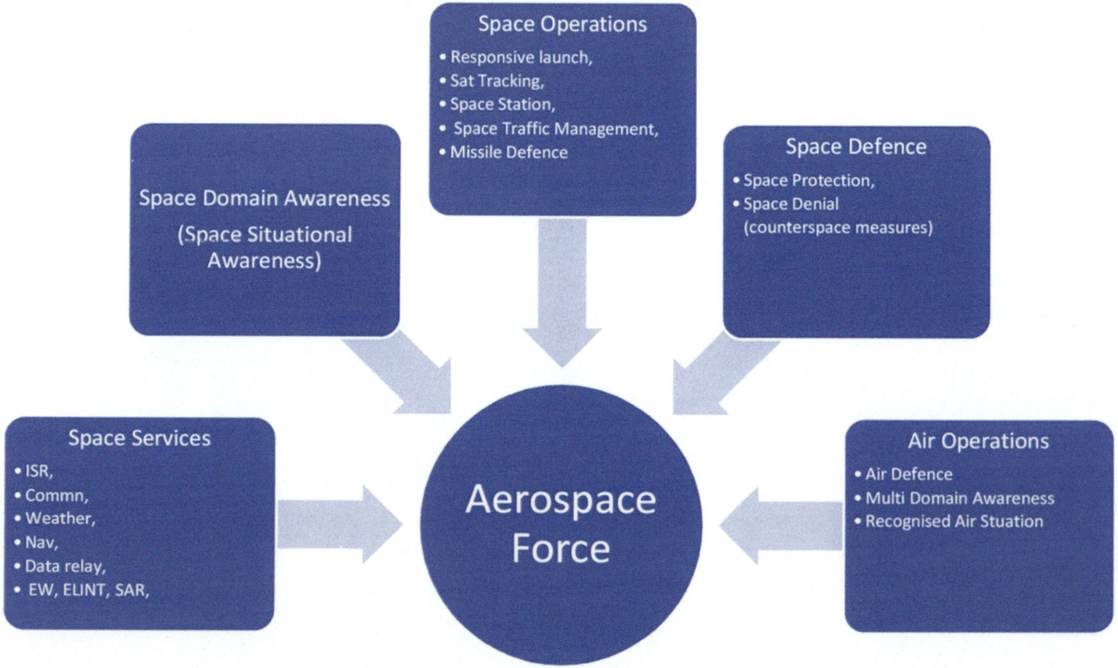

Source: Author's own creation.

SECTION I

IAF: A Glorious Past

1. A Sneak Preview of the IAF

Anchit Gupta

As Indian Air Force looks to the future in its centennial decade with the paradigm of modern warfare, which has changed considerably in this century and is likely to change further, one is often reminded of the great global military leaders' references to learn from the past. Two human instincts are the key reasons this proverb comes up repeatedly. First, human behaviour has remained the same forever; the primal instincts of self-preservation and fear do not change. Second, a constant belief that the current or future is different from the past makes us discount or, worse disregard the past, reinventing the wheel in the process. A chapter is too short to extract all the learnings from the past, but in this section, an attempt is made to focus on two critical aspects of any Air Force and how these evolved over the initial decades of the Indian Air Force's existence—Infrastructure and people setup (branches).

Technology, armament, communication, transportation, capabilities, and geopolitics have all changed since then considerably, leapfrogged. Nevertheless, our ability to extract learnings from the thought process remains relevant. One hopes the readers will grasp nuances around resource management, risk-taking, revelling in complexity, hard work, perseverance, and thinking out of the box. These are the most significant gifts that history can give us as we look to the future and the most extensive learning the readers can take away.

The Infrastructure Setup IAF Inherited in 1947 and How did it Evolve Till Then

A few questions have often baffled us. Why did No. 1 Wing, IAF come up after No. 2, No. 3 & No. 4 Wings, which were already in existence? Or why was the only war-fighting higher establishment of the IAF during the 1947 Kashmir War called No. 1 (Op) Group, and why did all the flying units reside under its Command? Why, of all places, were Poona, Palam and Agra selected to be the first numbered permanent wings of an independent IAF?

The Indian Air Force's structure at Independence owes its genesis to a combination of factors, key amongst which were the Royal Air Force's (RAF's) organisational structure in India, the tribulations of World War II, Britain's exit from India, and finally, the country's partition. It is the understanding of these factors and their consequences that help understand the evolution of the IAF's initial structure.

British Air Power in India before WW II

British apprehensions of the Russians turning up on the north-western borders of their Jewel are well known. While the Tsar refused to play along, the fiercely proud Afghan tribals did not take too well to the interlopers. Wars with the Afghans followed, resulting in the British setting a geographical limit to their physical presence. With the advent of air power in the subcontinent, they pumped in aircraft to stave off tribal threats in the North West Frontier Province (NWFP). This region remained their primary area of interest till the Japanese came knocking on their Eastern doors.

Figure 1.1: Headquarters, Royal Air Force, Shimla (or Delhi)

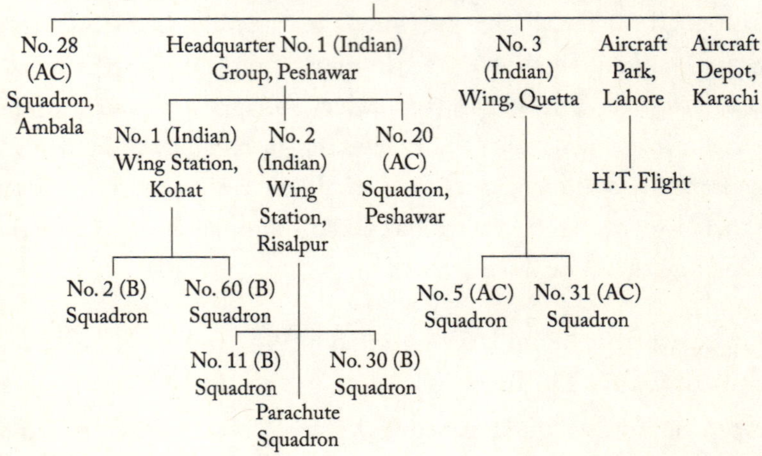

Source: National Archives of India.

Quetta, an RAF base initially, was abandoned after the devastating earthquake of 1935. Consequently, as World War II began, they had six permanent bases in the country—Lahore, Drigh Road (Karachi), Kohat, Risalpur, Peshawar, and Ambala, Ambala purely being a training base, was well removed from the frontline. In addition, it had accommodation for two flights at Miranshah and Fort Sandeman (also known as Zhob Fort).

RAF followed an established block structure comprising Commands, Groups, Wings & Squadrons such that each higher type comprised a few units of the smaller type—for instance, a few squadrons in a Wing and a few Groups in a Command. The Air Ministry in the UK managed Commands. The RAF structured Dominion Air Forces worldwide as Commands, and India was no different. The organisation setup was simple—a Command HQ in Shimla/Delhi (Summer/Winter) with one Group at Peshawar under it, a structure as of 1928 depicted in the image.[1] Even as the Indian Air Force formed in 1933 with a fledgling Squadron at Drigh Road (Karachi), the structure remained largely unchanged.

Peirse Era

Before the war, the British military focus had primarily been to control the restive Afghan tribes and were comfortably managing with the structure outlined above. Michael Pearson, in his book,[2] says,

> "In India, the RAF had always been the poor relation of the Army, dependent on the Indian Military budget for funding and subject to Army tactical control over operations that amounted to little more than flying outdated aircraft to support ground operations against restless tribes. Consequently, AHQ traditionally had little to do beyond rubber-stamping Army instructions."

The early 1940s changed all that. Michael Pearson puts this phase aptly—"In the space of four short months, this ramshackle "cushy billet" (referring to AHQ) found itself dropped uncomfortably into the hot seat of a state-of-the-art industrialised war in which the Army would rapidly come to appreciate that it quite literally could not operate without air support."

In late 1941, things raced. RAF had set up overseas Groups with a numbering pattern starting from No. 200. No. 221 Group at Rangoon was moved to Calcutta and put under Air Headquarters (AHQ) India command with the charge of all fighter and Bomber Sqns in North East India on December 15, 1941.[3] A few days later, on December 20, 1941, No. 222 Group, with control of RAF units in Ceylon and flying boat bases in the Indian Ocean, was put under the control of Air HQ India.[4] In March 1942, Sir Richard Edmund Charles Peirse, KCB, Distinguished Service Order (DSO), Air Force Cross (AFC), took over as AOC-in-C of Air Forces in India (now defined as India and Ceylon). During this period, Peirse made massive organisational changes encompassing the Indian subcontinent to build a viable structure around AHQ India, enabling him to launch offensive and defensive operations and create training and maintenance infrastructure.

Integrating India into the global RAF setup, effective May 1, 1942, Peirse renamed the No. 1 (Indian) Group at Peshawar as No. 223 Group, the role of managing the North-West remaining unchanged.[5] He also split the fighter and Bomber roles for No. 221 Group, passing the fighter operations role in North East India to No. 224 Group on April 1, 1942.[6]

Having covered the key risk areas of North-West and North-East India, Peirse set his eyes on the rest of the Indian Peninsula and ancillary functions. No. 2 (Indian) Group had been formed at Lahore on January 1, 1940 but had remained dormant.[7] No. 225 Group reformed at Bangalore on April 20, 1942, absorbing No. 2 (Indian) Group tasked with the air defence of southern India and the whole coastline from Bengal to Karachi. Peirse also set up No. 226 Group in May 1942 at Karachi to overlook supply and maintenance and No. 227 Group in June 1942 at Lahore to overlook training[8] across the entire area of the Command.

However, Peirse's boldest move was yet to come. Realising the geographical distance with North-East India from his base in Delhi and mindful that the Japanese offensive needed to be dealt with by the No. 221 and No. 224 Groups in the area, he created an AHQ Bengal at Barrackpore on April 20, 1942 to supervise the two Groups.[9] He did this without a formal Air Ministry approval, though after many deliberations, Air Ministry approved Perise's proposal, and a Command within a Command was born, perhaps for the first time. Air Vice Marshal DF Stevenson, who had formed the No. 221 Group just a few months earlier and then split it, was made the AOC of AHQ Bengal. In the current context, AHQ Bengal was operating akin to operations by AOC, and J&K today.

Figure 1.2: India Group Area Control, 1943

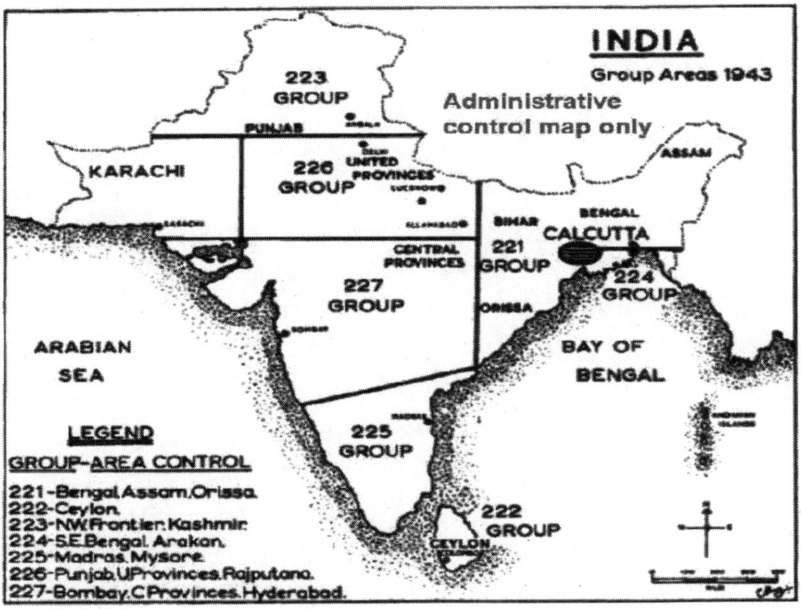

Source: "The Royal Air Force Medical Services", Volume 3, p. 635.

Such was the scale of expansion that it required upgrading the establishment. The AOC-in-C was authorisation as an Air Chief Marshal, and he was to be supported by a deputy AOC-in-C in Air Marshal rank. Richard Peirse and Guy Garrod, respectively, took up these roles in July 1942. When Air Chief Marshal Richard Peirse's tenure as AOC-in-C of Air Forces in India ended in November 1943, he had given shape to a genuinely Pan-India set-up under the "India Command." It now comprised one mini-Command at Bengal and seven groups. The map depicts the areas of responsibility of these groups.[10] The expansion of airstrips in India best explains the pace of the build-up of the infrastructure. In March 1942, there were only 16 airfields; by November 1942, this number was 148, and by November 1943, it was a staggering 285.[11]

In this brief period, IAF had grown to 7 Squadrons operating under 223 Group or 225 Group. The initial nucleus of IAF officers, though by now had been given staff postings in AHQ (Mukerjee, Awan and Majumdar), 223 Group (Mukerjee and Awan), and 225 Group (Mukerjee). Overlapping with most of the Peirse era, a newly minted Wing Commander Mukerjee was Wg Cdr (Operations) at AHQ India between November 1942 and August 1943, an experience that must have left him much wiser.

Burma Phase (1943-1945)

Despite this herculean effort, the India Command did not have enough strength to face the formidable Japanese forces. In January 1943, it had about 35 operational squadrons, with 18 of these with the 221 and 224 Groups facing the Japanese offensive in the Northeast.[12] The allied effort, augmented by Air Forces from the USA, Canada, Australia and New Zealand, was ready to take on the Japanese offensive. Such expansion of forces in the East of India's frontiers led to the formation of the South East Asia Command (SEAC) in November 1943 and consequently enforced another tweak to the structure of the Air Forces in India, with Lord Louis Mountbatten as its Supreme Allied Commander and an area that included India, Burma, Ceylon, Malaya, the northern islands of Sumatra, and, for offensive operations, Siam (Thailand). Its aerial component was the South East Asia Air Command (SEAAC), with its HQ at Colombo. It was shortly afterwards rechristened as the Air Command, South East Asia (ACSEA), a name that would harken tales of supreme courage for generations to come. Air Chief Marshal Richard Peirse once again found himself in the hot seat, moving from AOC-in-C, India Command to lead ACSEA as its first AOC-in-C, and Air Marshal Guy Garrod followed him as Deputy AOC-in-C ACSEA.

He again ushered in a series of organisational changes, keeping unity in Command paramount. He used the multi-tiered "command inside command" structure again, creating two new HQs, HQ Base Air Forces Southeast Asia (BAFSEA) and the Eastern Air Command reporting directly to him. He also kept No. 222 Group, which was controlling all operational squadrons in Ceylon (now called Sri Lanka), carrying out maritime duties under his direct control. In December 1943, No. 229 Group was created in Delhi in charge of Transport operations in the sub-continent. No. 12 Squadron, IAF was placed under this Group on September 15, 1946, when it became IAF's first transport squadron.[13]

BAFSEA directly controlled 225 Group (responsible for the air defence of southern India and the whole coastline from Bengal to Karachi), 226 Group (Maintenance), and 227 Group (Training). All Air Forces in the Indian subcontinent were placed subordinate to the ACSEA through BAFSEA, to ensure unity in Command. The term "Air Forces in India" associated with AHQ India was dropped. AHQ India's role was significantly reduced to managing one operational Group-223 only. After the restructuring, Air Vice Marshal Meredith Thomas CSI, CBE, DFC, AFC was appointed as AOC in March 1944. AHQ India retained the role of solely mentoring the IAF.

Allied Eastern Air Command straddled an area from Bengal to Siam and included the USAAF 10th Air Force under its control. As far as India was concerned, AHQ Bengal was placed under Eastern Air Command.[14] However, this was not before AHQ Bengal was renamed as Tactical Air Force (Burma) (also referred to as 3rd Tactical Air Force) on December 19, 1943.[15] Other than AHQ Bengal, Eastern Air Command had one more group operating in India. The No. 231 Group at Calcutta was raised for strategic air operations.

Figure 1.3: 6 Sqn, IAF with Air Marshal Sir John Eustice Arthur Baldwin

Source: Late Wg Cdr HK Patel.

AHQ Bengal/3rd TAF[16] retained control of the 221 and 224 Groups and remained at Barrackpore. However, to assist its standalone functioning, No. 230 Group (Maintenance) was formed at Barrackpore in December 1943. Later in February 1945, No. 228 Group (Administration) was placed under AHQ Bengal. Air Marshal Sir John Eustice Arthur Baldwin, KBE, CB, DSO, DL, was in Command of the 3rd TAF for over a year. Multiple Indian Air Force units moved to the Burma front and operated under 224 Group, 3rd TAF, and Air Marshal Sir John Baldwin (seen in the image with 6 Sqn, IAF at Cox Bazaar in 1944[17]).

An extract of the header of the monthly sortie report of No. 8 Sqn, IAF for July 1944 reflects this reporting structure.[18]

Figure 1.4: Sample Header of the ORB of IAF Sqns

From : Officer Commanding, No. 8 I.A.F. Squadron.
To : AC.SEA., 3rd TAF., 224 Group., I67 Wing.
Date : 7th July I944,
Ref : 8S/5I/INT-OPS.

SORTIE REPORT 6 - OPREP 205 - 7.7.44

Source: July 1944 ORB of 8 Sqn from National Archives of UK.

By the time Air Chief Marshal Richard Peirse relinquished Command of ACSEA on November 27, 1944, he had created an organisation with 11 Groups in India, as depicted in the figure below. Between his two tenures in direct or indirect control of India between April 1942 and November 1944, he radically transformed the Air Forces in India.

Post-WW II Reorganisation (June 1945-May 1947)

The structure, as mentioned above, continued till the war's end, with minor adjustments. However, the action remained in the East, with air operations in the Burma sector and those "over the hump." On June 1, 1945, with the war front narrowing, USAAF withdrew from the SEAC[19] dawning a phase of military management and reversion of sorts to the pre-SEAC organisation structure.

Figure 1.5: ORBAT of Air Command. ACSEA in early 1945 to the extent relevant to Indian Sub-Continent

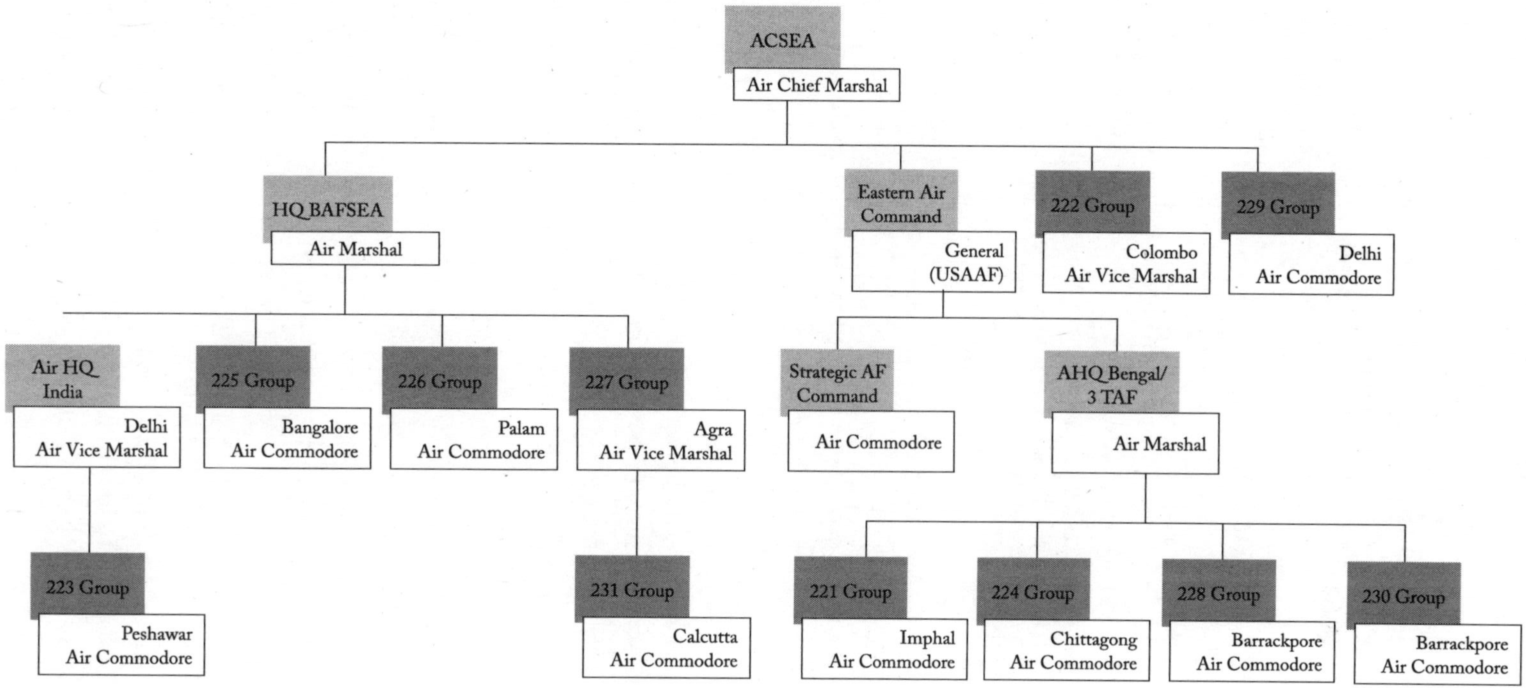

Source: Authors Creation.

Figure 1.6: Post-WW II IAF Plan

1. The Air Staff has appreciated the requirements of Post-War Garrison Air Forces in India to be 19 Squadrons and one Photo Recce Flight, together with certain ancillary flying units. The composition of these forces will be as follows :

Squadron Type.	R.A.F.	R.I.A.F.
Fighter.	4	6
Twin Engined Transport.	2	2
Multi Engined Transport.	2	-
Maritime	1	-
Light Bomber.	-	2
P.R. Flight.	1	-

Ancillary Flying Units.

1 Air Headquarters Communication Squadron.
3 Group Headquarters Communication Flights.
1 A.O.P. Squadron.
2 Drogue Towing Flights.
1 V.C.P. Air.

Source: National Archives of India.

As the war ended, altered threat perception, financial constraints, and the realigned world called for another reorganisation. The post-WW II threats in India were perceived to be the North-West province at one end, Bengal at the other, and the Deccan and southern areas along with the associated coastline as the third axis.[20] This assessment, as of the summer of 1945, saw the threat of seaborne attack as being remote and therefore not worthy of significant counter-deployments.

It was decided to reduce the air assets in a manner that would leave 20 flying squadrons in India, with ten each being from the RIAF and RAF.[21]

Interestingly, the RIAF's numbers included two twin-engined transport squadrons and another two light bombers. No. 12 Squadron, RIAF was the only squadron formed after these plans were implemented and was envisaged as a light bomber squadron on the Mosquito aircraft. However, it became its lone transport squadron due to a change in acquisition plans. It was only post-independence that RIAF raised its first bomber squadron. The new plan also entailed a Strategic Reserve Force of 18 RAF Squadrons based in the UK or the Middle East that could be brought to bear in India if the need ever arose. All efforts were also to be made to keep all airfields along the East-West strategic trunk route open.[22]

Figure 1.7: Re-constitution of Air HQ

Air Headquarters, (India).

1463/23.

Nos. 1 & 2 (Indian) Groups.
Headquarters 225, 226, 227, 228 and 229 Groups.
B.A.O.
B,P.O.
RIAF Record Office
RIAF Central Accounts Office.

23/1822,

O. 671 23/Feb.

UNCLASSIFIED(.) AIR HEADQUARTERS (INDIA)(.) {82}
ADMINISTRATIVE INSTRUCTION (No. to be notified later) 1946(.)
RE-CONSTITUTION OF AIR HEADQUARTERS (INDIA) ON POST-WAR BASIS
ARRANGEMENTS FOR PERSONNEL ADMINISTRATION(.)

INFORMATION(.)

Para.1. It has been agreed that with effect from 1st April 1946 command of the Royal Air Force in India and of the Royal Indian Air Force comma is to be vested in the Air Officer Commanding in Chief Air Forces of the India Command(.) This entails re-constitution of Air Headquarters India which with effect from the above date is to assume as an additional commitment under the command of the Air Officer Commanding in Chief responsibility for all formations and units in Base Air Forces South East Asia.(.)

Source: National Archives of India.

Two significant organisational changes were implemented with effect from April 1, 1946. The first of these saw BAFSEA being merged into Air Headquarters India. Air Headquarters was now made the nodal authority for all of India and was placed under the joint authority of the Indian government and the Air Ministry, reverting to the power it wielded before the formation of ACSEA.[23] Air Marshal Sir Charles Roderick Carr, KBE, CB, DFC, AFC, a New Zealander in service of the RAF, was Air Marshal Commanding HQ Base Air Forces South East Asia and took over the combined HQ on April 1, 1946 as Air Officer Commanding-in-Chief, Air Headquarters India based at Delhi.[24]

At the operational level, it was decided that the Air Forces in India would be organised into self-sustaining Groups whose headquarters would be co-located with those of the Army Commands and have the exact geographical boundaries.[25] The decision to co-locate was a direct result of the experience of ACSEA, where functional and administrative boundaries overlapped and were not always congruent with the Army Command boundaries leading to operational challenges. While the AHQ structure was made effective on April 1, 1946, the group reorganisation was put in motion in August 1945 itself and completed by May 1946.[26] Considering the military needs of the day, the 11[27] existing groups operating in the Indian subcontinent were morphed into four (Indian) groups, reverting to the nomenclature that existed before the Peirse era.

No. 223 Group at Peshawar was renamed back as No. 1 (Indian) Group on August 15, 1945[28] and subsequently subsumed the 229 Group at Delhi on its disbanding on March 31, 1947.[29] No. 1 (Indian) Group remains the oldest surviving establishment of the Air Forces in India, formed on November 1, 1928, and a progenitor to the current Western Air Command of the IAF. Raised to be congruent to the Army's Northern/North-West Army Command, the Group remained at Peshawar for operational reasons, even though the Army HQ was at Lahore.[30]

No. 225 Group at Bangalore (responsible for the air defence of southern India and the entire coastline from Bengal to Karachi) was again renamed the No 2 (Indian) Group on May 1, 1946. Later No. 226 Group at Palam disbanded and merged into the No. 2 (Indian) Group on July 31, 1946.[31] Southern Army Command was based in Bangalore at that time even though plans indicated Poona as the new headquarters location.[32] While the Southern Command moved to Poona on July 1, 1946, the No. 2 (Indian) Group never moved out of Bangalore.

No. 227 Group had moved to Agra in October 1944 and was redesignated as No. 4 (Indian) Group on May 1, 1946.[33] The Army's Central Command, with the charge of Lucknow, Delhi and Meerut districts, was based at Agra.[34]

No. 228 Group at Barrackpore was redesignated as the No. 3 (Indian) Group on May 1, 1946[35] and was expected to be parallel to the Army's Eastern Command, then based at Barrackpore,[36] with a debate about basing the headquarters at Ranchi or Lucknow. Eastern Army Command eventually moved to Ranchi on March 23, 1947, and so did the No. 3 (Indian) Group.

With the required Indian Groups having been formed, the Nos 221, 224 and 231 Groups were disbanded. Air HQ India was no longer required to supervise beyond modern-day India and Pakistan. Consequently, No. 230 Group evolved into the Air HQ Burma, later becoming Air HQ Singapore. Likewise, No. 222 Group was restructured to form Air HQ Ceylon.[37]

Thus, no Wings as we know them today were envisaged in the post-WW II plans for Air Forces in India. Instead, there were "Air Force Stations" under each group. Just as the Air Force reorganisation was completed in June 1946, the Indian Army decided to disband the Central Army Command at Agra.[38] With the Army's Central Command disbanding in October 1946, the No 4 (Indian) Group at Agra found itself without a parallel Army Command. A solution was found by downgrading the No. 4 (Indian) Group at Agra to the No. 4 (Indian) Wing. This Wing was moved under the control of the No. 2 (Indian) Group on July 15, 1946, but soon disbanded on October 1, 1946.[39] However, the establishment of the future No. 4 Wing, IAF at Agra, had been established to be revived when necessary.

Figure 1.8 shows the implemented structure as of early 1947.[40]

At the grassroots, the RIAF squadrons had started moving too. No. 1 and 9 Sqn (Peshawar), No. 3 and 7 Sqn (Risalpur), No. 10 Sqn (Chakeri), and No. 12 Sqn (Mauripur) were under the No. 1 (Indian) Group. No. 2 Sqn (Poona) and No. 8 Sqn (Kolar) moved under the control of No. 2 (Indian) Group, and No. 6 Sqn (Ranchi) was placed under No. 3 (Indian) Group. No. 4 Sqn, IAF was in Japan with the allied occupational forces.[41] Amongst the ancillary flying units—Target Tow Flights were formed at Poona and Karachi.[42] Each of the Groups had a communication flight,[43] and AHQ India Communication Flight was formed on January 1947.

Peshawar, Poona and Ranchi were expected to be the main stations under each of the groups, respectively.[44] Wg Cdr HS Ratnagar (1588) took over as the first Indian Station Commander of RAF Poona on May 21, 1947 and was referred to as RIAF Poona under his Command.[45] Poona was renamed as the No. 2 (Indian) Wing around this time, as it was under the control of the No. 2 (Indian) Group. However, the information supporting the date of such a change is conflicting.[46] Confusion around the date notwithstanding, this change did lead to India getting its second numbered Wing, based at Poona.

Figure 1.8: Post-WW II Plan for Garrison Forces in India

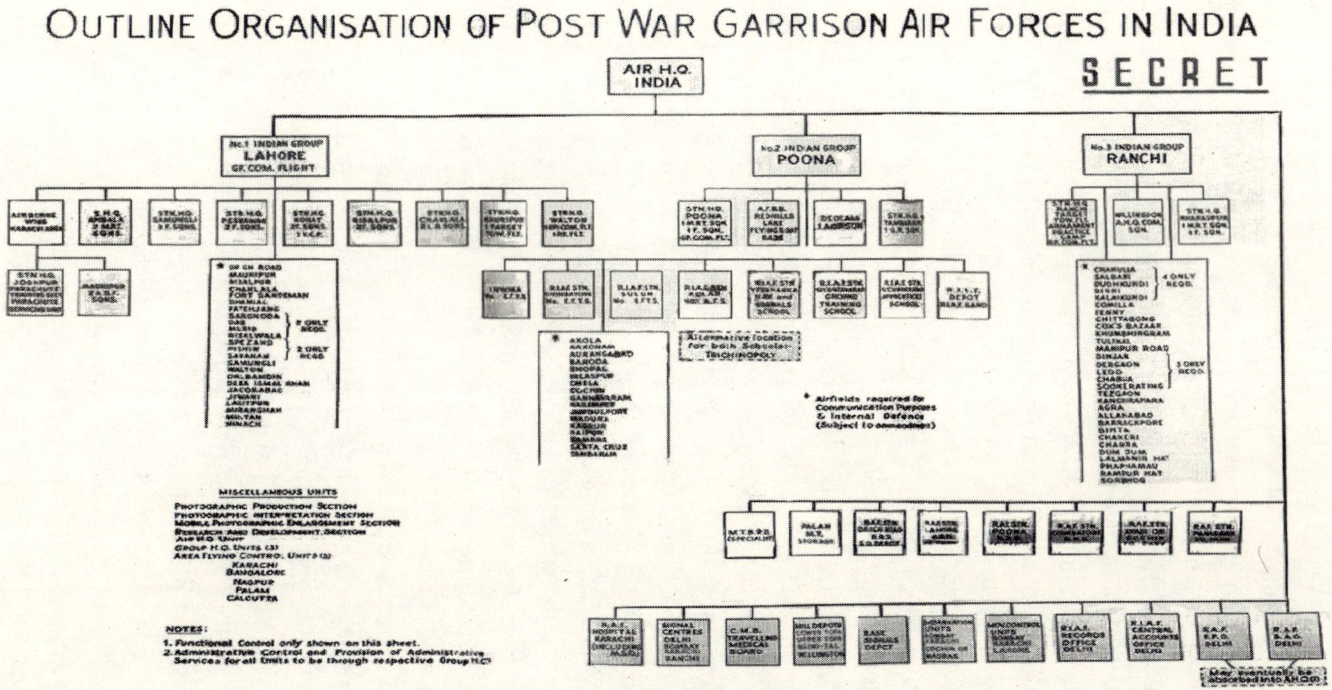

Source: National Archives of India.

British Exit and Partition (June 1947 Onwards)

British Prime Minister Clement Attlee, on February 20, 1947, announced the forthcoming transfer of power in India, and Lord Mountbatten was charged with overseeing it. In mid-June, the Armed Forces Reconstitution Committee was set up alongside the Partition Council to deliberate the armed forces division between India and Pakistan.

The impact of the first announcement on the Air Forces in India was far-reaching. Transfer of power meant that the ten RAF Squadrons to be placed in India would not happen, nor would they need to maintain bases for a strategic reserve, and keeping trunk routes open be a priority. This dramatic halving of units at the disposal of Air Forces in India led planners to take a complete U-turn on the structure so consciously put in place since the end of WW II, reverting to the adoption of functional groupings from geographical congruency with the Army. Interestingly, this debate continues to rage even today—though under the garb of Theatre Commands.

Air Commodore G Harcourt-Smith, Director of Organisation at AHQ, announced[47]—"The three IAF Groups were originally organised on a geographical basis corresponding with areas of the three Army Commands. It has now been decided to depart from this principle and to retain two Indian groups, one controlling all operational squadrons and units and the other responsible for the administration, training, and maintenance organisation of the RIAF."

Effecting the change, No. 3 (Indian) Group became redundant and was reduced to No. 3 (Indian) Wing on June 1, 1947.[48] No. 3 (Indian) Group, though, was still holding numerous units awaiting disposal. These units were nominally moved to the charge of the No. 3 (Indian) Wing that relocated to RAF Palam. Thereby making Palam, No. 3 (Indian) Wing. India got its third and final pre-independence Wing (4 Wing at Agra and 2 Wing at Poona having been raised earlier)—a twist of fate from the 1946 plans, which did not envisage any Wings in India. Implicitly, India did not have a No. 1 Wing as of Independence. When the Kashmir War (1947-48) necessitated the creation of a Wing at Jammu, it was given the so far unused number—1 Wing.

No. 1 (Indian) Group at Peshawar was made responsible for operational stations and squadrons, and the No. 2 (Indian) Group at Bangalore was to take up all training, maintenance, and administration units and stations in the country. Effective June 1, 1947, a reshuffle of all the units and stations under Nos 1, 2, 3 (Indian) Groups took place to enable this new reality.

Marshal of the Royal Air Force Samuel Charles Elworthy, Lord Elworthy, KG, GCB, CBE, DSO, LVO, DFC, AFC, was posted to India as SASO, No. 2 (Indian) Group in March 1947 in the rank of Group Captain. His biography has the following relevant exert to the changes in this period.[49] "When Sam arrived in Bangalore, 2 (Indian) Group consisted of only two frontline RIAF squadrons, 2 and 8, based at Yelahanka and Kolar, both close to Bangalore, where they were in the process of converting from the Spitfire XIV to the Hawker Tempest II. However, it was decided in June 1947 that there should be a major reorganisation of the RIAF: 3 (Indian) Group was disbanded, and 2 (Indian) Group lost its two squadrons and its station at Poona to 1 (Indian) Group, receiving, in turn, most of the latter's Training, Maintenance and Administrative units. It also assumed responsibility for all the university units. RIAF Kolar was closed down."

While this overhaul took care of the first announcement related to RAF's exit from India, the armed forces split between India and Pakistan was still being debated. On July 15, 1947, the Armed Forces Reconstitution Committee (AFRC) ratified that—No. 1 (Indian) Group would become the RPAF Air HQ and No. 2 (Indian) Group would remain in India.[50] With No. 1 Sqn remaining with Pakistan, the loss of the No. 1 (Indian) Group was a body blow to India.

Therefore, when August 15, 1947 dawned, RIAF had the following higher organisation structure at its disposal.

- Air HQ at Delhi
- No. 2 (Indian) Group at Bangalore
- No. 2 Wing at Poona, placed under the direct control of Air HQ
- No. 3 Wing at Palam was placed under the direct control of Air HQ
- No. 4 Wing at Agra, placed under the direct control of Air HQ

In the absence of the No. 1 (Indian) Group at the dawn of the Kashmir War on July 26, 1947, Air HQ, RIAF, waged war directly, in a departure from the usually accepted practice. At Air HQ, the responsibility of running the war fell on Group Captain Mehar Singh, who was the Director of Operations. On November 19, 1947, RIAF reformed the No. 1 (Opl) Group at Palam, and Air Commodore Mehar Singh, on promotion, was made the AOC of the Group and continued to run the operations in the Kashmir War. IAF would repeat the same revival on No. 1 Sqn later in 1953, thus bringing back to life both marquee establishments it had lost to Pakistan.

On September 15, 1947, No. 2 (Indian) Group was renamed as No. 2 (Trg) Group keeping in view its functional role. On November 4, 1947, Air Commodore Narendra took over as the first Indian AOC of the Group[51] from outgoing Air Commodore CD Adams, who had held the position since September 1946.

It was not until 1949 that the Indian Air Force changed its structure to that of an independent country. Effective February 1, 1949, Air HQ stopped being manned as a Command. For instance, Air Vice Marshal Subroto Mukerjee, who was SASO, Air HQ till January 31, 1949, was redesignated as Deputy Chief, though the role remained the same. Few months later, in July 1949, the Groups were upgraded to Command status, the role remaining unchanged. No. 1 (Opl) Group was renamed Operational Command, and No. 2 (Trg) Group was renamed Training Command.[52]

IAF—Branches Evolution

In his address on Air Force Day 2022, the Chief of Air Staff announced the creation of a new branch in the officer cadre for the first time since independence, though a significant reorganisation of the branch system was last done in 1971. This new branch represents a significant, much-needed reform. However, let us first return to 1932, when IAF was formed.

If one queued up to join the IAF as an officer in its inception, 1932, they would have been offered just one choice—to be a pilot. Since then, the IAF has come a long way. The IAF's branches have expanded along with the IAF's evolution as it continues to adapt and meet the needs of the modern battlefield. Today officer cadets have many more choices. The IAF boasts nine branches, and officer cadets can join as Pilots, Navigators, Ground duties (administration, logistics, accounts, education and meteorology), and technical officers into what they call "branches" of the IAF.

When the IAF was born in 1932, it had just a single squadron (1 Sqn). The General Duties Pilot, or GD(P) branch, as it was called then, was based on the lines that existed in the RAF. All other functions required to support flying were taken care of by airmen (initially called Hawai Sepoys). The headquarters, air bases, and all other aspects of managing the Air Forces in India were controlled by RAF in India. Hence the limited need for IAF personnel and, consequently, limited branches. The system continued for nearly a decade, and it was not till 1941 that the IAF felt the need to expand.

In the early years, the trainees who did not qualify to become pilots were commissioned into the Equipment (EQPT) branch to take care of logistics. Thereby EQPT became the 2nd Branch that IAF officers held. In the second half of 1939, the winds of war were blowing across Europe. Britain required manpower to deal with the demands of WW II and looked to its Indian colony, IAFVR, or the Indian Air Force Volunteer Reserve was set up, which led to a manifold increase in recruitment.

Nearly all the expanded IAF took part in WW II on the Burma front, some even in Europe. As part of IAFVR, apart from pilots, officers were commissioned in the Observers GD(O) and Air Gunner GD(AG) branches. Air observers or aerial observers were predominantly tasked with reconnaissance duties. The term was coined by the British Royal Flying Corps in WW-I and was maintained by its successor, the Royal Air Force. An air observer's brevet was a single wing with an O at the root.

Just like any intake, some do not make it to pilots. Therefore a few of the IAFVR folks were commissioned into ground duties. Ground duties then were called Administration and Special Duties (A&SD). Hence the Branch was called A&SD. Special duties included Air Traffic Control (ATC), photography, and cypher, for instance.

Between 1939 and 1942, IAF saw a massive expansion, growing from the size of just one to as many as six squadrons. Numerous training institutions for officers and airmen were set up to accommodate this increased size. It was here that the proliferation of other branches took place across the officer cadre in the 1942-43 timeframe. It was natural that the first choice of officers for these roles were the Airmen (Hawai Sepoys) already playing the part. This transition eliminated training time and retained experienced manpower. The IAF did not see the need and therefore did not have any establishments to induct or train for ground duties.

The branches that got set up in this period were the education branch, accounts branch, a specific branch called Balloon, and four branches in the technical field—Signals, Armament, Electrical and Engineering. Unknown to most in the IAF, there was a fifth technical branch called Radar, referred to as T/Rad. Nevertheless, it had merged into signals around 1947 and therefore was forgotten.

The Balloon branch formed as an independent branch at first to look after the balloon barrages erected around vulnerable points to trap low-flying enemy aircraft, a concept used extensively during World War II in Europe, but its utility waned soon after, and the branch was discontinued in 1945.

Such expansion of force and services created challenges in recruiting trained manpower, and the IAF had to rely on the services of other government agencies as well. For instance, IAF did not have any Meteorology (Met) expertise or manpower. Before the 1940s, Met was handled by RAF/IMD. In 1943, IAF started to have commissioned officers in the MET branch. All these officers were deputed from IMD. Direct recruitment into MET did not happen till much after 1947.

Similarly, air traffic and aerodrome management skills needed to be in order. IAF deputed "Aerodrome officers" from civil aviation for a while in the 1940s to meet the needs. They were part of the A&SD Branch. As a result of these arrangements, the officer cadre in the IAF outside of pilots tended to be short service commission and significantly older. For instance, many officers of the ground duties branches were commissioned as pilot officers well into their 1940s.

IAF also had a distinct Legal branch with officers commissioned for the role. This branch was merged into A&SD around 1949. In 1946, the system of Observers was stopped, and navigators as a stream was introduced. The difference between them is a change of era. So GD(O) became GD(N). Erstwhile GD(O) officers underwent a conversion course.

At its peak, just before the 1971 war, there were as many as 14 branches in the IAF. This system of branches continued till September 1, 1971, when a reorganisation took place under Air Chief Marshal PC Lal. Technical Branches were consolidated into two branches. GD was replaced with the word flying. So GD(P) became F(P), and GD(N) became F(N). A&SD was renamed ADM (Administration) and predominantly had three duties—Administration, Air Traffic Control, and Fighter Controller. EQPT was renamed LGS (Logistics). ARMT + ENG became Aeronautical Engineering (Mechanical) or AE(M), and SIGS + ELECT became AE(L). MET, EDN, and ACCTS continued as is.

IAF did not have its own medical and dental officers who were from 1941 onwards deputed from Army Medical Corps (AMC). However, on such deputation, the office was given a commission in the IAF under the "medical" or "dental" branch. The first MED officers were commissioned in January 1941. Dental came in much later, in 1956.

The branch structure has remained the same since 1971, until today. The new Weapon System branch will combine four streams—surface-to-surface missiles, surface-to-air missiles, Remotely Piloted Aircraft (Drones), and Weapon System Operators. This is an essential step in making IAF future-ready as it recognises the need to recruit, groom and grow talent in the organisation and focus on these streams.

APPENDIX 1: PIB Release of November 4, 1947

Ministry of Defence,
Public Relations Directorate,
New Delhi, November 4, 1947.

Press Note

AIR COMMODORE NARENDRA TO COMMAND NO.2 GROUP RIAF.

NEW DELHI, Nov. 4 - Group Captain Narendra has been promoted to the rank of Air Commodore in the Royal Indian Air Force. He took over command of No. 2 Group RIAF, Bangalore from Air Commodore C.D. Adams, RAF, who left for the United Kingdom today.

No. 2 Group RIAF, Bangalore, which comprises the majority of the Ground Training Schools and all units of the Royal Indian Air Force in Southern India, to the extent of 5,000 men, has from its formation in 1944 been commanded by an officer of Air Rank of the Royal Air Force.

APPENDIX 2: PIB Release of July 26, 1949

PRESS INFORMATION BUREAU (DEFENCE WING)
Government of India,

PRESS COMMUNIQUE.

The Government of India have decided to rename the two major Air Force "formations" directly under the Air HQ, India, which have been known hitherto as No.1 (Operational) Group and No. 2 (Training) Group, as Operational Command, RIAF, and Training Command, RIAF, respectively.

The chnage in the nomeclature has been effected in order to raise the status of the two formations in conformity with their present functions. The designation of the commanders of the two formations with their headquarters at palam and Bangalore, will hereafter be Air Officer Commanding, Operational Command, RIAF and Air Officer Commanding, Training Command, RIAF.

Notes

1. Source: National Archives of India.
2. The Burma Air Campaign, 1941-1945, 2006.
3. https://www.rafweb.org/Organsation/Grp07.htm
4. https://www.rafweb.org/Organsation/Grp07.htm
5. Source: National Archives of India.
6. https://www.rafweb.org/Organsation/Grp07.htm
7. Source: National Archives of India.
8. https://www.rafweb.org/Organsation/Grp07.htm
9. The Burma Air Campaign, 1941-1945, 2006.
10. Source: Samuel Cuthbert Rexford-Welch. 1954. *The Royal Air Force Medical Services*, Volume 3.y
11. The Burma Air Campaign, 1941-1945, 2006.
12. Wesley Frank Craven, James L. Cate,.1948. "The Army Air Forces in World War II: The Pacific, Guadalcanal to Saipan", August 1942 to July 1944.
13. "Monthly Operational Record Book", No. 12 Sqn, IAF for the period September 1946.
14. https://www.rafweb.org/Organsation/Cmd_O3.htm
15. https://www.rafweb.org/Organsation/Cmd_O3.htm
16. This establishment was again renamed AHQ Bengal/Burma on 4 December 1944 and again as AHQ Burma on February 27, 1945.
17. https://www.bharat-rakshak.com/IAF/history/ww2/veterans/1035-hoshang.html
18. AIR-27-124, National Archives of United Kingdom.
19. Far East Air Operations, 1943-1945, John Grehan, Martin Mace, 2014.
20. National Archives of India.
21. Source: National Archive of India file named—"Post War Air Force Organisation" page 67 at the link https://www.abhilekh-patal.in/jspui/handle/123456789/2734801
22. Source: National Archive of India file named—"Post War Air Force Organisation", p. 30, at https://www.abhilekh-patal.in/jspui/handle/123456789/2734801
23. Source: National Archive of India file named—"Post War Air Force Organisation", p. 44, at https://www.abhilekh-patal.in/jspui/handle/123456789/2734801
24. http://www.rafweb.org/Biographies/Carr_CR.htm
25. Source: National Archive of India file named—"Post War Air Force Organisation", p. 31, at https://www.abhilekh-patal.in/jspui/handle/123456789/2734801
26. Source: National Archive of India file named—"Post War Air Force Organisation", p. 50, at https://www.abhilekh-patal.in/jspui/handle/123456789/2734801
27. A 12th Group, No. 233 Group, was also created in Bombay for Operation Roger (Takeover of Phuket) but was never operationalised and disbanded in June 1946.

28. Source: RAF Flying Units and Support Units since 1915 by Ray Sturtlvant.
29. *Vayu Aerospace & Defence Review* V/2012.
30. Source: National Archive of India file named—"Post War Air Force Organisation", p. 18, at https://www.abhilekh-patal.in/jspui/handle/123456789/2734801
31. https://www.rafweb.org/Organsation/Grp07.htm
32. https://indianarmy.nic.in/
33. https://www.rafweb.org/Organsation/Grp07.htm
34. https://www.britishmilitaryhistory.co.uk/docs-india-1930-1947-central-command-india/
35. https://www.rafweb.org/Organsation/Grp07.htm
36. https://indianarmy.nic.in/Default2.aspx?MnId=60ZkZs9dEb2z796rutmOaA==
37. https://www.rafweb.org/Organsation/Grp07.htm
38. https://www.britishmilitaryhistory.co.uk/wp-content/uploads/sites/124/2020/10/Central-Command-India-History-Personnel.pdf
39. Source: National Archive of India file named—"Establishment of No4 (Indian) Group and No. 4 (Indian) Wing", at https://www.abhilekh-patal.in/jspui/handle/123456789/2732258
40. Source: National Archive of India file named—"Post War Air Force Organisation", p. 9, at https://www.abhilekh-patal.in/jspui/handle/123456789/2734801
41. Review of Monthly ORBs of all the squadrons from the National Archives of the UK.
42. Source: https://www.abhilekh-patal.in/jspui/handle/123456789/2734807
43. http://www.joebaugher.com/usaf_serials/1943_2.html
44. Source: National Archives of India.
45. Source: wwww.bharat-rakshak.com
46. While the ORB of Poona from MoD History Division uses the term 2 Wing from May 1947 onwards, communication in National Archives material, Squadron ORBs continues to address it as RAF Poona till August 1947.
47. Source: https://www.vayuaerospace.in/Issue/202005311704580334.pdf
48. RAF Flying Units and Support Units since 1915 by Ray Sturtlvant.
49. Richard Mead. 2018. *'SAM' Marshal of the Royal Air Force the Lord Elworthy: A Biography*.
50. Bharat Kumar, *An Incredible War: IAF in Kashmir 1947–48* (New Delhi: KW Publishers, 2014).
51. PIB release of November 4, 1947 refers to the No. 2 Indian Group being commanded by an air rank officer since 1944, confirming the link to the past. See Appendix 1.
52. PIB release of July 26, 1949. Refer Appendix 2.

2. IAF Through Wars: A Story Telling

Bharat Kumar

While the Indian Air Force came into being on October 8, 1932,[1] when the same was notified in the Gazette of India and the first batch of Indian cadets undergoing flying training at Cranwell were commissioned on that day, 'A' Flight of No. 1 Squadron was raised only April 1, 1933, at Aircraft Depot, Karachi, with Flight Lieutenant Cecil Arthur Bouchier, DFC, as its Flight Commander. The newly commissioned pilots, the standard-bearers of a new fighting Service, joined the squadron only on May 11, 1933. The Depot Commander initially did not want Indians in the officers' mess, but with Bochier taking a firm stand, he relented and permitted the use of the mess by the Indian officers for a *probationary period.* Bouchier did not reveal his 'fight' with the Depot Commander when he addressed these young officers on their arrival at the unit. Bouchier described this address in his autobiography as follows:

> "When my first young Indian officers were seated in my office, I said I wanted to talk to them about the standards we, the standard-bearers of their new fighting service, must set in everything we do, on duty, off duty and in the mess. I told them that, with regard to the aircraft and engine maintenance and inspection, this was 100% in Royal Air Force and second to none in the world, and I wanted, with their help, to see to it that cleanliness, maintenance and inspection in our RIAF would be 150% if that were possible. Extra 50%, I said, was insurance against the day the RAF connection and supervision would be withdrawn, and the squadrons of the RIAF would have to stand on their own feet and maintain their own standards. When that day came, it was possible, I

> said, that the 150% standard might gradually fall. But so long as it did not fall below 100% of the Royal Air Force, they would be all right, and their lives as pilots would be long and happy ones."[2]

His young officers, who during their stay at Cranwell had excelled in the air with two of them vying for the flying trophy[3] and dominating on the sports field, did not let their Commanding Officer down but proved to the world with the highest possible standard of professionalism and excellent leadership which has been emulated by the generations of 'Indian Air Warriors' that has followed them since then. Bouchier, during his visit to India in 1959, commented: "The Indian Air Force is what it is today because of one thing only—the imagination, the courage and the loyalty of the first little pioneer band of Indian officers and airmen, for they were the salt of the earth ... they have built a great fighting Service ..."[4]

Similarly, despite extreme discrimination, the ground crew excelled in all spheres and surpassed their counterparts by a wide margin. Bochier was correct in his assessment as the Indian Air Force has been an epitome of excellence, as demonstrated during various wars in which it has been involved and today is considered one of the finest amongst the world's air forces.

This chapter looks at the excellence displayed by the Indian Air Force in various wars since its inception. Indian Air Force has been involved in the following operations/wars:[5]

- Pre-Independence Era
    - Operations in North-West Frontier Province (NWFP)
    - First Burma Campaign
    - Second Burma Campaign
- Post-Independence Period
    - Indo-Pak War in Kashmir 1947-48
    - Sino-Indian War 1962
    - Indo-Pak War 1965
    - Indo-Pak War 1971
    - Operation Pawan 1987-1989
    - Kargil War 1999

Operations in North-West Frontier

The British had been involved in operations in NWFP since 1848. The RAF was inducted for air support tasks immediately after the arrival of the first two RAF squadrons in 1916. The flying environment in this mountainous desert was challenging due to hazardous weather, high operating altitudes, and aircraft limitations. An RAF pilot needed many months of experience in local flying conditions before he could be considered 'operational'.[6] Indian pilots trained with 20 Squadron, RAF for three months in 1936. The Indian Flight operated independently from Miranshah in September 1937. It flew 337 hours in one month—a feat that had not been matched by any of the RAF flights until then.[7] This Flight flew 1400 hours in three months and maintained 100 per cent serviceability[8] and this ensured that from then onwards the Indians were considered at par with their RAF counterparts. In September 1938, Majumdar led a flight manned entirely by Indian personnel and created another record. This record was broken by the flight led by Flight Lieutenant Aspy Engineer in May 1939 logging 410 hours in a month with just four aircraft!

From August 1939 onwards, the IAF was given the responsibility of supporting operations in NWFP and this task continued till India's independence. The tribals targeted the aircraft both from below and from above. Mehar Singh and Arjan Singh along with their gunners were shot down in September 1938 and October 1941 respectively. All of them managed to drudge back to Miranshah, though, after some harrowing experiences. The decisive role played by the IAF ensured that the region was comparatively peaceful between 1939 and 1947. Aspy Engineer was one of the few pilots to be awarded the DFC for his performance in operations in NWFP.[9] In addition, three Indians were mentioned in despatches.[10]

First Burma Campaign

No. 1 Sqn was the first Indian squadron to be inducted into Burma and moved to Tungoo on February 1, 1942. 28 Sqn RAF, which was co-located with it at Ambala had moved there three days earlier. On its arrival, the 'Tigers' found their sister squadron completely demoralised and in total disarray. The Japanese attacked Toungoo the very next day but failed to do any damage to the assets of 1 Sqn. Squadron Leader Majumdar was so enraged by the attack that he, on his own, decided to attack the suspected Japanese launch airfield with his Lysander—a slow, high-wing monoplane army cooperation aircraft with a fixed undercarriage that had not been designed for bombing. It had no chance against far superior Japanese fighters. But that was not going to hold Majumdar back. The aircraft was loaded with two 250 lb. bombs on the borrowed racks on the aircraft's wheel spats. After a quick handling sortie in this configuration, Majumdar, escorted by two buffaloes attacked Mae-Haungsaun, the Japanese airfield in Siam and caused extensive damage there. The next day, he led his entire squadron to the same airfield, but this time unescorted. With this daredevil attack, Indians now stood out for their courage, daring and innovation. Thereafter, the squadron got down to its role of army cooperation and tactical reconnaissance. It also successfully attacked Japanese airfields. On March 1, Majumdar and his gunner[11] crash-landed in the jungle while on a reconnaissance mission. They managed to get back after trekking through the jungle for four days and were back in action immediately. Just before its return, the squadron also helped retrieve two Hurricanes that had been abandoned at Mingaladon by one of the RAF squadrons. The superlative performance of the squadron was recognised when the C-in-C, Lord Wavell flew in personally to congratulate the squadron on its professional excellence—a rare honour. Majumdar was awarded DFC for his daring performance.

In April 1943, 2 Sqn, IAF with its Hurricanes supported the First Chindit Operation. It was tasked to locate out-of-contact Chindit groups. It meant an extremely high quality of reconnaissance while flying at treetop heights for prolonged durations and looking into the jungles—and not at the jungles and spotting the Chindits who invariably took cover on hearing any aircraft, making the job of spotting even more difficult. The pilots had to keep a sharp lookout for any movements below the continuous green canopy of the Burmese jungles and for enemy aircraft around them. The advantages of aerial over ground reconnaissance of speed, the economy of effort and the extensive area covered were clearly visible. These advantages have been proven in every conflict. After pinpointing them, they were to lead transport aircraft to these observed locations. A normal sortie was of

3 ½ hours' duration; normally, each pilot flew two sorties a day. After its stellar performance, the Squadron returned to India after 41 days.

Second Burma Campaign

The IAF grew from just one to nine squadrons during WW II with all of them making significant contributions to the Allied war effort—the IAF's tenth squadron (No. 12) was formed in December 1945. The IAF was tasked with every possible role typical of any air force.[12] 1 Sqn was back in Burma in February 1945 and was based in soon-to-be-besieged Imphal. On April 10, Squadron Leader Arjan Singh while returning to Imphal late in the evening spotted a large column of the Japanese heading towards Imphal. He warned the base which scrambled all available aircraft. Arjan Singh quickly got his aircraft turned around and was airborne along with his entire squadron and attacked this force during the twilight dusk period—some of the aircraft had to use landing lights to spot attackers. This major attack was successfully foiled causing heavy Japanese casualties.

The main role of the IAF squadrons was fighter reconnaissance. These squadrons came to be known as "the Eyes of the 14th Army" and members of the 6 Sqn led by legendry Mehar Singh were dubbed: "the Maungdaw Twins," "the Buthidaung Twins," "the Kaladan Twins" and "the Arakan Twins"—the more famous name. The credit for these should go to the pilots who showed a phenomenal reconnaissance sense and capabilities.[13] The degree of professional excellence in reconnaissance can be gauged from three examples. 4 Sqn successfully located lost South African troops in a dense forest with some of the trees over 180 feet tall.[14] Massilamani located the cooking vessels of the Japanese under a thick jungle. Finally, most pilots could assess the means of transport by looking at the jungle tracks—they were as good as, if not better than, the professional tribal trackers.

The IAF squadrons were known for their very high-flying effort—2 Sqn flew a record of 740 hours in one month. Indian squadrons were understaffed but this did not affect the flying effort. Each IAF squadron also produced a record number of photo prints. Air Marshal Baldwin, during his visit to 6 Sqn asked Mehar Singh, "You only have five pilots besides you, how can you do the job?" "Sir, you leave that to me, I am the Squadron Commander," was the reply!

It was also in 6 Sqn that on February 15, 1944, Flying Officer JC Verma got the better of the Japanese Oscar and became the first Indian to score an aerial victory. There was also another probable kill by Flying Officer Dodler Ranga Reddy but the same was not reported for some unknown reasons.[15] As should be expected, there were casualties and some forced landings mostly due to enemy ground fire. Notwithstanding the constant threat from far superior Japanese aircraft and extensive ground fire, the pilots pressed on with their tasks. Flight Lieutenant Moolgavakar's almost drowned when his aircraft went on its back after it had force-landed on a beach. He was back in the air the very next day.

The quality of leadership displayed by the Indians was exemplary. One such example is that of Mehar Singh taking off a Hurricane that had forced landed in a field with a bent propeller and sent the original pilot in a Harvard aircraft. The contributions of the IAF in the Burma Campaign must be measured, not by the tonnage dropped by it or by the number of aircraft shot down, but by its ability to keep operating, in extremely difficult and challenging circumstances, in demonstrating to their army colleagues that they would be available whenever and wherever there was the need for them. The British government recognised the IAF's contributions by prefixing 'Royal" to its name with effect from March 1945.[16]

Indo-Pak War in Kashmir 1947-48

The Indo-Pak War in Kashmir 1947-48 was the first and the longest war (438 days)[17] independent India has fought to date. In this war, air power played a decisive role and if it was not for the Indian Air Force, Kashmir would have been lost to Pakistan in 1947 and the history and geography of India would have been quite different. No Air Force has had to deal with major military aggression under such adverse circumstances and in terrain unprecedented in modern warfare and sometimes at altitudes at which no air wars had been fought earlier.

Pakistan launched 'Operation Gulmarg' on October 22, 1947, but this information was passed to the prime minister only on the night of October 24. The Defence Committee of the Cabinet (DCC) met the next morning but the proposal to send Indian forces into Kashmir was not agreed. Governor General Lord Mountbatten opposed this move till the instrument of accession had been signed by the Maharaja. After the Maharaja of Kashmir acceded to India, the DCC finally decided on October 26 to airlift an Indian battalion to Srinagar in the IAF and civil Dakotas despite vehement and strong opposition by Mountbatten and the Service Chiefs who considered this an undoable venture. The challenging airlift went through early next morning and the aircraft managed to land at Srinagar airfield and saved it from the raiders who had reached Baramulla, 35 miles from Srinagar. Mountbatten later admitted that in his war experience, he had never come across an airlift of this order being successfully undertaken with such slender resources, and at such short notice.[18] The airlifts continued, and a full brigade was flown in within a short period.

The next day two Spitfires and a Harvard landed at Srinagar airfield whose runway length was less than 1,000 yards. There was a delay in the ground party fetching up due to a fatal accident, but the two pilots managed to refuel[19] and turn around the aircraft on their own and flew operational missions on required bases till the ground party's arrival on October 31. In the meanwhile, the buildup of air assets continued at Srinagar. On October 28 itself, Spitfires from Ambala and Harvards from Srinagar strafed enemy positions and checked the raiders' advance towards Srinagar and thus helped the Army to hold their own against a numerically superior enemy. This air support from Ambala and Srinagar ensured that the raiders were kept away from Srinagar airfield. In addition, Tempest commenced operation from Amritsar till their induction into Srinagar on November 7.

On November 3, raiders ambushed an Indian company led by Major Somnath Sharma[20] who fought back the raiders to the last man last round. The situation was critical as the safety of Srinagar airfield was in jeopardy. Spitfires were scrambled—they had to use a piece of the lone map of the area hanging in the Brigade Commander's office. The attack was successfully repelled and Srinagar airfield as well as Kashmir was saved.

On November 7, the Battle of Shalateng, perhaps the most decisive battle of Kashmir, took place. An aircraft spotted a big raiding column advancing towards Srinagar. In the ensuing battle, the raiders were surrounded on two sides by the Army while one side was patrolled by aircraft. The raiders suffered 300 casualties and had to retreat. The tide finally turned in India's favour. The Brigade Commander commented: "the IAF, in this crucial engagement and during following up, played a decisive role."[21]

Besides supporting the Army by carrying out reconnaissance, interdiction and close air support, the Tempests also supported the besieged garrison at Skardu by dropping canisters full of atta and other food items as well as attacking the raiders surrounding their fort. Unfortunately, this effort was too little and too late and Sakrdu had to surrender.

In the only aerial engagement of the War on November 4, 1948, two Indian Tempests intercepted a Pakistani Dakota dropping supplies; they were able to score some hits on it, but the Dakota managed to get into Pakistani territory and the Indians had to give up their chase.

Dakotas made a stellar and very significant contribution to the war in Kashmir. Besides airlifting the troops and materiel into the Valley, their main contribution was supporting the besieged garrison in Poonch which had a brigade, and approximately 40,000 refugees besides residents to be catered to. A strip for operation for Dakotas was carved out at Poonch. Dakotas continued to land there though they were constantly under enemy artillery fire. They even managed to transport artillery guns there at night. It was a back-breaking job, but the goods were delivered. Without a doubt, Poonch could not have survived without air maintenance. Similarly, other logistics requirements were fully met in every theatre where the Army demanded, air support.

"Dakota Bomber" was another Indian innovation which helped to keep the Pakistani gunners quiet if the aircraft were overhead. The accidental bombing by a Dakota Bomber of 'Muree' (instead of Muzaffarabad bridge) in Pakistan almost became an international incident.[22] Daring casualty air evacuations by the Dakotas kept the Army's morale up. Flight Lieutenant Ghadiok landed on a football field to fly out the casualties. Flying Officer Barty, with a suspect starboard engine, went ahead and landed at a field just fit for Auster aircraft and flew out with the wounded and thus saved their lives. Both flew these missions without proper prior clearance from their higher headquarters.

Once Leh was threatened, Air Commodore Mehar Singh flew a Dakota there on May 24, 1948. It was indeed a remarkable feat with an unpressurised Dakota aircraft, with no de-icing equipment and without oxygen available to the pilot and crew, crossing over uncharted mountain ranges at heights that the aircraft was not considered capable of going over. Thereafter, flights to Leh were a regular feature. Leh was thus saved by flying in reinforcements whenever required.

The IAF had to operate in Kashmir with several restrictions that prevented it from performing to its full potential. Some of these restrictions included the prohibition of attacking targets across Pakistan—even targets like bridges with some of their portion in Pakistan; enemy not to be attacked unless fired upon—this restriction was imposed during the last month before the ceasefire. The IAF was indeed a saviour of Kashmir in this war, not once but multiple times.

Sino-India War of 1962

It is a wrong perception that the IAF did not take part in the Sino-Indian War of 1962. While the combat fleet was fully deployed by mid-October, the government had ruled out its use in August 1962. Corps Commander, Lieutenant General Kaul did request offensive air support before the outbreak of hostilities, but the request was vetoed by Army Headquarters. On the other hand, transport aircraft and helicopters had been supporting the Indian Army both in Ladakh and in NEFA even before the adoption of the 'forward policy'. This policy could not have been enforced without the constant support by the IAF. The meagre resources of the IAF were one of the factors that limited the quantum of forces that could be deployed and sustained.[23] Were it not for the excellent work done by the transport and helicopter crews, there was no way the Army could have sustained itself during peacetime, leaving aside fighting the Chinese.

The air supply was the lifeline of the troops. Their requirements were either landed or dropped. The tempo of air support in the Eastern Sector started increasing from September 1962 onwards and reached its peak during November and December. For example, 11 Sqn flew 434 hours in

August while its effort went up to 2038 hours in November but reduced to 1149 hours in December after the ceasefire. The initial airlift capacity rose from 20-30 tonnes per day at Gauhati to 150-200 tonnes per day by the middle of October—an increase of nearly ten times.[24] Similar was the case with other units.

Overloading of transport aircraft and helicopters was the norm. Two Otter squadrons transported one brigade to the Walong sector.[25] Flight Lieutenant MK Chandrasekhar operating from the makeshift Teju airstrip had to walk over the sitting soldiers to get to the cockpit.[26] Flight Lieutenant KK Saini evacuated 30 soldiers in a Mi-4 from Walong while Flight Lieutenant PR Marathe did one better by picking up 37 soldiers from Tawang. Can one imagine a pilot officer sitting on the lap of the AOC-in-C in an Alouette which now had nine occupants on board?[27]

The flying continued from first to the last light of the day with numerous aircrew logging over 100 hours in a month. The shortages of aircrew compelled the Dakotas to be flown with a navigator acting as copilot and the fighter pilots manning the copilots' seats in Mi-4s. The helicopters did commendable work in casualty air evacuation missions during and after the conflict. Squadron Leader Williams evacuated a casualty in a Bell 47G at night—the helicopter was not fitted with night flying instruments and the casualty illuminated the instrument panel with a torch while the lone pilot flew the helicopter. Mi-4s also carried out a few night casevac missions.

Besides the IAF, services of civil aircraft were utilised for transporting personnel and materiel to the Eastern Sector. In addition, the American C-130s chipped in from November 3 but they only brought troops and equipment to Tezpur and, after the ceasefire, to Leh.

The terrain, the operating altitude and the weather posed challenges that no other air force in the world had faced till then. But the IAF aircrew faced these challenges and delivered the goods. They also innovated when so required. Dropping/transporting artillery guns in parts, and transportation of a refuller in a Packet aircraft by completely deflating its tyres to fit it into the aircraft, use of Mi-4s in photo reconnaissance roles are a few examples. Vampires and Canberras also carried out a few reconnaissance missions.

Ladakh was entirely dependent on air maintenance. It had its own challenges with airfields like Leh, Thoise, Chushul, Fukche and DBO being some of the highest airfields in the world. Various posts were air-maintained by fixed-wing aircraft and landing sorties by helicopters. The number of posts increased exponentially after August 20, increasing air maintenance tasks. The aircraft came under enemy ground fire at DBO and most of the DZs in the Ladakh sector, but the aircrew pressed on regardless. The aircraft also carried out reconnaissance sorties to pinpoint and assist the withdrawing forces and dropped supplies wherever required. Ladakh was served by An-12s, Dakotas, Packets (including jet-pack Packets—the first of these landed at DBO on July 23, 1962) and IL-14s.

The IAF knew what was in store for it even before the outbreak of hostilities and was prepared for the same. The establishment of a post at Galwan on July 5, 1962, was bitterly opposed by the Chinese. It was surrounded forcing India to air maintain it by helicopters. The personnel of the post were turned over by helicopters right under the Chinese nose—it was indeed a daring feat. On October 4, Squadron Leader SK Badhwar and Flight Lieutenant KR Narayanan, after completing the task at Galwan, had to land near Hot Springs due to an engine problem and were immediately surrounded by the Chinese. Showing a great presence of mind, they managed to restart the engine and fly away safely and land elsewhere. The helicopter did come under the Chinese ground fire. The post was finally run over when the Chinese launched their offensive on October 20.

The air maintenance task increased manifold after November 3, when Zoji La closed down, and the entire responsibility of transporting war material to Ladakh devolved on the IAF. It is to the IAF's credit that the troops did not suffer any shortages in this theatre. The Chinese had their eyes on Chushul Airfield (14,230 ft altitude) even before the hostilities. They encircled it on July 10, 1962. They, however, had to withdraw under Indian protests.[28] They attacked the airfield with light tanks on October 21, wiped out three outposts, controlled the Spangur gap, and posed a direct threat to the airfield. The only way to defend the airfield was by armour which the Indians did not have. The IAF went into action and managed to load AMX-13 tanks into An-12s at Chandigarh—a technical feat by any standard—and flew them across to Chushul—once again a flying marvel.[29] Thus, the Chinese threat was neutralised, and Chushul was saved. The tanks and artillery played a significant role in the defence of Chushul and the credit for their positioning should rightly go to the IAF.

During October-November 1962, the IAF airlifted double the average load lifted during the previous nine months, which speaks of its commitment and dedication. The air effort by the An-12s and IL-14 was about four times during October and November as compared to the earlier months.[30] The effort could have been higher but for lack of demand from the Army in the Western Sector. It is because of this stupendous air effort that no forward Indian position suffered from a lack of food, ammunition, or clothing. Such stores were air-dropped on the withdrawing troops wherever they were required and thus many lives were saved.

Indo-Pak War of 1965

The Indo-Pak War of 1965 was the first one in which both Air Forces confronted each other. The war was preceded by Pakistani actions in Kutch in April 1965 and where aerial photographs taken by Flying Officer Barbara exposed the Pakistani much-denied claim of the use of American weaponry.[31] To fulfil its aim of annexing the entire J&K, Pakistan launched Operation Gibraltar on August 5, 1965, and sent in Razakars and Mujahedeen to cause disruption and destruction in the J&K. To meet this threat, the IAF innovated by modifying its Mi-4s into armed helicopters.[32] These helicopters bombed, rocketed, and strafed the intruders and thus foiled Pakistan's plans successfully.

After the failure of Op Gibraltar, Pakistan launched Op Grand Slam in the Chhamb sector on September 1. The IAF went into action within less than 40 minutes from the go-ahead for the first Vampire formation to get airborne and attempt to thwart the Pakistani advance—the quickest reaction time by any Air Force in the world; and it did succeed in its mission, though three Vampires were lost in the process. For the next four days, both sides confined their operations within the J&K and in this period, midget Indian Gnats turned into Sabre-slayers. After government clearance, the IAF launched its counter-air strikes against

Pakistani airfields at the first light on September 6. The high quality of the leadership was evident when Wing Commander OP Taneja ordered Squadron Leader S Handa to strike Pakistani citadel Sargodha and that too without escorts, at mid-day because they had failed to do so during the pre-dawn strike. The mission was highly successful. It was also during that day's dawn strike that Squadron Leader AB Devayya flying a Mystere took on a far superior F-104 supersonic aircraft and shot it down—sadly, he crashed into the ground during the aerial combat. The IAF, thereafter, switched to interdiction and close air support missions. Canberras continued attacking enemy airfields at night—they successfully attacked Peshawar on the last day of the war—the day political clearance was accorded.

Wing Commander 'Pete' Wilson led the most daring attack against Badin's radar. His Canberra formation was un-escorted and attacked in broad daylight. Wilson fired delivering his rockets at the radar radome from below instead of diving from the top. Such an act had never been performed earlier. India was indeed the victor, and the war was not a 'draw' as dubbed by some analysts. India was able to achieve the assigned military objectives while Pakistan failed to do so and was thus a loser. The IAF played a major, significant, and decisive role in this victory.

Indo-Pak War of 1971

Unlike the previous wars, independent India had adequate warning of the same and was fully prepared when Pakistan launched its offensive with pre-emptive strikes at the Indian airfields on the evening of December 3, 1971—it miserably failed to achieve much success. Even earlier, the IAF gave an indication of the forthcoming results when its Gnats shot down three PAF Sabres on November 22 during the Battle of Boyra.

On the Western front, the main achievements of the Indian Air Force included a strike against Karachi Oil Farm on December 4 by Wing Commander DM Conquest's Hunter formation, the decimation of Pakistani armour thrust during the Battle of Longewala on December 4-5 by Hunters of 122 Sqn operating from Jaisalmer, and the IAF's support to the Indian Army in Shakargarh sector by S-22 aircraft operating from Adampur, and at Husseniwala and Sulemanki by S-22s from Halwara.

The IAF carried out extensive interdiction and provided close air support to the Indian Army along the entire front. Successful attacks on Attock Oil Refinery, Sui Gas Plant, and the powerhouse at the Mangla Dam besides the oil farm at Karachi practically destroyed Pakistan's entire energy resources. The IAF had established a favourable air situation very early during the war by targeting Pakistani airfields.

On the Eastern front, the IAF established air supremacy within three days by bombing the Dacca runway and provided extensive and unlimited close air support to the Indian Army advancing on various axes. The heli-bridging operation at Sylhet (December 7) by transporting troops behind the enemy lines under enemy fire during day and night and the Meghna heli-bridge (December 11 to 15) in which more than a brigade was heli-lifted across the mighty Meghna River were historical helicopter operations by the IAF. Paradrop of a battalion group at Tangail by a force of six An-12s, 20 Packets and 22 Dakotas and a resupply drop the next day, facilitated the capture of Dacca. This was followed by forcing the Pakistanis to surrender on December 16 as a direct result of effective and remarkable aerial attacks by MiG-21s and Hunters on the Governor' House on December 14.

The IAF demonstrated its innovation and flexibility during the war through the innovative use of MiG-21s and Su-7s in the night strike role against Pakistani airfields supported by a MiG-21 to aid in their recovery—these were misconstrued to be Russian Airborne Warning And Control System (AWACS); the use of Vampires for night interdiction and close air support role at heights above 16,000 feet in Kargil sector; deployment of modified armed Harvards against Mujhadeens in the J&K; and using An-12s as bombers against Pakistani targets—except for the raid over Skardu, the rest of the missions were at night. The IAF's contribution was decisive and historic and ensured a quick and decisive victory.

Operation Pawan 1987-1989

Operation Pawan was independent India's first and only out-of-country operation that commenced as a peacekeeping operation but soon got converted into a peace-enforcing one. Air power played a significant role in every facet of Operation Pawan. It was preceded by Operation

Poomalai on June 4, 1987, in which five An-32s, escorted by four Mirages, air-dropped humanitarian aid over Jaffna.

After the Indo-Sri Lanka Accord was signed on July 29, 1987, the IAF transport aircraft were positioned that very evening at various designations to induct the Indian Army into Sri Lanka early the next morning—the IAF response was even better than the much acclaimed Operation Cactus (to counter the coup in Maldives) in 1988. Nearly a hundred thousand sorties by transport aircraft and helicopters were flown during the operation and that too without the loss of even a single aircraft. Jaffna University Heli-drop under intensive Liberation Tigers of Tamil Eelam (LTTE) fire was the turning point of the operation and was carried out after the LTTE went back on the agreement. The combination of utility and armed helicopters enabled the Indian Peace Keeping Force (IPKF) to perform its role. The IAF was involved in almost every action by the army units against the LTTE. The transport fleet ensured air maintenance and sustenance of the entire IPKF. Were it not for the IAF, Indian Army would have suffered far greater casualties and would not have been able to achieve what they did.

Kargil War of 1999

The IAF commenced flying ELINT and photo reconnaissance missions soon after the discovery of Pakistani intrusions across the LoC in the Kargil sector. It launched "Operation Safed Sagar," on May 26, 1999, after political clearance was accorded. The conventional attacks by fighters as well as strikes by armed Mi-17s were given up after the loss of two fighters and one Mi-17 due to MANPADS. Bombing in the medium-altitude release was resorted to which ensured aircraft safety from MANPADS. Besides causing physical damage, the air strikes severely lowered the defender's morale and their will to fight. The effectiveness of the strikes compelled Pakistan to ask India to stop the use of air power in the very initial stages of the war. Airborne escorts successfully deterred the Pakistan Air Force (PAF) which only carried out combat air patrols within Pakistan. The destruction of the Muntho Dhalo logistic base practically broke Pakistan Army's back. The IAF used laser-guided bombs (LGBs) for the first time—Tiger Hill was the most prominent target where LGBs were used.

The fact that there was not a single location recaptured by the Indian Army that had not been targeted and softened by the IAF before its capture amply speaks for the IAF's contribution. But for the decisive role of the IAF during Operation Safed Sagar, it is doubtful that intruders could have been cleared off the Indian territory well before the onset of winter. The effective use of the IAF ensured that Pakistan had to plead for an unconditional ceasefire.

War Against Terror

Till 2019, the IAF had not been permitted to launch retaliatory strikes against Pakistan which has been pursuing cross-border terrorism. The Pulwama incident on February 14, 2019, in which 40 CRPF personnel were killed proved to be an inflection point and the IAF was ordered to strike deep inside Pakistan. On the night of February 25/26, the IAF Mirages struck a terrorist training camp at Balakot in Khyber Pakhtunkhwa in Pakistan killing at least 300 terrorists there. The PAF retaliated by launching a strike with a large package of F-16s and JF-17s. The strike failed to achieve its objectives but did lose one F-16 while also shooting down an Indian MiG-21. The successful strike by the IAF conveyed an unambiguous message to Pakistan that if there are any such incidents in the future, India would not hesitate to strike deep inside Pakistan at a time and place of its choosing. The message seems to have gone home and is a big step in India's fight in the war against cross-border terrorism.

Conclusion

War is an act of force to compel our adversary to do our will and to secure our will we must disarm the enemy. For this purpose, it is essential to have adequate force, if possible, with the latest technologies and, of course, well-trained and motivated personnel. The force must have full freedom of action and its entire might must be brought to bear against the enemy. However, in the real world, some restrictions are bound to be there, and the leaders have to not only follow them but also evolve suitable strategies and tactics to achieve the assigned objectives within the limited duration of modern wars.

A perusal of the various wars that the IAF has been involved in since its inception will indicate that it has been able to achieve its assigned objectives each and every time though the adversary enjoyed some technological advantages, the training and leadership ensured that this disadvantage was neutralised to a large extent by better training, tactics and motivation. As someone said, wars are the 'examinations' that not only test the quality of the force but the results are based on the achievements of the assigned objectives. As already mentioned, the IAF has always successfully achieved its assigned objectives—even in the Indo-China war of 1962, the transport and helicopter fleets delivered more than what was expected of them.

The Indian air warriors, by their professional excellence, valour, bravery, courage and leadership of the highest orders in the most challenging environments as displayed continuously in various wars have ensured that the IAF today occupies a very high stature amongst the world's Air Forces. This is evident by most of the advanced Air Forces wanting to exercise with it today. One is more than hopeful that the IAF would have an even bigger stature in the future and will be able to successfully deter/defeat any adversary who may try to challenge it.

Notes

1. *The Gazette of India*, No. 4, Notification 564, dated October 8, 1932.
2. Cecil Bouchier, *Spitfires in Japan: From Farnborough to the Far East*, BRILL/ Global Orientals, Netherlands, 2005, p. 156.
3. Amrjeet Singh and Bhupinder Singh were the contenders for the flying trophy or Groves Memorial Prize as it was then known. Aspy Engineer who joined the next batch went on to win the coveted prize. The British were so rattled by a native's victory, they changed the eligibility criteria and only the British could then onwards compete for the prize. Considering the flying abilities of persons like Majumdar, Mehar Singh, Arjan Singh and Prithipal Singh they would have been top candidates for this prize if they had been permitted to compete for it.
4. Bouchier, n. 2, p. 36.
5. Goa Operation 1961 and Operation Meghdoot 1987-till date have not been included.
6. Chaz Bowyer, *RAF Operations, 1918-38* (William Kimber, London, 1988), p. 169.
7. Somnath Sapru, *Combat Lore: Indian Air Force 1930–45* (KW Publishers, New Delhi, 2014), p. 50.

8. Pushpindar Singh, *The Himalayan Eagle, History of the Indian Air Force* (Society for Aerospace Studies, New Delhi, 2007), p. 47.
9. KN Dutt, *A Coin of Indian Metal, The Life of Wing Commander KK Majumdar* (The Christian Literature Society for India, Bangalore, 1949), p. 136.
10. These were Squadron Leader S Mukerjee, Flight Lieutenant MK Janjua and Sergeant Kartar Singh.
11. Havaldar Rustomji.
12. These diverse tasks included interdiction, tactical reconnaissance, close air support, strikes against sampans, smoke laying, artillery direction, leaflet dropping, 'Nickle drop', escorting shipping and Dakotas and even being pathfinders for the RAF Spitfires, etc.
13. Other pilots were equally competent in reconnaissance.
14. Operational Record Book of 4 Squadron as quoted in Bharat Kumar, *The Beginning: A History of Indian Military Aviation 1901-1947* (IMR Media, Gurgaon, 2021), p. 541.
15. Ibid., p. 554.
16. The prefix "Royal" was dropped on India becoming a Republic, i.e., on January 26, 1950.
17. The IAF was with the IPKF in Sri Lanka from July 30, 1987 to January 9, 1989 (528 days). However, the IPKF operation cannot be strictly speaking termed as a war.
18. Bharat Kumar, *An Incredible War: Indian Air Force in Kashmir War 1947-1948* (KW Publishers, New Delhi, 2007), p. 52.
19. Due to the non-availability of refuelling facilities at Srinagar, fuel for the fighters used to be decanted from the incoming Dakotas into jerrycans.
20. He was the first recipient of Param Vir Chakra.
21. Bharat Kumar, n 18, p. 71.
22. Ibid., p. 181.
23. In peacetime, 18,000 and 25,000 tonnes of supplies were required annually to supply the NEFA and Ladakh areas respectively; 70 per cent of this total was air-dropped. This requirement went up to 600 tonnes a day against the IAF's capacity of 400 tonnes. The British assessed the annual air-drop requirement as 153,000 tonnes and annual landed tonnage as 95,000 tonnes.
24. SN Prasad, et al., *History of Conflict with China* (History Division, Ministry of Defence, New Delhi, 1962), p. 354.
25. As narrated by Air Marshal J.S. Rai and quoted in Bharat Kumar, *Unknown and Unsung: Indian Air Force in Sino-Indian War of 1962* (KW Publishers, New Delhi, 2013), p. 243.
26. As narrated by Air Commodore MK Chandrasekhar and quoted in Bharat Kumar, n. 14, p. 209.

27. As narrated by Wing Commander RK Sinha and quoted in Bharat Kumar, n. 14, p. 232.
28. Ibid., p. 261.
29. Ibid., p. 264.
30. Operational Record Book of No. 44 Squadron as quoted in Bharat Kumar, n. 14, p. 277.
31. The IAF was not committed in Kutch except for Barbra's mission.
32. Bharat Kumar, *The Duels of the Himalayan Eagle: The First India-Pakistan Air War (1-22 September 1965)* (IMR Media, Gurgaon, 2015), pp. 18-22.

3. Helicopter Saga of the Indian Air Force

Nitin Sathe

Introduction

Although the design and development of a vertical lift, heavier than air machine began well before the aeroplane, it was the aeroplane which first took to the skies in December 1903. Thereafter, it took almost 36 years for the helicopter to arrive on the scene when the Germans designed and developed the Focke-FA-61 and used the subsequent models to transport the senior brass during the Second World War, also utilising it for reconnaissance and direction of artillery fire.

The very fact that the helicopter came on to the aviation scene so late tells us that it was a complex machine to develop and fly. Strategists and scientists of that era opined that it was more important to develop the fixed-wing aeroplane and therefore, the development of the helicopter was stunted to a large extent. Treating this machine as a secondary requirement continued right up to the 1960s, but the successful use of these machines in the Vietnam conflict made even the nay sayer's realise the importance of this noisy, vibrating and unstable platform.

The IAF, born out of the seeds of the RIAF, was a small fighter-oriented force at the time of independence. Lack of funds, lack of futuristic thinking and the fact that helicopters hadn't yet come into their own ensured that the Indian armed forces kept pushing the projected need for these machines to a later date.

Whilst the projection of the requirement of these machines was made as early as 1949 by a high-powered committee, the helicopters first arrived in India from the United States of America in the form of the Sikorsky

S-55 only in 1954. By this time, the Indian armed forces had also drawn some lessons from the US helicopter deployment in the Korean war where the first of the Combat Search and Rescue (CSAR) and Casualty Evacuation (CASEVAC) missions were successfully carried out.

Post training on the S-55, the first of the helicopter pilots were posted to the newly raised '104 HU' and this unit became operational in 1957. This was the time that trouble on the northern and eastern borders with China had commenced; and the Army was in dire need of support for its troops deployed in the far reaches which could only be done by helicopters.

The growing military requirements in the run-up to the 1962 conflict with China as well as the requirement of heli-lift for floods and VIP duties saw the fleet of 4 helicopters being extensively utilised almost all over the country. The experience gained here was to be put to good use in the war with China.

1962 Indo-China War

While the transport support to the troops all along the Chinese border continued to the far-flung advanced landing grounds in the build-up to the war, the helicopters also had a major role to play during the hostilities. A large number of troops were transported into Walong in the northeast corner of our country and supply drops to the forward posts manned by our poorly equipped troops were achieved under enemy fire.

The first helicopter casualties also occurred during this war when the flight commander of 104 HU-Squadron Leader Vinod Sehgal's helicopter was shot by the Chinese near Tsangdhar. The Chinese took the almost intact aircraft as a trophy but Sehgal and his passenger, Major Ram Singh, are believed to have been killed in cold blood by the ravaging enemy. The second aircraft flown by the CO of 105 HU, Squadron Leader AS Williams which went looking for the downed helicopter was also shot down by the Chinese. Fortunately, Williams survived and avoided capture despite the fact that he too received bullet injuries.

By the start of the hostilities, Mi-4 helicopters from Russia had been received and were also utilised to carry out casualty evacuations and supply drops in Tawang, Walong and Ladakh sectors.

1965 Indo-Pak War

The importance and effectiveness of the helicopter was again reaffirmed during the 1965 war. Mi-4 helicopters were inducted into Srinagar and used against the infiltrators in the valley by smart and timely modification of the machines to drop 20 lb bombs and fire 0.5-inch guns with a fair amount of success. The helicopters were also used in CASEVAC, supply drop and recce roles during the conflict. According to figures available, almost 2.5 lakh kg of the load was dropped and air-landed along with 500 troops; 1,227 bombs dropped and 7,000 rounds expended during this conflict by the Mi-4's alone, flying a total of 966 hours in 1297 sorties.[1] Post this conflict, the IAF went in for an increase in the helicopter inventory so as to provide the requisite support in peace and war to our army. Let us delve into history and understand the yeoman service that IAF helicopters have done in the yesteryears by looking at salient aspects of their contribution to the 1971 conflict, the operations in the Siachen Glacier and the IPKF operations in Sri Lanka.

Figure 3.1: The Helicopter Finally Comes of Age: 1971 Indo-Pak War

Source: Air Cmde Ram Mohan Sridharan.

The 1971 war finally saw the helicopter fleet of the IAF proving its metal and reiterating to the strategists how important they were in the roles envisaged during the war. While the western front only saw the helicopter operating in more standard roles like CASEVAC, recce and patrolling, the eastern front saw the most amazing feat achieved by these machines and the men who flew them. The credit for the same must go to General Sagat Singh, the veritable and dynamic IV Corps Commander and Group Captain Chandan Singh, who, as station commander Jorhat, commandeered the transport and helicopter air operations in the Eastern Theatre.

For the first time in the history of IAF helicopters, Special Helicopter Borne Ops (SHBO) was carried out, wherein, waves upon waves of Mi-4 helicopters dropped troops and war-fighting equipment across the Meghna River in East Pakistan, forcing the Pakistani forces to capitulate and surrender. This was an audacious and daring plan, and how it made history needs to be told.

As per the original Army plan for the offensive in the east, three divisions were tasked to attack from north, central and south of the western boundary of East Pakistan with clearly defined primary and depth objectives. IV Corps, operating from the east had to do a similar attack from the east, thereby annihilating the Pakistani forces by the sheer volume of the attack alone.

Planning for the IV Corps operations had begun as early as May of 1971, with General Sagat Singh, the Corps Commander given the go ahead by General JFR Jacob, the Chief of Staff Eastern Command. Gen Jacob was busy with the clandestine training of the Mukti Bahini in as many as ten camps along the border, and left the planning and execution of the offensive with Gen Sagat. Sagat, an intelligent commander, realised that the operations from the east would be thwarted by the imposing Meghna River which was, at places, almost 19 km in width.

The river ran in a north-south direction along the eastern border, and south of Dacca, joined the Padma River which drained into the Bay of Bengal through the large riverine and mangrove-infested delta. Whilst the Padma River provided a natural tier of defence to the west of Dacca, the Meghna protected the capital city from the east. Movement of their own troops in this foreign land due to the forested terrain interspersed with rivers was going to be tough and the planners were aware of the difficulties these rivers posed to the progress of operations.

Figure 3.2: Bangladesh Political Map

Source: Istock Photo, at https://www.istockphoto.com/vector/bangladesh-political-map-gm544475614-97866077.

Threatening, or an attack on Dacca was never an objective given to any of the Indian forces, either by the Chief of Army Staff in his orders to the Eastern Army or subsequent orders to the GOCs by the Army Commander himself. Sagat, in his wisdom, thought of the possibility of threatening Dacca to bring about an early end to the war. This needed the operations to progress beyond the river Meghna. The only way to achieve this was to get the IAF to provide an 'air-bridge' over the river and facilitate the crossing of a sufficient number of troops and loads to carry the fight towards the capital city from multiple directions.

The Army did not have the required wherewithal; and hence the capability to take such a large force across a water body of this size. If stranded at the river, the troops of IV Corps would be sitting targets for the Pakistani Air Force as well as their Infantry; and this needed to be avoided at all costs. Sagat turned to Chandan Singh and asked him to work out feasibility of such an airlift with the resources available. Both the dynamic leaders were in agreement that if this plan worked, the war in East Pakistan could be brought to a quick closure.

Having carried out an assessment, Chandan Singh reported to Sagat that the IAF choppers were in a position to carry out the air bridging operation. SHBO training at the Mi-4 unit commenced in all earnest on orders from Chandan. The army units under the command of Sagat sent their troops for joint training and this helped the soldiers to practise their part of the task of loading, offloading as well as emplaning and deplaning operations. Minimal time over the Drop Zone (DZ) was of the essence and the entire operation needed to work like clock-work.

Chandan also realised the vulnerability of the choppers to enemy fire during such operations and decided to train the crews on SHBOs by night. This was essential to improve the survivability of the choppers as well as to maintain a fair degree of surprise and deception.

Very soon, the pilots were trained and ready to take on some mock exercises which were executed well, giving the commanders the much-needed confidence to execute this audacious plan. The Air Force HQ, using all the planning tools it had, was of the opinion that the choppers in the east were, at best, capable of a company lift; and this was soon to be proved wrong. Chandan, Sagat and Squadron Leader Pushp Vaid—the flight commander of the Mi-4 unit located at Kumbhigram flew in a Chetak helicopter and carried out a clandestine recce of the proposed landing sites and selected the ones that provided adequate cover and concealment as well as were well out of immediate reach of Pakistani troops.

The Chetak had a providential escape during this recce mission itself, when it was fired at with small arms. General Sagat suffered a minor bullet-graze injury to his hand while the co-pilot, Flying Officer Sidhu suffered a more severe bullet wound to his knee and needed medical attention. Despite this, the mission was accomplished and the chopper returned to base with 38 bullet holes!

The Helicopters with their crew and their Army counterparts now waited for the balloon to go up and receive orders for the 'real''live' missions. As D-day drew closer, with the war plans activated, 8 helicopters of the 110 HU at Kumbhigram were positioned at the Corps HQ at Teliamura while the rest of the serviceable choppers were disbursed at other small landing grounds. With the war formally declared on December 3, the choppers were moved to Kailashaher.

Figure 3.3: Phases of Operations

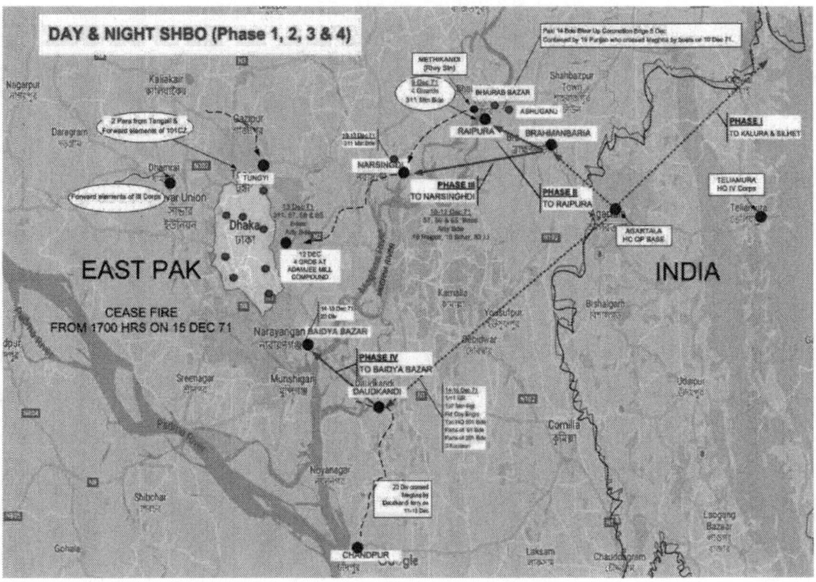

Source: Air Commodore Ram Mohan Sridharan (Retd).

The first air bridging operation was planned for the DZ at Sylhet on December 7, with a task to heli-lift 4/5 Gorkha Rifles. As the SHBO operations found success, additional missions were planned and the operations shifted further south. A fair amount of tactical mistakes on both sides coupled with poor intelligence led to some amount of confusion and uncertainty amongst commanders and decisions taken in this fog of war eventually turned out in favour of the Indian forces. It is estimated that the heli-bridging operation brought an early end to the war by at least 8 days. The success of the Gorkhas in Sylhet earned them battle honours, albeit at a loss of almost 25 per cent of their strength.

The air bridging was essentially carried out in four phases along the eastern border of East Pakistan. At the end of every phase, operations shifted southwards from bases selected in close proximity to the holding formations inside enemy territory. With this, the exposure time in the enemy area was reduced to the minimum. The entire sortie flown with tactical routing was generally accomplished within 35 to 40 minutes in all phases; the aircraft having to fly inside enemy-held territory for about half that period at best. The first SHBO was successful and 600 odd troops of 4/5 Gorkhas and 13,000 kg of load was air-landed on the other side of Meghna. The Gorkhas immediately went into action and engaged the two brigade strength holding the built-up area of Sylhet.

The second phase of operation commenced from Agartala into the captured territory of Brahmanbaria from where troops of 4 Guards and 311 Mountain Brigade were air-landed at Raipura and Methikandi on December 9, 1971. The aim was to fight the enemy strongholds at Bhairab Bazar and Ashuganj and keep the half-destroyed bridge over the river at Ashuganj intact to facilitate the further move of our troops towards Dacca. These operations were carried out mostly by night over two days with success. The operations continued from Brahmanbaria from December 10 to 13, wherein troops of three brigades (57, 59 and 65) and some artillery pieces along with some remnants of 18 Rajput and 10 Bihar were inducted into Narsingdi.

By this time, the war was drawing to a close and Pakistan appeared to be capitulating; and by December 15, the Gorkhas at Syhlet had ensured a localised surrender of the two brigades after a bloody battle. The last of the SHBO missions were planned on December 14/15 wherein troops of 1/11 Gorkha Rifles, 197 Mountain Regiment, Engineers along with remnant troops of 61 and 301 Brigade and two companies of 3 Kumaon were across the Meghna. Largely due to the success of the SHBO, troops were now well poised to threaten Dacca and this also ensured that no Pakistani reinforcements could fetch up to defend the Garrison. In fact, the first artillery shells to land inside the capital town was fired from one of the guns transported by helicopters.

In totality, the operations saw 6,000 troops and 20,000 kg of war-fighting material transported by the helicopters of the IAF. The Mi-4 was a delicate machine, and with extensive usage, required the technical staff to work overtime through the war to keep them fighting fit; and for this, our valiant airmen need special mention. Historians have rightly said that the role of the IAF helicopters in East Pakistan was the most important factor which led to the Pakistani army yielding to the Indians in just 13 days. They also go on to say that if it wasn't for the dynamic leadership of General Sagat and Group Captain Chandan Singh, the war would have ended differently.

Figure 3.4: The Chetak and Cheetah Operations in the Siachen Glacier

Source: CO 114 HU, Air Force.

This story is dedicated to Wing Commander SP Puranik, the Commanding Officer of 114 HU, who, in 1984, led his unit into a war that continues even today. Incidentally and sadly, Puranik lost his son Siddharth in the same operation 16 years later in 2000. 'Nik sir' as he was known as in IAF circles, breathed his last on February 25, 2023 at Secunderabad.

Siachen Glacier was a small piece of land whose importance was not understood when the new country of Pakistan was carved out by the British. The cartographers, in their wisdom, felt that there was no need to clearly demarcate the border in the higher reaches of the Himalayas where no human actually ventured to go due to the harsh terrain and weather.

Little did anyone think that this small triangular piece of land barely a few kilometres wide and 70 km in length (covering an area of 2,553 sq km) that was home to the glacier, would become a bone of contention in the years to come and the longest battle over its occupation still rages on as we complete 40 years of its occupation by the Indian armed forces.

For India, keeping the Pakistanis out of the glacier was important since it would have allowed China and Pakistan to open up a road connection through the Chinese-occupied territory of Aksai Chin. Over time, both sides understood the importance of this piece of land; and started to plan to occupy it to gain a tactical, strategic and psychological advantage. Pakistan started with small expeditions which included foreign nationals into the area and then followed it up with military recces under operation code-named 'Abadeel'. It was the Indian Army which finally beat their counterparts in the race to occupy the glaciated heights of Siachen in what came to be called as Operation 'Meghdoot'.

To support our own troops, helicopters were an inescapable necessity and the Cheetah helicopter was found to be the most suitable since it could operate, although with minimal load, at heights of above 15,000 feet and land on small helipads made next to the border posts created by the army. These helicopters became the lifeline of the Siachen operations as the army presence swelled up to almost 5,000 men deployed at heights where only skilled mountaineers attempted to go.

Figure 3.5: Siachen Glacier and NJ9842

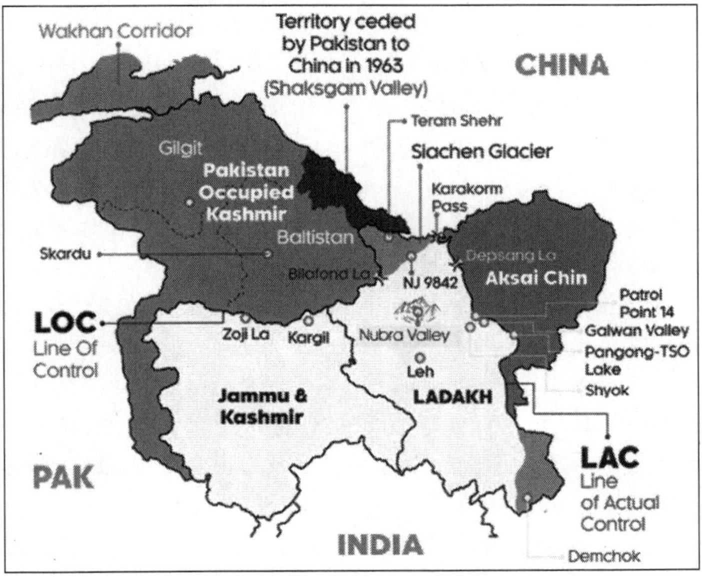

Source: Organiser.org https://organiser.org/wp-content/uploads/2023/02/50a49f38-ce64-45d2-b1ba-5331f421e0ac.jpeg

But before that, the first chopper to land in the glacier was in fact, the heavier Chetak. On October 6, 1978, one Chetak was tasked to land on the glacier at what came to be called the 'track junction' helipad at 17,400 feet to drop some supplies. Thereafter, sorties in this area were only flown on as required basis in support of the numerous mountaineering expeditions sent in the area till 1984.

The Cheetah helicopter began operations as soon as the troops started taking up posts in the area. Flying and living conditions were not at all easy for the pilots and technicians as well as the helicopter itself. To brave the cold condition during flying, pilots had to wear obsolete heavy winter clothing, which was uncomfortable and restricted movement. Also, they had to suck oxygen from tubes (called the Hookah!) in the absence of a dedicated oxygen system while the heating system in the aircraft was, at best, below par. Besides this, the lack of oxygen, white-out conditions and the sheer risk factors involved compounded the difficulty levels.

Missions in the glacier start at sunrise and end by mid-morning due to deteriorating weather as well as turbulence after 1200 hours. The aircraft, therefore have to be made ready by the technicians in darkness, well before first light. Servicing these machines in dark and freezing conditions was yet another daunting task for our airmen who had to get out of their beds around 3 am every day to get the helicopters ready for their never-ending missions. Today, we have much better living conditions, better winter clothing, good weather forecasting, good food and improved basic amenities at the forward airfields of Leh, Thoise and Base Camp which have made operations safer and tolerable.

The single-engine helicopter was operated in pairs to enhance safety. While they flew at max all up weights possible, manoeuvring in the rarefied atmosphere in the narrow valleys needed exceptional flying skills. Pilots posted to the unit had to undergo special 'glacier clearance' before they were allowed to captain the aircraft in these operations. Flying in these conditions also led to a large amount of stress on the helicopter components and constant technical monitoring of the machine was the need of the hour. And, to top it all, during landing at forward helipads, pilots were often greeted with shelling and firing from the other side leading to further stress.

The weather in the high reaches is unpredictable and it is extremely risky to fly missions post noon after which, thundershowers, blizzards and snow storms are a common phenomenon. Poor instrumentation in the helicopter meant that the pilots had to practice visual and 'seat of the pants' flying, (pure 'manual' flying) an art which has seen a decline in the recent years with modern technology and gadgetry helping safer flying and recovery.

In these conditions, there was hardly any room for error and pilots mastered this art of flying at the margins of all envelopes—be it human, aerodynamic or power related. They were the best of the best; (they still are!) the skills acquired here came in handy throughout their careers.

114 HU, which operated ex-Jammu in the initial stages of Op Meghdoot was permanently relocated to Leh a few months into the operations, and has been flying in the area ever since. For almost four decades now, the unit has operated a permanent detachment at Base Camp. Today, they operate alongside Army aviation aircraft leading to better synergy and bonhomie between the two Services.

Over time, the Cheetah aircraft has been replaced with the new improved re-engined and redesigned 'Cheetal' (Modification carried out by Hindustan Aeronautics Limited, Bangalore-HAL) which has better-carrying capacity than that of its mother aircraft. The presence of HAL-produced Advanced Light Helicopter (ALH) and the medium-lift Mi-17 class of aircraft in the area has augmented the efforts needed to keep the troops fighting in this highest battlefield in the world well-fed, well-armed and above all, motivated.

The men who guard our land borders in this area always await the sweet sound of the Cheetah christened 'Macchar' (Mosquito) by the troops. Besides getting them some fresh rations, water, ammunition, etc., the helicopter brings with it much-awaited letters from loved ones and also helps to evacuate and save the lives of comrades who have fallen prey to the vagaries of nature or odd shrapnel from the enemy fire. Many machines and lives have been lost to the risky glacier operations and this is a tribute to all the valiant soldiers who have made the supreme sacrifice in keeping our country safe.

One cannot end this piece without describing an incredible event that happened in June 1990 which brings out some magnificent aspects of soldiering in this part of the world. Two helicopters were on a mission to drop supplies at one of the highest and the most difficult places in the glacier named 'Amar'. One of the helicopters developed a technical snag in its engine after landing and had to be switched off. (Switching off the engine at that altitude isn't permitted since the engine may not be able to start again.) The crew of the defective helicopter were rescued to safety by the second helicopter while the unserviceable machine remained on the helipad in sight of the enemy.

Time was at a premium and it was decided to attempt to repair the helicopter and fly it back. It wasn't any ordinary repair though. The engine of the Cheetah that weighed 182 kg had to be replaced! That, plus a whole lot of tooling, cranes and technicians had to be taken on-site for this incredible mission done with enemy shelling going on. The aircraft, at that altitude, can carry barely 75 kg of load at a time. A lot of innovations needed to be done to get the heavy engine to the helipad.

The ground party along with their tools were first dropped at 15,000 feet to get them acclimatised before they found their way to the helipad. The unserviceable aircraft on the helipad had to be manually lifted by the troops of the Sikh Light Infantry guarding the post and moved to another site so as to make way for the rescue helicopter to land. How they did it is another incredible story in itself. Around the flat piece of ground where this helicopter was parked for an engine change, the troops created a wall of snow and ice blocks so that it remained out of the vision of the enemy who, otherwise, would have made it impossible for the technical activity to take place unhindered.

To fly in the engine, the weight of the helicopter was reduced by removing the seats, doors and even the tail skid! Next, they filled in just as much fuel for a one-way mission to the helipad where fuel in jerricans was pre-positioned for a quick refuelling. The battery too was removed after starting the engines! Despite all these efforts, the aircraft, flown by the Commanding Officer of the Unit, Wing Commander Mahendra Goli, was way above its load limits.

The CO's superior flying skills ensured a safe landing on the helipad and the engine was offloaded by the army jawans in quick time. One can only imagine how the technicians would have got the unserviceable engine off its mountings after the removal of dozens of secure bolts, pipelines and accessories; and, thereafter fitted the new one in those freezing conditions. The aircraft was flown back by two young pilots just after a cursory ground run and leak check; wherein, in normal situations, the aircraft would have had to be air-tested for its air-worthiness before being ferried. This was a special case and special dispensations were given for the mission to succeed. It was, no doubt, a lesson in 'jointmanship' and an unbelievable achievement which proved that our armed forces can achieve the seemingly impossible when the chips are down.

When one visits the Helicopter Unit at Leh, a bright board greets every visitor, "*We do the difficult as a routine … the impossible may take a bit longer*". This statement more than sums up the helicopter operations in the Siachen Glacier.

Figure 3.6: Entry to Siachen Glacier

Source: CO 114 HU.

Figure 3.7: Helicopter Operations in Op Pawan, Sri Lanka

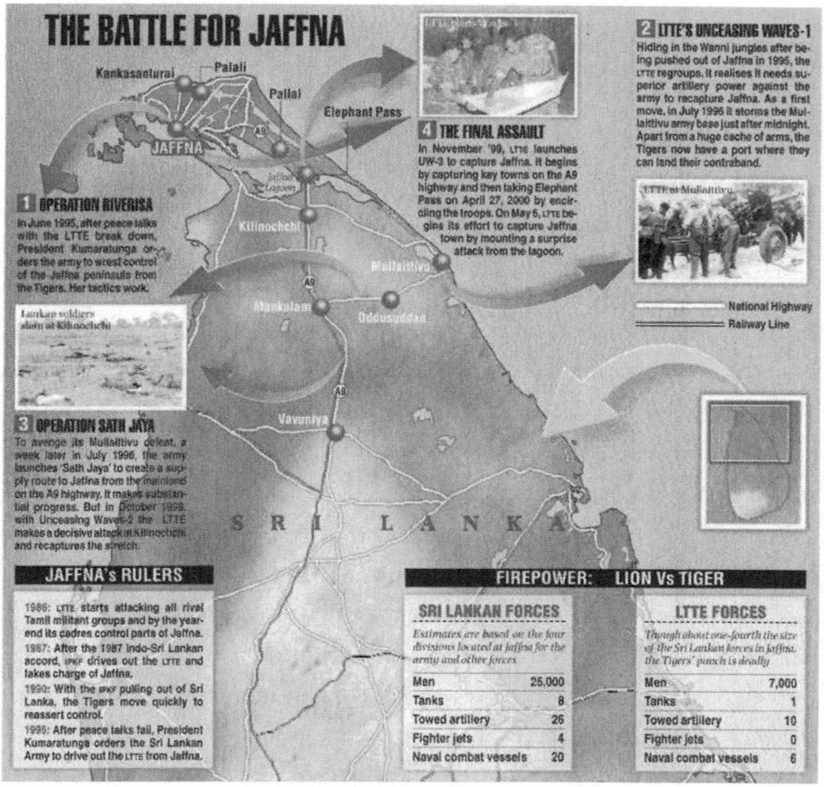

Source: *India Today*, at https://www.indiatoday.in/.

The Liberation of Tamil Tigers Elam (LTTE), a Tamil militant separatist group commenced fighting for a separate Hindu homeland for the Tamils in the north eastern part of Sri Lanka after its formation in the 1970s, led by their versatile leader, Velupillai Prabhakaran. With time, the atrocities against the local Sinhala population increased, trying to coerce the government into capitulation. The situation soon became bloody and threatened to go out of hand, and in response, the Sri Lankan army troops were moved in to restore peace. The threatened LTTE cadre, in retaliation, started attacks on the army leading to further mayhem and bringing the country into international limelight. The shock waves of the militancy were also being felt in nearby south India as well as in Delhi and the Indian government opened up diplomatic channels to bring about a quick end to the internal strife which seemed to be heading for civil war. When it became clear to the Sri Lankan government that it was not possible to thwart the rebels, they approached the Indian government to send in 'Peace Keeping' troops. Quickly, In response to this request, the first two Indian Peacekeeper battalions arrived on the island nation in mid-1987, post-signing of the Indo-Sri Lanka peace agreement.

By October of the same year, not finding success in the operations, a decision was taken to disarm the militants by force; and this was the beginning of Operation 'Pawan'. Whilst the IAF fighters were used minimally for escorting transport aircraft and a few photo recce missions, this operation saw the extensive use of fixed-wing transport aircraft and helicopters. While troops were ferried in from mainland India using transport aircraft, the helicopter usage in operations was more extensive and fraught with danger.

The Mi-8 was the workhorse and played a crucial role during these operations while the Chetak and Cheetah of the army and IAF were used for communication and other allied roles. The Mi-25 helicopter gunships were inducted slightly later (February 1988) for offensive tasks along with the Mi-8 which also had some armament delivery capability. In addition, the Chetak Anti-Tank Guided Missile (ATGM) helicopters were utilised for a few missions to fire the obsolete wire-guided AS-11-B1 anti tank missiles into the militant-infested jungles, albeit only for their deterrent value.

By the time the issue was resolved and the de-induction of troops took place in July 1989, the Mi-8 fleet had flown over 35,000 sorties, lifting over 100,000 troops and 5,700 tonnes of load, a no mean task by any standards. Despite minor battle damages due to small arms fire, this task was achieved without the loss of any machine. The augmented rotary wing effort of Chetak and Cheetah of the Army and the IAF flew around 500 sorties, lifting 600 troops and 25 tonnes of load whilst the Mi-25 attack helicopters flew 500 sorties in the offensive role.

The operations in Sri Lanka by helicopters can be divided into two phases which were in keeping with the phases of the operations planned by the army. Phase-1 commenced with the LTTE taking up armed action against the Indian Army in October, resulting in the first of the casualties on our side. This phase saw some heavy fighting and was more akin to conventional infantry operations of war.

The aim of Phase 1 of the operations was to wrest control of Jaffna; and along with that, destroy the main militant hideouts and logistic pads in the jungles around the town which was home to the training camps as well as the leadership. The overall concept of the operation involved capturing Jaffna, sealing off the northern peninsula to cut off the escape routes over land and sea, and having done that, clearing the areas around Jaffna.

The LTTE was well fortified and had laid a large number of booby traps to cause maximum attrition to the Indian forces. Move over land or by sea routes was not possible for our troops since the area was under the control of the militants and therefore, helicopter SHBO missions were planned to induct the troops into the area. In the first mission in early October 1987, a night SHBO was planned in conjunction with a multi-pronged advance and attack by ground forces at the Jaffna University. The 10 Para Commandos (now Special Forces) and the Sikh Light Infantry soldiers made up the two-company heli-lift to be done by 4 helicopters in five lifts each.

The aircraft were to land in the heavily defended Jaffna University stadium, but all the troops as planned could not be landed due to various reasons. Bloody battles commenced as soon as the first of the troops touched the ground; the LTTE appeared to have received inputs of the plans, and lay in wait to counterattack. Whilst the helicopters were also fired at, they did not suffer much damage during the first two waves of the mission. One helicopter with 20 commandos had to return to base unable to find the DZ and more confusion prevailed on the ground at the launching base as regards who were to go in the next wave leading to further delays.

The LTTE had assessed the repeated landing and take-off direction of the Mi-8's and were quick to reposition their heavy machine guns and RPGs by the time the Mi-8's came in for the third wave. Pilots did report the RPG flashes which were way off mark, but the machine guns scored multiple hits on all the aircraft. Luckily for the crew, there was no major damage except for a hydraulic leak in one helicopter, and all the aircraft were flown back to Palay Airfield—the mounting base for the mission. Luck surely was on the IAF side since none of the aircrews were injured, but the Army lost about 30 odd men that night with several more wounded. The four helicopters were out of action for the next few days and our engineering staff did a very good job to get them online to participate in the fighting which was to continue for the next four weeks with retaliatory attacks by the LTTE.

Although we claimed success after prolonged fighting for almost a month, it was at a huge loss of 350 casualties and 1,100 injured out of the 20,000 troops that participated in this particular phase of operation. Post-operation analysis brought out a lot of lessons and led to a change of approach and tactics by the leadership. Of the lessons learnt as given below, some were more or less applicable to the whole of Operation Pawan.

- A joint briefing is a must for better coordination. In the first phase, the air force component commander wasn't available for the planning and briefing for the mission. This led to a fair amount of confusion.
- Maps of the entire area of operations were not available for the troops as well as the pilots flying the missions. Whatever maps were available with the Sri Lankan army were in short supply. Tourist maps were used by the helicopter crew for some missions. Mapping of some areas of interest was done later by the Mirage 2000 aircraft. More of this effort could have been made available to get hot intelligence

as required for all the missions over areas to find out the LTTE strongholds.

- Recce of the landing site was done from a higher altitude to be safe from enemy fire and this led to inadequate knowledge of the terrain and the Landing Zone itself. Lessons from the 1971 Meghna operations could have been gone through to help in intricate planning of this SHBO.
- Jointness is required between operating forces right from the planning stage itself. Post mission analysis revealed that the Task Force Commander of the IAF was not very clear about the objectives and plans of the army.
- Tactics to fly and land in enemy-held territory weren't worked out and practised. The take-off and landing directions of the helicopters in this mission remained fixed which led to the LTTE getting potshots at the machines by the third mission. Also, the tactics used by the helicopters needed to match with the overall plan of the ground forces and this was not done.
- Lack of intelligence was another issue that came to the fore. While each agency had a chain of intelligence gathering, the lateral exchange was not defined and sometimes, major gaps were left during sharing of information. Adequate use of fighter aircraft and satellite photography could have been resorted to, to get information on the LTTE deployment and hideouts.
- There was a poor system of communication with higher HQ especially in respect of the IAF. The operations were not monitored at the operations room of Southern Air Command which was responsible for the overall conduct of operations. Satellite communication and radio relay through transport aircraft flying over the area of operations could have led to better command and control.
- Related to the above, the compatibility of some of the radio sets held by the IAF and the army wasn't good and this led to a further lack of communication. After this incident, an air officer was positioned at Jaffna as the task force commander to coordinate and exercise full operational control over all IAF operations in Sri Lanka. A joint operations centre was also set up to ensure better communication

between the forces and the higher HQ's and also for lateral communication between operating units.

Post this phase, after Jaffna fell, the LTTE dispersed into the jungles of Vavuniya and Batticaloa and their tactics changed from conventional to guerrilla. Hereon, they avoided direct confrontation with the Indian Army troops but continued to use ambushes, booby traps, IEDs and mines to cause attrition. The LTTE also stopped their movements by day and used the cover of darkness to move through the jungles they knew so well. Fighting these cadres who moved in small groups in these dense jungles at night without adequate maps and good intelligence was an uphill task for the army, and therefore, the IAF helicopters were again tasked with a multitude of missions during the second phase.

One of the soldiers who took part in the operations describes the difficulties faced, "We did not know who we really were fighting. It was difficult to even discern a Tamil from a Tiger (LTTE Cadre). Anyone above 10 years of age-be it a boy or girl could be carrying weapons. We had casualties when a small girl took out a weapon from under her clothing and shot at point-blank range!"

The Mi-8 fleet was soon augmented with fresh aircraft and crew from the mainland. The Mi-25's were also called in for offensive support for Phase 2. The Mi-8's, modified with pods, carried out rocket firing besides their usual role. The Chetak ATGM aircraft was used to fire missiles. On the Army side, besides fresh re-deployment, additional troops were flown in from the mainland to bring about a quick end to the war. It was the Mi-25 helicopter which proved its worth during this conflict, especially in the second phase of operations.

Attack Helicopter Operations

125 Squadron, based at Pathankot in Punjab was tasked to move to the island just after cessation of the disastrous Jaffna University operations. The squadron was trained to fight alongside the Army, albeit in the anti-tank role and was soon to be bloodied in the deadly operations. Besides the lethal Scorpion missiles used for anti-armour, it could fire the 57 mm rockets, had an accurate 12.7 mm four-barrel Gatling gun and could

drop 250 kg bombs; these area weapons were put to good use during the conflict.

The LTTE feared the Mi-25 and code-named it the 'Mutulai' which is Tamil for crocodile. The presence of the machine overhead made them run for cover even without a single shot being fired. The Mi-25, besides being assigned specific targets, also went on 'show of force' missions and provided an escort to heliborne missions, helping to keep the enemy heads down.

The first mission flown by the Mi-25 on November 6, 1987 dropped 4 bombs over an LTTE hideout and destroyed it. These aircraft were thereafter utilised for taking on moving vehicles, boats, bunkers, jetties, campsites and ammunition dumps every effectively. Identification of a friend or foe was easy since only the LTTE cadre moved about while the civilian population stayed indoors in the battle area. Some media reports, however, wrote about many civilians and innocents killed during these attacks.

> "The effectiveness of the Akbar's (as the Mi-25 was called) particularly in the search and strike role, can be best judged by the radio intercepts and interrogations. The fact that this weapon system forced the LTTE to move only by night is itself an indication of its effectiveness. This way it also helped in bringing about a shift in the initiative from the LTTE to our ground troops. Besides causing severe casualties, this helicopter had a tremendous psychological impact on the LTTE. The extensive damage caused to them, particularly to their fortified strongholds, greatly assisted and perhaps hastened the process of forcing the LTTE to abandon Phase 1 of direct confrontation with the IPKF and switch to Phase 2 of guerrilla tactics", writes Air Vice Marshal AK Tiwary.[2]

Operations in Sri Lanka lasted for 967 days, and the Indian side, though able to almost annihilate the LTTE, lost 1,200 men and had 3,000 plus injured which is rather heavy for a 'peace keeping' operation. Operation Pawan, over the years, has drawn a fair amount of criticism after post mortems carried out by chair-borne experts; but one cannot, and must not take away anything from the valiant soldiers of the Indian armed forces who fought fearlessly to restore peace in a country which wasn't even theirs.

Conclusion

Today, the armed forces the world over are looking at employing pilotless helicopter drones during war, taking over some of the high-risk tasks hitherto being done by manned machines. But, that, for the IAF, is still a long way off. The helicopter fleet of the IAF has grown into a formidable force that carries out operational missions as a routine, day in and out. The Indian Air Force today, boasts of 35 units, manning almost 400 helicopters. A majority of the helicopter fleet is of Russian origin, with the medium-lift Mi-17 series making up maximum strength. The attack helicopter units have been augmented with the state-of-the-art 'Prachand' Light Combat Helicopter produced indigenously and also the US-made AH-64. The heavy lift capability has been enhanced by bringing in two units of Boeing Chinooks whilst the utility helicopters have been augmented by the HAL-manufactured Advanced Light Helicopter (ALH) 'Dhruv' which has replaced some of the ageing light helicopter fleet of Chetaks/Cheetah helicopters. The IAF today has plans to induct replacement helicopters for high-altitude operations, and, with a push to self-sustainment under the 'Atmanirbhar Bharat' policy, we will soon see more indigenously manufactured helicopters inducted in our growing inventory.

Helicopters have proved it over and over again that, whether it be peace or war, they will continue to play a pivotal role in the outcome of future operations. The ubiquity and flexibility of the platform make it a versatile machine capable of carrying out a multitude of tasks, something that has been proven time and again through history.

Notes

1. Arunav Sinha, "Silent but resilient IAF choppers fought the 1965 war", *TOI*, October 2, 2015, at https://timesofindia.indiatimes.com/city/lucknow/silent-but-resilient-iaf-choppers-fought-1965-war/articleshow/49189186.cms, accessed on January 22, 2023.
2. AK Tiwary, "Helicopter Operations in Sri Lanka", *Indian Defence Review*, Vol 27(3), October 31, 2012, at http://www.indiandefencereview.com/news/helicopter-operations-in-sri-lanka/, accessed on January 22, 2023.

4. IAF's Airlift Capability: Face of the Nation

Rajeev Sachdeva

> "No matter how good the armed forces are, they are of no value if they cannot be in the right place at the right time and in the right numbers."
>
> —Adm James R. Hogg, USN

The Versatile Transport Fleet

The Indian Air Force (IAF) provides unique war-fighting capabilities that are essential to joint operations. Within the basket of both offensive and enabling air power capabilities, the ability to rapidly focus combat power and resources where required, offers any nation a first-mover advantage. Frequently and especially in the opening stages of a conflict, air power may be the main manifestation of combat power that is brought to bear against an adversary. One of the critical components of this capability is the ability to rapidly position and sustain forces at a place and time of one's own choosing.[1]

This pivotal capability is an essential ingredient of modern operations and supports the desired effects to deter, dissuade, or destroy the adversary. While other forms of military power have some degree of inherent mobility, the scale of flexibility and responsiveness that the IAF's air transport and helicopter fleets provide is essential for driving the desired outcomes in war, less-than-war situations and routine military deployments and sustenance in diverse and hostile terrain such as the ones in which the Indian Army is deployed.

A critical component of combat power is the ability to rapidly position and sustain forces at a place and time of one's own choosing.

These attributes of speed, reach, flexibility, versatility, the concentration of force and responsiveness are provided by the IAF's Transport fleet. Carriage of military equipment between theatres for routine deployments, reinforcement and evacuation of stranded personnel and diaspora from troubled spots around the globe is a demonstrated role of the IAF. Over the years and with the gradual accretion of platforms and capabilities, the IAF has developed world-class expertise in diverse force multiplier roles. Among these are Special Operations, Air-to-Air Refuelling (AAR), Airborne Warning and Control Systems (AWACS), Intelligence, Surveillance and Reconnaissance (ISR), Casualty Evacuation (CASEVAC), Search, Rescue, Mercy Missions and airborne command platforms for national leadership.

Dynamics of Transport Operations in the Indian Sub-Continent

The aim of military air transport is to provide mobility and logistics support to the armed forces.[2] The primary task of transport forces is to provide airlift and logistics support for other military units both between and within theatres of operation, including the immediate vicinity of the battlefield. Air mobility has always been the key to major conflicts. Neither surface forces nor offensive air forces can move with speed in the absence of commensurate logistics and air mobility support provided by the transport fleet.

India has one of the most diverse landscapes and climatic variations spread across its geographical expanse.[3] To the south, we have a vast coastal region along with island territory. To the west, we have deserts, and even salt pans and marshy land. Northeast has lush green hilly regions and mountain ranges with an average height of 5,000 to 10,000 feet. To the north, we have the mighty Himalayas, mountains with an average height of 20,000 to 25,000 feet. To defend this vast territory, we can't afford a separate specialised force for each region, the soldiers, in rotation, guard the boundaries in all regions.

The IAF has a special role to play, not just in wartime, but even in peacetime. The Army operates in areas that have no rail or road connectivity with the mainland. To provide them with their daily needs, the IAF works 24 x 7 and *'Air Maintains'* their inaccessible post in the north, the northeast and even in the south for our island territory of Andaman and Nicobar Islands throughout the year. The volume of peacetime load that is air-dropped or air-landed annually is unapparelled to any military in the world.[4]

It is mandated that the attributes of speed, reach, flexibility, versatility, concentration of force and responsiveness are provided by the IAF's air transport fleet. Air logistics, carriage of military equipment between theatres for routine deployments, reinforcement and evacuation of stranded personnel and diaspora from troubled spots around the globe is the main task of the Transport fleet of the IAF.

The Geography of the Tasking. Along with the IL-76 and the C-17, the major load of the tasking of the transport fleet as depicted below has been with the An-32 and Avro aircraft:

(a) Air Maintenance, both in the North and the North East.
(b) Coastal requirement.
(c) Para trooping.
(d) Island territories connectivity.
(e) Connectivity of the major hubs of military stations.
(f) Logistics air bridging.
(g) Strategic asset movement.
(h) HADR, both internal and International.
(i) Strategic troop movement.
(j) Communication of the senior leadership.
(k) International requests.
(l) Both ab-initio and operation training.

Air Transport Capability

Air transport operations are classified under two broad headings:[5]

Strategic Airlift. A strategic airlift is the carriage of passengers or cargo between theatres (Inter-theatre) or to any place within the area of interest. Strategic transport role is resorted to support a broad strategic or operational goal and it includes:

(a) **Projection of Capability.** This capability is of particular importance to a state, which aspires to project its influence beyond its borders.

(b) **Evacuation of Personnel.** This includes evacuation of stranded citizens/military personnel from trouble spots around the globe. Indian Air Force, during the Gulf War, had set a world record with its large-scale evacuation from Kuwait and Lebanon.

(c) **Reinforcement and Re-supply of Forces Deployed.**

(d) **Support for Own Forces in Global Exercises.** The IAF has in recent times acquired the capability to operate across the globe. Its fighters regularly take part in joint exercises in Europe, Africa, Middle East and across the Atlantic in Alaska with foreign Air Forces, a capability acquired with the induction of the IL-78 flight refueling aircraft. In addition, IL-76 and AN-32 aircraft have been used for airlift operations to enable move of our fighter units for these exercises.

Tactical Airlift. Tactical or theatre airlift is the carriage of passengers and cargo within a theatre (Intra-theatre). A tactical airlift is resorted to for rapid and responsive movement within an area of operations to meet specific tactical goals. Aircraft performing tactical airlifts have traditionally been smaller, shorter-range aircraft such as the An-32, C-130 or C-27. Tactical operations are broadly classified under two heads, namely, Tactical Combat Missions and Tactical Support Missions.

(a) **Tactical Combat Missions.** These missions are flown in direct support of own forces, such as:

- (i) **Air Landed Missions.** Delivery of troops and equipment by transport aircraft into prepared or semi-prepared airfields in or close to the battlefield.
- (ii) **Air Dropped Missions.** Paradrop of troops or airdrop of tactical mission payloads into the battlefield if no suitable airfield is available for air-landed missions.
- (iii) **Special Forces Missions.** Insertion/extraction of special forces either air landed, or air dropped.

(b) **Tactical Support Missions.** Tactical and special missions are flown, not for direct military action but in support of military action like:

- (i) Air-to-Air Refuelling Operations.
- (ii) Airborne Warning and Control Functions.

(iii) Search and Rescue.
(iv) Casualty Evacuation Missions.
(v) Air Maintenance-tactical re-supply.

History would have been Different but for the Transport Fleet

> "I have come here to congratulate you on your remarkable work in saving Kashmir and creating confidence among the people of India in their country's strength. Without you Kashmir could not have been saved."
>
> —Pt. Jawahar Lal Nehru to IAF Dakota Crew

The First India-Pakistan Conflict

On October 27, 1947, the oldest transport squadron, 12 Sqn, was tasked to carry out the first-ever air landed operation in a battle zone conducted by independent India. It was an operation that saved Srinagar and laid the framework for what the state of Jammu and Kashmir looks like today. Three Dakotas carrying troops of the First Battalion of the Sikh Regiment (1 SIKH) touched down in Srinagar in the nick of time to save the airfield from imminent capture by advancing *lashkars* (tribal armies) embedded with regulars from the Pakistan Army.[6]

Another crisis was developing at Poonch, which was literally under siege as lashkars and the Pakistan Army shelled the town incessantly with their howitzers. Poonch would have fallen by early 1948 had it not been for hastily building a *kuccha* airstrip that supported a risky but possible landing by Dakotas to sustain the besieged town through air landed and air dropped operations, with induction of light artillery into Poonch that offered a befitting response to the enemy firing, an operation that was executed by day and night in extremely hazardous operational conditions.

In early 1948, Pakistan also launched Op Sledge to seize the areas of Skardu, Kargil and Zozila, and ultimately wrest control of the Leh Valley. To foil this attempt even as a column of Indian troops attempted to breach the Zozila pass and open the second land route from Manali, Air Commodore Mehar Singh led the first airlanded task force into Leh as Dakotas and opened an airbridge to Leh by ferrying in 250 soldiers of Second Battalion of 4th Gorkha Rifles.

Airborne Assault to Capture the Poongli Bridge

One of the key catalysts of the collapse of the Dacca garrison in December 1971 was the psychological impact of the Tangail airdrop. 2 Para was tasked to launch an Airborne Assault to capture the Poongli Bridge on the river Jamuna in East Pakistan. Six An-12, two Caribous, 20 C-119 Packets and 22 Dakotas were engaged in this assault and captured the Poongli bridge giving the advancing Indian Army, the manoeuvrability to side-step the strongly held main road to Dacca and advance right up to Mirpur Bridge at the gates of Dacca.[7]

Innovative use of Transport Fleet for Bombing

To augment its bombing capability, the IAF worked for years and thus employed An-12 transport aircraft for bombing during the 1971 conflict to disrupt Pakistani formations attempting to cut Kashmir from the rest of India and several thousand Pakistani casualties, and heavy losses of their armour were reported. The concept to deploy An-12s for bombing was first mooted in 1967 and this innovative idea was encouraged by the then Chief of the Air Staff, Air Chief Marshal Arjan Singh. The aircraft's rear 35mm turret gun was activated and a rear radar was installed. The aircraft was configured to carry 28 to 36-500-pounders for carpet bombing.[8]

Out-of-Area Contingencies

The coup d'état attempt in 1988 that threatened to overthrow the government of President Gayoom in the island republic of Maldives, presented the IAF's transport fleet with an opportunity to showcase its capabilities in the first joint out-of-area-contingency operation that was launched by India in response to an SOS from a friendly neighbour.[9] The air landed assault on Hulule airfield in the Maldives, code-named Op Cactus, was launched by the Indian Air Force and Indian Army on November 3, 1988, to foil the coup and rescue the President of Maldives.

Strategic Airlift

The Successful evacuation of 1,11,711 Indian citizens from Iraq, Kuwait and Jordan in 1990 by operating 488 refugee flights over a period of 59 days by Air India and IAF has been a world record. Similar missions were carried out from Lebanon in 2006 (Operation Sukoon), Libya in 2011 and Yemen (Operation Rahat) in April 2015. Operation Rahat, involved the deployment of C-17 aircraft of the IAF and Air India's aircraft to airlift thousands of people in distress.[10]

Strategic airlift from the war zone during the Ukraine crisis in February 2022 of over 3,000 citizens in 'Op Ganga' in just six days is reflective of our commitment to the Indian diaspora that being a rising global power. IAF undertook evacuation from Afghanistan by C-17 and C-130 aircraft seamlessly with minimum support to the aircraft once they left India. In four days close to 700 personnel were flown out of Kabul safely.

Humanitarian Assistance and Disaster Relief (HADR)

Also, termed as mercy missions by aircrew across the world, the IAF's transport fleet has always been an early responder during disaster relief operations at home and overseas. The Tsunami that hit the Andaman and Nicobar Islands and all the nearby island-states around India including Sri Lanka and Indonesia on December 26, 2004, proved to be a test bed for the transport fleet.[11] Not only did the IAF render speedy relief to India's own island territories that were devastated, it also swung into action with the spare capability to join rescue efforts in Sri Lanka and Indonesia. Whether it is the repeated and effective responses to earthquakes, floods and forest fires, or the more specific responses to the Bhuj,[12] Kashmir or Nepal earthquakes,[13] the increasing sophistication of airlift platforms such as the C-130 and C-17, have allowed the IAF's transport fleet to emerge as a powerful instrument of diplomacy and statecraft.

Special Operations and Force Multipliers

Of all the contemporary air transport capabilities that any leading power must possess, Special Operations[14] have seen significant accretion in the IAF. The IAF regularly trains in near realistic conditions and has the capability to execute a swift brigade-sized airborne assault in large formations of over 40 aircraft with a mix of all types, the An-32, IL-

76, C-17 and C-130 bunched together. IAF force multipliers based on air transport platforms such as AAR, AWACS, AEW, Communication Intelligence (COMINT) and Electronic Intelligence (ELINT) act as tri-Service enablers that allow operators to plan and execute missions that were hitherto considered complex and complicated to execute. They have literally changed the way full-spectrum operations are planned and conducted. By plugging in easily to the IAF's Integrated Air Command and Control System (IACCS),[15] IAF's 'Eyes in the Sky' or AWACS offers significant value to both offensive and air defence operations and acts as an excellent situational awareness and decision-making tools for the effective conduct of the entire range of offensive and enabling air operations.

Covert Special Operation missions by C-130 in recent years of pulling out our embassy personnel and their equipment from Herat in an Engine Running Ops was a shining example of Out of Area Contingency (OOAC) Spl Ops undertaken with less than 24 hrs notice. Another mission on August 19, 2021 was a high-risk limited intel operation undertaken immediately after the fall of Kabul. Landing past midnight on NVGs in an uncontrolled air space avoiding a number of near air misses with UAVs, the only call the crew remember as they approached the dark airfield was, "Land at your own risk". Both these aircrew earned gallantry awards for these extraordinary missions. In a daring operation carried out on the intervening night of April 27-28, 2023, an Indian Air Force C-130J Super Hercules aircraft rescued 121 personnel from a small airstrip at Wadi Sayyidna, about 40 km north of Khartoum, in strife-torn Sudan.

Casualty evacuation is a crucial, task in contemporary wars and conflicts as the 'golden hour' can be the difference between life and death. This particularly holds good in potential conflict zones in hostile terrain that stretches across thousands of kilometres along the LoC and LAC. Most effective when conducted in tandem with the IAF's and the Indian Army's helicopter fleets, this role involves the availability and positioning of aircraft with specialised medical facilities at forward airfields to create a 'medical bridge.' While most transport aircraft of the IAF can be modified for this role, it is the C-17 in its medical evacuation (MEDEVAC) and ambulance configuration that can be a game-changer in both conflict and natural disaster scenarios.

Assistance during Pandemic

On February 27, 2020, 76 Indians and 36 foreign nationals from Bangladesh, China, Madagascar, Maldives, Myanmar, South Africa and the USA were evacuated from Wuhan (China).[16] The aircraft also carried medical supplies as a symbol of goodwill to China. IAF's C-17 also brought back 58 Covid-stranded Indians from Iran on March 10, 2020. During 'Operation Sanjeevani'[17] over 1,500 sorties, 3,000 hours and 2 million km, a distance akin to going around the Earth 55 times is a testimony to how busy the IAF has been in its COVID-19 mitigation efforts distributing life-saving medical equipment and oxygen cylinders, due to its massive logistical muscles.

Fig 4.1: Ways Means and Ends

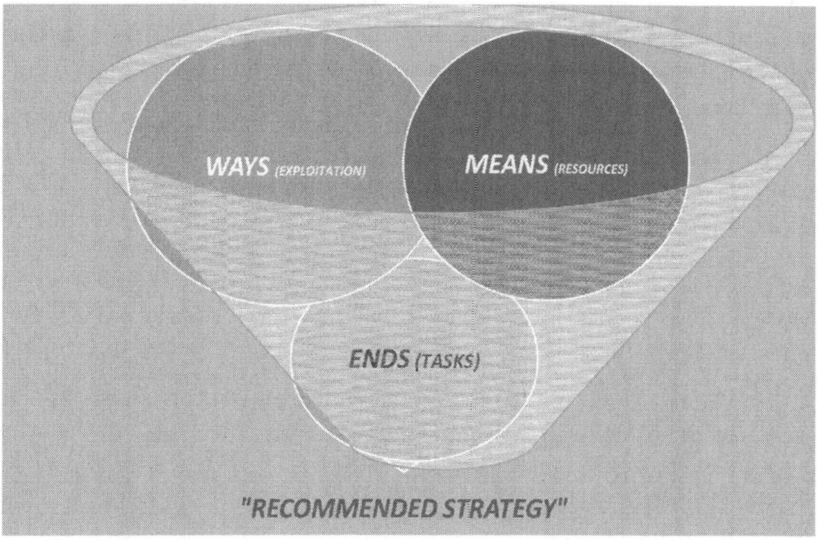

Source: Author's creation.

Tasking, Exploitation and Resource Utilisation

Means (Resources)

The transport fleet has over 250 aircraft of eight design variants in its inventory and they are from Russia, Ukraine, Germany, Britain and the USA, and at induction had 56 Avro (British), 115 An-32 (USSR - now

Ukraine), 17 IL-76MD (USSR - now Russia), 56 Dornier (German - under license by HAL), six IL-78—(USSR - now Russia), 12 C-130J (USA), 11 C-17 (USA) and contracted for 56 C-295MW (16 Airbus Spain + 40 Tata Sons India).[18]

Ways (Exploitation)

The rate of consumption and thus the exploitation of the available flying hours of the entire fleet depends on the task in hand, trained aircrew and maintenance support philosophy. The life of an aircraft and its components depend on either, number of flying hours or the number of landings or on a calendar basis or conditional and thus can be exploited accordingly. Despite an increase in the tasking, if the exploitation rate has been sub-optimal and has never been commensurate to the flying hours available till the life expectancy of any fleet, it could be either due to the life being *Un-exploitable* (Operational and HR Reasons) or the *Maintenance Philosophy* (Spares Management and Supply Chain Reasons) were not in sync with the *Operational Capability* (Specified Aircraft Life).

Ends (The Task)

Since independence the transport fleet of the IAF has been undertaking the tasks of *Troop Movement* and *Air Logistics*, however, the task has been exponentially increasing decade by decade and so has the demand for this potent fleet. The transport fleet routinely undertakes thousands of missions for air logistics, moving thousands of tonnes by air landing and air dropping for the sustenance of the Indian armed forces, Para military and the state governments both in the North and the North East. This task, for the last four decades, has been entrusted only to IL-76MD and An-32 fleet, however, after the induction of C-17 aircraft, the bulk load both ways, has been taken over by this strategic aircraft.

The East, North, South and the island territories are connected to the mainland through regular couriers and the IAF conducts hundreds of scheduled couriers transporting lakhs of passengers per year. The transport fleet is also engaged in planned annual exercises conducted by the three Services and during the entire phase of the exercise, as a potent strategic fleet, has the capability to launch thousands of missions both by day and night, airlifting thousands of tonnes of load and personnel.

Natural disasters come uninformed but timely succour is provided by this very transport fleet for relief, rescue and rehab, both within the country and for international requests. IAF has flown hundreds of missions transporting relief, men and material within the country and also supported friendly foreign countries including Bangladesh, Myanmar, Iraq and Indonesia. Maldives, Nepal, Bhutan and once USA. For Supply Chain Management, the transport aircraft regularly move essential aircraft spares and rotables between Base Repair Depots (BRD), Equipment Depots (ED) and Movement Control Units (MCU). The fleet also flies hundreds of missions every year across international borders to friendly foreign countries.

Capability Upgrade of the Fleet

In the 1980s, due to accidents and age, the legacy fleet of Packet Fairchild, Caribous, Dakotas and Otter aircraft were phased out, leaving only the An-12 and Avro fleet to fill the void created by the grounding of Caribou and Packet aircraft. Avro aircraft, with its primary role of communication, was inducted into Air Maint for Leh, Thoise, Kargil and for drops in the Arunachal sector. The aircraft was also deployed for Para Trooping and Search & Rescue with a permanent detachment at Carnicobar. The transport fleet of the IAF underwent a capability upgrade in the mid-1980s when 17 IL-76MD aircraft, 115 An-32 and three dozen Dornier DO-228 aircraft joined this potent fleet. After another 30 years, the fleet and the capability were again upgraded with the induction of 11 C-17 Globemaster-III and 12 C-130J Hercules aircraft, which joined the legacy and ageing fleet of the IL-76, An-32 and the Avro aircraft thus augmenting the strategic lift capability of IAF, presumably for the next three decades and soon 56 C-295MW will join the versatile fleet.[19]

A mix of 20:60:20 ratios of Heavy, Medium and Light airlift capability is required to accomplish both the strategic and tactical airlift tasks. The medium-lift capability provides greater flexibility to switch roles and keep the fleet size trimmer to accrue cost-cutting benefits. The IL-76 and An-32 will need to be replaced in the coming years. Atmanirbharta in transport aircraft manufacturing has commenced with the manufacturing line being set up in India for C295MW.

Preferred Operational Strategy

It is mandated that the attributes of speed, reach, flexibility, versatility, concentration of force and responsiveness are provided by the IAF's air transport fleet. Air logistics, carriage of military equipment between theatres for routine deployments, reinforcement and evacuation of stranded personnel and diaspora from troubled spots around the globe is the main task of the transport fleet of the IAF.

Action to satisfy the felt need to replace the Avro, An-32 and IL-76 aircraft was initiated by the IAF a decade ago and has fructified in the form of 56 C295MW aircraft. It is important that the mix of the legacy fleet and the C-295MW are deployed with utmost care so that the tasking capability of the IAF enhances and there is smooth induction of the C295MW into the transport fleet of the IAF.

Strategy Dynamics with C-295MW

Capability voids in the medium-lift would be visible after a decade when the legacy fleet, for need of spares, could slowly start to reduce. 56 C295MW would then require a boost, either by increasing the numbers or by inducting the MTA, the RFI for which has already been floated by the IAF. Employment of C-295MW becomes very critical or else voids in tasking would be glaring into the IAF as soon as the medium-lift capability starts depleting. A pragmatic utilisation of the depleting Avro, An-32 and IL-76MD along with the rising numbers of C-295MW is the need of the hour and is recommended in the subsequent paragraphs. In the next decade, the first 16 C-295MW could be available in three years as they are being ferried in straight from Airbus Spain and the rest 40 would be in a joint venture in India, the first aircraft has been flight tested on May 8, 2023, in Spain. These aircraft would gradually complement the legacy fleet.

C-295MW was approved by the Cabinet Committee on Security (CCS) as the Avro replacement but has the capability of undertaking the roles of An-32 aircraft as well needs to be inducted into the roles being performed by the An-32 and IL-76MD aircraft as well, because a replacement of 115 An-32 and 17 IL-76MD is yet to get CCS approval. All three aircraft could be number plated by the time all the C-295MW are inducted. C-295MW is an 8-tonne class aircraft and possesses an operational capability higher than both the Avro and the An-32 aircraft and thus should start filling the voids created both by the Avro and the An-32 aircraft. Till the time a replacement for An-32 reaches the procurement stage, C-295MW would have to play a double role and accomplish the task both for the Avro, depleting An-32 and the IL-76MD.

Utilisation Rate and Tasking of C-295MW

The first 16 aircraft, which will be rolled in by the Airbus industry of Spain have to be inducted both for the communication duties and the air maintenance in the Northern sector. However, till the An-32 are available, the air maintenance in the Eastern sector and the air bridging task could remain with An-32. The communication duties could be with the Avro, and Dornier aircraft, with C-295MW joining in gradually. A robust spare support and trained aircrew should be available for round-the-clock operations of the C-295MW. The Airbus Original Equipment Manufacturer (OEM) has not specified a life and thus the exploitation could be maximum, provided the rate of spares inflow and trained aircrew are available for such missions and will be the need of the hour, because the workhorse An-32, IL-76MD and Avro aircraft would complete 50 and 70 years respectively.

Strategy for Air Maintenance in the North

The main requirement for air maintenance in the Northern sector is that of the movement of heavy load, passengers and that of Airdrop in remote areas. Till the C-295MW fit into the operational plans, a mix of An-32 and IL-76MD could be best utilised alongside the C-17 aircraft for air maintenance task. An-32 can remain in drop mode and be employed only for drops, whereas, the IL-76MD could be kept in a double-decker mode for the carriage of only passengers per mission. Downtime of An-32 and IL-76MD could be reduced if the configurations are not disturbed and it matters if the availability reduces due to the depleting fleet. The C-17 aircraft should be employed for the mix of heavy loads and passengers. C295MW should be gradually brought into this role with the aim of replacing the An-32 and IL-76 in the valley.

Strategy for Supply Chain Management

Every year crores of kilograms of spares move in and out of the MCUs, EDs and BRDs of the IAF. The mode of transportation are service aircraft, service vehicles, Indian railways, civil flights and commercial vehicles and all these modes take away the ever-reducing revenue budget of the IAF. The fleet is depleting and so is the revenue budget, thus an efficient Supply Chain Model as an Air Bridge to connect all the EDs, MCUs and BRDs for spares and rotatable movement is the need of the hour.

On September 17, 2022,[20] the Government of India launched the 'National Logistics Policy' wresting on four pillars: 'Integration of Digital System (IDS); Unified Logistics Interface Platform (ULIP); Ease of Logistics (ELOG); and System Improvement Group (SIG)'.

A similar concept could be adopted by the IAF logistics air-bridge, through the medium of Integrated Material Management On-line System (IMMOLS) and Air Force Net. A nodal agency could compile the data of spares ready to move and in collaboration with the operations team plan out a weekly courier to connect all the bases using the "Shortest route software of Operational Research", being used by cargo airlines like Blue Dart, etc. This could be the most efficient and professional air bridging concept with a nearly 100 per cent strike rate every week giving the best value for money by the employment of a few An-32/C295MW for the entire supply chain of the IAF and would also raise the tonnage per hour (TPH) of flight. This could reduce/eliminate the requirement for other sources of transportation which would render a huge revenue budget savings.

Communication Configured Capsule

C-295 is a military aircraft with a ramp configuration like an An-32 and is being used for all military operations like the Para and load drops across the world. To utilise the C-295 against both the Avro and the An-32, the pre-fab communication configured capsules must be such positioned, preferably with the present Communication Flights, so that the communication duties could be performed by any of the aircraft engaged even in operational roles, like the air maintenance.

Aircrew and HR Management Strategy

A realignment of the aircrew between the squadrons and platforms would enhance the availability of aircrew for round-the-clock operations of strategic aircraft. An optimal HR management would also ensure good flying for all pilots. As per the aircraft availability, the An-32 and Avro Sqns would soon start having surplus aircrew and they can be realigned and better managed so that adequate flying hours are available for the junior aircrew and enough aircrew are available for the strategic aircraft for round-the-clock operations. Aircrew management software are freely available and could also be integrated into the system in the same way as professional and profit-making airlines do.

Conclusion

The IAF has in the recent past demonstrated the Strategic Lift Capability both during major exercises and also during operational commitments within India and overseas. In the next decade, the Strategic Transport Fleet of the IAF is upgrading after 40 years and will give a boost to the legacy fleet. It is possible to systematically bridge the perceived voids which will emerge once the 5-tonne class of aircraft complete 50 years of its life in the next decade. A pragmatic strategy with which the predictable operational gap could be bridged and not adversely affect the operation capability of this potent fleet is the need of the hour. The manning levels are more than adequate for the number of aircraft available today or in the next three decades thus induction rate and the training schedules should be maintained to sustain the operation capability of the transport fleet. The game plan lies in the management of the aircrew, spares and synchronising them with the ever-increasing task of the IAF.

Notes

1. Rajeev Sachdeva, "The Versatile Transport Fleet of the IAF", SP Aviation - IAF Special: Transport Fleet, September 2022, at https://www.sps-aviation.com/story/?id=3185&h=The-Versatile-Transport-Fleet-of-the-IAF, accessed on October 8, 2022.
2. BK Pandey, "World's Top Multi-role Military Transport Aircraft, SP's Aviation, May 2021, at https://www.sps-aviation.com/story/?id=2922&h=Worlds-Top-Multi-Role-Military-Transport-Aircraft.
3. Geography of India, at https://en.wikipedia.org/wiki/Geography_of_India, accessed on January 10, 2022.
4. Suryakant Chaffekar, "Why the IAF's Peacetime Operations are Bigger than any other Country", *The Print*, October 7, 2020, at https://theprint.in/opinion/why-the-iafs-peacetime-operations-are-bigger-than-any-other-country/517963/, accessed on November 3, 2020.
5. NATO Air Transport Capability *An Assessment*.
6. Arjun Subramaniam, *India's Wars: A Military History 1947-71* (HarperCollins Publishers India, 2016), p. 105.
7. Soumyadip Mullick, "1971 War: How Army Para-Dropped Infantry into East Pak", *The Statesman*, December 12, 2020, at https://www.thestatesman.com/bengal/1971-war-army-para-dropped-infantry-east-pak-1502940334.html, accessed on June 26, 2021.
8. Gulshan Luthra, "IAF's Innovative use of Transporters as Heavy Bombers", India Strategic, April 2013, at https://www.indiastrategic.in/topstories1980_IAF_use_transporters_ _bombers.htm, accessed on March 13, 2021.
9. JV Singh, "Out of Area Contingencies", Geospatial World, January 4, 2014, at https://www.geospatialworld.net/article/logistics-extending-the-reach/, accessed on March 23, 2021.
10. Shreya Pareek, "Did you know that the largest Air evacuation in history was done by India?", The Better India, February 18, 2015, at https://www.thebetterindia.com/15179/heres-need-know-largest-air-evacuation-history-india/, accessed on March 31, 2021.
11. "27 October 1947: The Spectacular Rescue of Kashmir", *Indian Defence Review*, Reflections of the Past.
12. Josy Joseph, "Earthquake hits India", rediff.com, January 2021, at https://www.rediff.com/news/2001/jan/26quak24.htm, accessed on April 7, 2021.
13. All India, Press Trust of India, "Nepal Earthquake: Indian Air Force, Army made 2223 sorties, rescued 11200 People'" NDTV, June 6, 2015, at https://

www.ndtv.com/india-news/nepal-earthquake-indian-air-force-army--2223-sorties-rescued-11200-people, accessed on May 16, 2021.

14. Anil Chopra, "Air Elements in Special Ops", *Indian Defence Review*, June 6, 2020, at http://www. indiandefencereview.com/news/air-elements-in-special-ops/, accessed on May 3, 2021.
15. Indrastra Global Editorial Team, "India's Integrated Air Command & Control System (IACCS): A NCW Milestone", September 28, 2015, at https://www.indrastra.com/2015/09/ANALYSIS-IACCS-257.html, accessed on May 27, 2021.
16. Shreya Dhodiyal, "The Distance IAF Has Covered In Fight Against Covid-19", News18, May 27, 2021, at https://www.news18.com/news/india/55-times-around-the-globe-thats-the-distance-iaf-has-covered-in-fight-against-covid-19-3781889.html, accessed on June 7, 2021.
17. Special Correspondent, "IAF Airlifts 6.2 tonne Essential Drugs to Maldives", *The Hindu*, April 2, 2020, at https://www.thehindu.com/news/national/iaf-airlifts-62-tonne-essential-drugs-to-maldives/article31240436.ece, accessed on April 2, 2021.
18. List of active Indian military aircraft, at https://en.wikipedia.org/wiki/List_of_active_Indian_military_aircraft.
19. "India Formalises Acquisition of 56 C-295 Aircraft", *The Defence*, September 24, 2021.
20. "PM launches National Logistics Policy", September 17, 2022, at https://www.pmindia.gov.in.

SECTION II

IAF: Future Trajectory

5. Air Power as a Tool of Comprehensive National Power

Anil Golani

> "The IAF is the only military institution exclusively devoted to military operations in the aerospace continuum for national defence as well as protecting our national interest, which is expanding with the growth of the economy and expansion of trade and commercial interests where they can best—or only—be pursued through the aerospace continuum."
>
> —Air Cmde Jasjit Singh

Introduction

Just like human beings, nation-states also aspire for status and power that can be wielded as and when required to achieve desired outcomes. History is replete with examples of the great rise and fall of empires and nation-states. The emergence of new technologies, connected businesses, and a reliance on global trade with faster and easier connectivity across the world, both virtual and physical, have only exacerbated the challenges for the leaders of the world. The tools of power are undergoing a change with technological developments, as can be witnessed by the role and influence that information warfare wields over ongoing conflicts, including the prolonged Russia-Ukraine war that has completed a year and has no end in sight. While economic power might be perceived as being at the heart of national power, no nation can protect itself without military power. This realisation continues to reiterate itself as many European nations and a pacifist country like Japan witness a significant increase in their defence budgets. Alliances and pacts have their limitations, and any nation aspiring to wield power and influence can only ignore its military capability at its own peril. An analysis of past conflicts proves that militarily stronger opponents do not necessarily emerge victorious, thereby leading to the assumption that there are various intangibles that comprise components of national power.

The concept of Comprehensive National Power (CNP) has both a Western and a Chinese construct. However, Ray Cline of the CIA came up with an index based on the formula Pp = (C + E + M) x (S + W) where C stood for critical mass (population + territory), E and M for the economic and military capability of the nation, S for strategic purpose, and W for the will to pursue the national strategy. Kautilya's *Arthashastra* also talks about the concept of CNP as the *Saptanga* model, which comprises seven constituent elements of the state. The analogy is that of a growing organism, where *Sapta* is seven and *ang* denotes the different body parts that need to grow in harmony. Kautilya ascribes the greatest importance to *Swarnim* or the ruler, and also has a place for *Mitra*, which denotes a friend or ally. Thereby, the ruler along with friends and allies play an important role in an increasingly divisive world that remains interdependent.

While hard power has traditionally been used to coerce or change the behaviour of other states to one's advantage, Joseph Nye coined the term 'soft power' in the 1980s to refer to the ability of a country to persuade others to do what it wants without using force or coercion. Leading by example and with a sense of legitimacy, soft power sought to influence others through cultural values, political systems, and foreign policy. Finally, in 2005, Nye came up with the concept of 'smart power,' which related to a variable amalgamation of soft and hard power options across the tools of statecraft. Nation-states would therefore need to employ all the tools of statecraft at their disposal to ensure peaceful growth and prosperity for their citizens. The use of Diplomacy, Informational, Military, and Economic (DIME) components would need to be seamlessly segued through a national strategy with a strong political will to implement the same.

The aim of this chapter is to analyse the role of air power as a tool of CNP in the Indian context.

Military

Well into the second aerospace century, the world has witnessed the efficacy of air power come of age. Whether acting independently or in support of other military instruments, the contribution of air power in the service of the nation in all past military conflicts has been amply demonstrated. While no arm or service can win a conflict on its own, it is an undisputed fact that without the use of air power, the outcome of any conflict is unlikely to be favourable. The participation of the IAF in all conflicts post-independence, from the liberation of Kashmir in 1947 to the Kargil war and the Balakot strike in 2019, is well documented. The first-ever conflict for the liberation of Kashmir brought to the fore the need for rapid deployment of the Army, which was facilitated by the Dakotas of 12 Sqn, the only IAF transport squadron at the time. If the IAF had not airlifted the Indian Army's 1 Sikh Regiment to Srinagar on that fateful day, the map of Kashmir would have been different. More than seven decades later, the rapid response of the Indian Army in its deployment in eastern Ladakh after the Galwan crisis in 2020 was facilitated once again by the more potent airlift capability of the IAF. The sustained operational deployment and a 24×7 air defence readiness have been able to deter the adversary from any further misadventures and have also displayed national intent to be aggressive in protecting national interests. The noticeable difference in India's political resolve, which has hitherto pandered to China's sensitivities, has been noticeable. The statement of Dr. S. Jaishankar, India's External Affairs Minister, bears testimony to this fact, "peace and tranquillity in the border areas clearly remain the basis for normal relations. From time to time this has been mischievously conflated with the sorting out of the border question."[1]

The IAF's fledgling transport fleet made a herculean effort to support the Indian Army during the Chinese invasion in 1962. A saga less talked about due to the ignominious defeat faced by the nation coupled with the decision to not use the combat capability of the IAF. The 1965 Indo-Pak conflict witnessed the first full-scale employment of air power by the IAF, which was still in the process of consolidating itself and operating six different types of fighter aircraft from four different nations. Many drawbacks noticed by the IAF during this conflict were consolidated during the following years, leading to greater synergy in inter-service coordination. The 1971 conflict witnessed the IAF gaining air superiority in the Eastern Theatre, leading to unfettered support for the Indian Army and the fall of Dacca (now Dhaka). The attack on the Governor's House in Dacca on December 3, 1971, by MiG-21 aircraft of the IAF led to the capitulation of East Pakistan and its surrender the next day. In the Western Theatre, the Hunters of the IAF played a crucial role in the Battle of Longewala by thwarting the enemy armour offensive. Even though the airspace over the Western Theatre was heavily contested, the IAF, with its close air support to the Indian Army offensive and strategic strikes over the energy sources and transportation system, played a leading role in the liberation of Bangladesh.

When the Indian Army was taken by surprise at the scale of Pakistani intrusion in the Dras-Kargil sector in the summer of 1999, the entry of the IAF immediately altered the nature of the conflict. Adapting to the situation, the IAF carried out a number of innovations by integrating laser-guided bombs, Commercial Off the Shelf (COTS) Global Positioning System (GPS) on MiG-27 aircraft and carrying out air attacks with the limitations of not crossing the line of control, paving the way for a hasty retreat by the intruders. The use of air power in this conflict shattered the myth of air power being escalatory, and the credit for this must go to the political as well as the IAF leadership that ensured the same, winning accolades for waging a battle at hitherto unprecedented heights amidst challenging conditions.

Political

For all the air operations carried out by the Western Air Forces, the essential rationale has hovered between creating primary strategic effects and direct political coercion.[2] While the strategic effects have been questionable, from Libya to Iraq and Afghanistan, the use of air power as a tool to decapitate terrorists through drones and manned aircraft has been successful to an extent. However, the political leadership needs to understand the capabilities and limitations of air power, and when used without the conjunction of friendly forces on the ground, the results could indeed be questionable. Public opinion, collateral damage, and post-conflict stabilisation strategies are some of the issues that need to be deliberated upon before utilising this potent instrument of national power, lest it becomes counter-productive in the long term. A good example of political coercion in the region was the employment of the IAF in carrying out surgical strikes against the terrorist training camps in Balakot in February 2019, which have deterred any major terrorist attacks since then. This was a prime example of an approach that effectively used its diplomatic and military power in unison to ensure that world opinion was in favour of India.

The contribution of air power through the IAF and civil aviation has been stellar in building the nation and achieving political ends in the growth of the nation. When the present government created the union territories of Jammu and Kashmir and Ladakh in 2019, the IAF played a stellar and silent role away from the public glare by airlifting central police personnel to the region to ensure security. More than 100 sorties were flown in ten days, airlifting approximately 12,000 personnel before August 5, 2019, when Article 370 was abrogated. The contribution of the IAF during national elections, carrying personnel and ballot boxes to inaccessible areas and ensuring universal adult franchise has been exemplary in nation-building ever since independence. The use of the IAF as a non-kinetic and non-lethal tool in Left Wing Extremism (LWE) infested areas has helped the political leadership demonstrate its will to deal with the problem, which is indigenous in content and character, unlike the terrorism and insurgency that plague the border states. Combating LWE requires a multi-pronged and multi-dimensional comprehensive strategy comprising all the instruments of national power, in which the IAF, in its utilisation of air power towards supporting the administration and the paramilitary forces, plays an important role. Carrying relief and supplies to some of the most inaccessible areas in the north and north-eastern parts of the country, the IAF has been the face of the nation that brings succour to its citizens. From casualty evacuation missions to rescuing people during floods and other natural disasters, dousing fires in urban as well as jungle and hilly areas, and aiding in search and rescue, the IAF has always been at the forefront. The IAF has assisted the Border Roads Organisation

(BRO) in airlifting critical equipment to clear roads and build bridges over inaccessible areas.

Diplomacy

The inherent attributes of speed, mobility, flexibility, and rapid response invariably position air power as the first responder and instrument of choice for political leadership in times of crisis. Whether it involves the evacuation of the Indian diaspora during the Gulf War, evacuation of personnel from strife-torn Yemen and Afghanistan, or the rapid deployment of Humanitarian Assistance and Disaster Relief (HADR) missions across continents as is being witnessed after the recent earthquake in Turkey and Syria, air power has been effectively and efficiently used to project national power. When Russia launched its military offensive against Ukraine in February 2022, it was some deft Indian diplomacy coupled with air power that came to rescue the many stranded Indian students and citizens and brought them home safely. When the world was struck by the covid pandemic in 2020 and 2021, India's vaccine diplomacy brought much succour to the neighbouring states. Air power was instrumental in saving lives domestically and internationally. Indian air power was used to rescue the Indian nationals stuck in Iran during the pandemic, an IAF C-17 delivered medical supplies to Wuhan, China, as a goodwill gesture, the same flight was used to rescue many foreign nationals stuck in China. The IAF carried out these missions while the situation in eastern Ladakh was building up in mid-2020. The IAF simultaneously carried out strategic airlifts of military personnel for deployment in the forward areas. Aerial diplomacy through the IAF has added an unprecedented capability to the nation that has been utilised time and again with alacrity and precision, bringing accolades to the country and justifying its status as a responsible and emerging power that is ready to help when the need arises, irrespective of geography and past affiliations.

The participation of the IAF in multiple bilateral and multilateral exercises with friendly foreign countries not only builds bridges and strategic partnerships but also demonstrates its capability, intent, and resolve. These exercises help promote regional and international peace, security, and stability through the means of air power. The participation of the IAF in United Nations peacekeeping (UNPK) operations across the world has been exemplary and stellar. The Indian aviation contingents have always managed to stand out with their professionalism, good and balanced risk-taking abilities, and commitment to the cause (UNPK), despite what others interpreted as flawed mandates.[3] These roles and missions performed professionally by the IAF further India's national interest. The ability to project military force with speed and precision and assist statecraft has been enabled by the IAF and amply demonstrated time and again.

The swift action taken by the IAF in conjunction with the other two services during Op Cactus in 1988, air landing Indian troops in Male, was instrumental in rescuing the president, thereby foiling the coup and restoring peace. These actions leave a lasting impact on the psyche of the affected nations, adding to the intangible benefits that accrue to national power and prestige. The timely relief and succour provided during the 2015 Nepal earthquake by the IAF, when the first aircraft got airborne within a couple of hours after the earthquake, was vitiated by the inept and insensitive handling of the tragedy by the electronic media. On the contrary, in all probability, the relief provided to Turkey by India has the potential to change the outlook of the country towards India, which it was finding difficult to do considering its close association with Pakistan and its inability to delink the Kashmir issue in its bilateral relations with India.

An active role played by the IAF with transcontinental capabilities during non-combat evacuation exercises in the past, from Yemen to Afghanistan, reassures the Indian diaspora about national power, its capability, and the political will to execute the same when required. The IAF has been at the forefront, whether it has involved rescuing mountaineers and trekking expedition personnel from other countries or airlifting 374 tonnes of fresh water to the Maldives in 2014 when there was a drinking water crisis in the Male due to a breakdown of their RO plant. Apart from being a net security provider in the region, the IAF had reached across to the United States as well during natural calamities when Hurricane Katrina struck the country in 2005, bringing much-needed relief. The IAF transport fleet even airlifted cheetahs from South Africa and relocated them in the jungles of Madhya Pradesh in central India.

Economic

The aerospace-military industrial ecosystem is a national strategic asset that has traditionally been state-owned. However, with the proliferation of technology, economic reforms, and burgeoning private industry, including scores of start-ups, this industry has the potential to transform the nation from being import-dependent to a country that is not only self-reliant, or '*Aatmanirbhar*,' but also a major exporter of aircraft and a Major Repair and Overhaul (MRO) hub for many fleets. The recently concluded Aero India 2023 saw the participation of more than 800 defence companies, including Micro, Small and Medium Enterprises (MSME), showcasing their technologies. The '*Bandhan*' event, aimed at forging and renewing partnerships between business entities, witnessed 53 major announcements, nine product launches, and three Transfer of Technologies (ToT) worth approximately Rs 80,000 crore. Defence Ministers of 32 countries, Air Chiefs of 29 countries, and 73 Chief Executive Officers (CEOs) of global and Indian Original Equipment Manufacturers (OEMs) attended the event. India has set itself the target of increasing its defence exports from US$ 1.5 billion to US$ 5 billion by 2025. Air power is set to play a key and leading role in this endeavour, which would lead to the transformation of India into a US$ 5 trillion economy, by generating growth, job opportunities, and technological prowess in the sector through indigenous design and development and joint development with foreign OEMs. Foreign Direct Investment (FDI) in the defence aerospace sector is likely to increase manifold in the coming years as the traditional aerospace conglomerates realise that, in case they want to do business with India, there is no other route except to 'Make in India' and thereby 'Make for the World'.

The order placed by Air India with both Boeing and Airbus for a total of 470 aircraft with options for 370 more is the largest deal ever signed in aviation history. This deal would create and sustain jobs in the US, India and France. The deal is expected to generate employment, creating direct and indirect jobs for approximately two lakh people in India over the next few years. Moreover, the creation and addition of aviation infrastructure and increased connectivity, wherein the airline promises to connect every city in the country, would lead to all-round growth and development. Hailed as historic by US President Joe Biden and French President Emmanuel Macron, the deal is an important marker of the growing strategic ties between India and the United States and India and France. According to a report published by the Centre for Asia Pacific Aviation (CAPA), "India is, perhaps on the cusp of a long-awaited and historic change—it may finally be set to take its place as the global aviation market of the 21st century."[4] With almost every national and regional airline expected to order more aircraft in the next two to three years, the growth of civil aviation with its potential to leverage national power only adds heft to the growing stature of India in the evolving and changing world order.

The Russia-Ukraine conflict exposed the lack of resilience of the global supply chain for energy as well as defence spares, specifically for India with its reliance on Russian aircraft and weapon systems. This realisation reiterated the importance of self-reliance and propelled the nation towards policy changes that are going to ensure that the first option for procurements would necessarily have to be indigenously designed, developed and manufactured, followed by 'Make in India' through FDI coupled with ToT.

Education

Training and education play a vital and leading role in empowering the professional soldier. Air power has always been sensitive to technology, and the need to learn and adapt has been critical in the employment of air power. The IAF has laid great emphasis on this as human resources become an important and intangible variable when calculating the power of its force. The training and education of air warriors and their career progression are largely dependent on their professional qualifications and merit. It is invariably going to be the man behind the machine who makes the difference in an even contest. With India's growing engagement and strategic partnerships, there has been a significant increase in the number of personnel from the Air Forces of friendly foreign countries undergoing courses of instruction in India.

The lack of adequate opportunities and the lack of adequate facilities for research and education at the postgraduate and doctoral levels in the country resulted in a chicken-and-egg situation that prevented the domestic aerospace industry from achieving its true potential. The congruence of the military, academia, and industry is vital to the growth of national power. The establishment of Rashtriya Raksha University (RRU) as an Institute of National Importance through the RRU Act passed by the Indian Parliament in October 2020 underscores the importance of education. Furthermore, during Aero India 2023, Airbus signed a Memorandum of Understanding with the Indian Institute of Science (IISc) Bengaluru to expand the country's access to aerospace education and research.

Future Roadmap

To further strengthen air power as a component of CNP, there are a number of measures that could be undertaken to transform its capability and effectiveness. First, investment in domestic research and development, indigenisation, and 'Make in India', or '*Aatmanirbharta*,' with indigenous as well as foreign OEMs would require a significant boost and thrust that sustains in the near-to long-term. This would significantly reduce the gap between the capability desired by the air force and the capability supplied indigenously. Technology-enabled tools that would ensure unhindered operations in a hostile environment and ensure secure communications for effective command and control. Space is increasingly becoming the fourth frontier of war, and the utilisation of the space domain in all aspects of human endeavour, whether in peace or war, has become inescapable and essential. Merging operations between air and space among different stakeholders through a combined and common grid that would share the required information on a need-to-know basis has become essential. The fusion of the air and space domains has been facilitated by technology and the ever-increasing use of the space domain for navigation, imagery, surveillance, communications, meteorology, cyber, and command and control. The burgeoning aerospace industry in the country will require more and more trained personnel, and the nation has to create the required infrastructure and training establishments to meet this challenge.

An understanding of the precepts of aerospace power, its attributes, strengths, and limitations by the leadership of the country, and the options that this vital instrument of power provides in order to preclude its use from becoming counter-productive, is absolutely essential. The onus of providing these sovereign options rests with the practitioners of air power, academia, and the think tanks of the country.

Conclusion

With a growing economy that is set to leapfrog India into the world's largest economy in the coming years, the power and influence that the nation wields on the global stage are only going to increase. This, however, will not be uncontested as the nation is plagued with unresolved boundary disputes with two nuclear-capable and hostile neighbours. To protect its sovereignty and national interests and to ensure peaceful growth and development, the nation would need a strong and potent military capability. India, the largest democracy in the world, has time and again validated the resilience of the system that rules and governs the country. India's parliamentary democracy has stood the test of time, and the leader of the party in power is akin to a conductor of a symphony who needs to ensure that all the components of national power play in harmony. Air power, as an adjunct of military power, is an important and inalienable component of national power that has been successfully used by the nation-state across the spectrum of conflict, no war, no peace, natural and humanitarian disasters, internal disturbances, and nation building to protect the national interest, project both hard and soft power, and empower the nation. Air power, therefore, remains one of the principal elements of a modern nation's ability to reinforce its strategic planning.[5]

Air power requires boldness in execution, and there are a host of intangible ingredients like employment doctrine, training, and leadership that govern its efficacy. Nevertheless, the inherent attributes of speed, flexibility, transcontinental reach, precision, and firepower make air power one of the most dynamic and preferred options of CNP for political leadership. Its use, however, is fraught with challenges, and the options for utilising this instrument of power, whether on its own or in collaboration with other instruments of national power, need to be carefully deliberated upon before pulling the arrow out of the quiver.

Notes

1. Rezaul H Laskar, "In blunt message for China, Jaishankar talks of India's new normals in posture", *Hindustan Times*, October 18, 2022, at https://www.hindustantimes.com/india-news/in-blunt-message-for-china-jaishankar-talks-of-india-s-new-normals-in-posture-101666095105089.html, accessed on February 12, 2022.
2. John Andres Olsen (ed.), *Routledge Handbook of Air Power* (Routledge, 2018), pp. 233.
3. Rajesh Isser, *Air power in Irregular & Hybrid Conflicts: The Indian Context* (The Book Line, New Delhi 2017), p. 89.
4. "After AI, IndiGo & other airlines set to order 1,200 planes: CAPA", *ET Brand Equity*, February 17, 2023, at https://brandequity.economictimes.indiatimes.com/news/business-of-brands/after-ai-indigo-other-airlines-set-to-order-1200-planes-capa/98003650, accesses on February 18, 2023.
5. Sanu Kainikara, "The Art of Air Power Sun Tzu Revisited", Air Power Development Centre, Canberra Australia 2009, Strategic Assessments, p. 18.

6. Future of Combat Aircraft

Anil Chopra

In August 2022, videos surfaced that indicated that the USA was testing its technologies for a new 'seventh generation' fighter jet.[1] The aircraft will be developed in parallel with the sixth-generation fighter, which has yet to reach the roll-out stage. This was to be the second project in the Next-Generation Air Dominance (NGAD) program. Many new technologies have already evolved, and therefore the two projects could move in tandem. A somewhat similar approach was used when some technologies evolved for the F-22 Raptor were ported to the F-35 Lightning II. Artificial Intelligence (AI) and quantum computing will hasten the process. Neural networks are predicting future combats and setting 'combat operational' requirements. AI will support airframe design, material selections, and combined-cycle engine design and compatibility. Sixth-generation fighter capabilities have already been defined. Some of the technologies for these may be at a rudimentary stage initially. The same advances will be ported to the seventh-generation fighter. The approach will be modular, and the aircraft could be quickly reconfigured for totally different missions. The aircraft will be optionally manned. Aircraft could fly at hypersonic speeds at near-space altitudes, well above the current air defence systems. The aircraft will work in a totally networked environment. Aircraft will mostly use energy weapons and can strike space-based targets. It will be able to carry hypersonic weapons comfortably. Such a plane will, of course, be very costly to acquire and maintain.

Fifth-Generation Aircraft

The fifth-generation aircraft technologies are well-defined and in place. They are the most advanced fighters currently in service. The first aircraft in this category, the Lockheed Martin F-22 Raptor, made its first flight in 1997 and was formally inducted into service in December 2005. This generation of aircraft has been fielded only by the big three: the USA (F-22, F-35), Russia (Su-57) and China (J-20). Many more are under development. Typical characteristics of these aircraft include high agility, all-aspect stealth, advanced integrated avionics with a low probability of intercepting active electronically scanned array (AESA) radar (LPIR), high situational awareness through networking with other platforms and sensors, and the ability to 'super-cruise' (supersonic flight without afterburner). The munitions have to be carried internally to retain stealth. The airframe and engine design have reduced reflecting surfaces. Higher manoeuvrability is managed through thrust vectoring engines. The aircraft weight is reduced through the use of advanced composite materials, which are also less reflective of radar waves. External transmissions are kept low, and systems like infrared search and track and other important sensors are used to keep the approach to the target stealthy. Fibre-optic signalling is extensively used to reduce weight. Sensor fusion improves 360° situational awareness. Secure data links support platform-to-platform information flow, and the aircraft could act as a mini-AWACS at the tactical level. A modular approach allows for easier and more frequent upgrades.

Most fifth-generation aircraft are single-seaters. But the higher cockpit load and aircraft capabilities have often pushed operators to desire the two-seat configuration. In addition, fifth-generation aircraft have high life-cycle costs. The stealth requires frequent maintenance. These facilities cannot be set up at many air bases. Integration of fifth-generation aircraft with unmanned platforms in buddy roles is still in the evolutionary stage, while the same is mostly being done with fourth-generation fighters. Some fourth-generation fighters like the Rafale and Super Hornet have imbibed fifth-generation technologies such as advanced AESA radars and avionics, sensor fusion, and reasonable frontal stealth. Hence, these jets are categorised as 4.5 generations.

Under Development Fifth-Generation Fighters

The 'Flygsystem 2020' was a planned Swedish Air Force project to develop a fifth-generation low-observable fighter jet to replace the JAS

39 Gripen. Saab AB was asked to carry out a study on future combat air capabilities and to develop new concepts and technologies.[2] While the study continues, Sweden joined Italy and the United Kingdom in the tri-nation 'Tempest' program. Tempest is a UK-led program imbibing sixth-generation technologies and sensors for networked combat, unmanned aircraft, and for air dominance in future conflicts. Tempest is meant to replace the Italian and British Eurofighter and the Swedish Gripen from 2035.

Table 6.1: Flying Fifth-Generation Fighters

Type/ Country	First Flight/ Service Entry	Numbers Built	External/ Internal Points	Payload kg	Thrust Vectoring	Radar Range 1M²TGT
J-20 China	January 11, 2011/ September 28, 2017	208	4/6	11,000	30,000lbs	160 km
FC-31 China	2012	2	6/6	28,000	None	NA
F-22 USA	1997/2005	195	4/8	8,500	26,000lbs in dry/ 35,000lbs with reheat	240 km
F-35 Variants USA	2006/2016	875+	6	8,160	28,000lbs in dry/ 43,000lbs with reheat	150 km
Su-57 Russia	2010/2019	16	14/8 internal	11,000	35,000lbs	390 km

Source: See Annexure A.

The Turkish Aerospace Industries (TAI) began its ambitious fifth-generation fighter program TF-X in 2011. Sweden's SAAB AB was initially chosen to provide design support. Reports also claimed probable cooperation with South Korea, Indonesia and Brazil. In 2015, it was decided to go solo and make totally indigenous aircraft. As per TAI CEO Temel Kotil, TF-X (similar in design to the F-22) will be rolled out by March 2023. It will make its first flight by 2025, and enter service in 2029. The assembly-line pictures reveal that the twin-engine aircraft is in an advanced stage of construction.[3] Turkey was one of the partners in the F-35 program and contributed to the funding of the development, with a commitment to 100 F-35A. However, Turkey was removed from the program because it insisted on purchasing the Russian S-400 air defence system despite the US raising an objection. It not only cost Ankara the stealth fighters but also the industrial base benefits of being in the program.[4] The aircraft will initially use two General Electric F110s for test flights but will later replace them with indigenous engines to be developed by TAEC.[5]

Japan began evolving its indigenous stealth jet fighter, the Mitsubishi X-2 Shinshin. The prototype rolled out in mid-2014 and made its first flight on April 22, 2016. Later, it was decided to bring in international partners to replace its fleet of F-2 multirole fighter aircraft, a Mitsubishi license-produced variant of Lockheed Martin's F-16. Japan's now-designated F-3 stealth fighter jet would be a sixth-generation aircraft led by a Japanese team. They could be in collaboration with contenders such as Lockheed Martin, Boeing, Northrop Grumman, or BAE Systems.[6] This Future Fighter (F-3) Program could take around 15 years. The target is to build 100 aircraft that will complement the 147 F-35As already under induction.

DRDO-HAL AMCA

The Advanced Medium Combat Aircraft (AMCA) is the fifth-generation Indian program for the Indian Air Force and the Indian Navy (IN). The aircraft is being designed by the Aeronautical Development Agency (ADA) and will be manufactured by Hindustan Aeronautics Limited (HAL). The 25-tonne, single-seat, twin-engine, multi-role aircraft will be developed in two stages. The AMCA Mk1 will have partial stealth, and the Mk2 will have full stealth and will imbibe sixth-generation technologies. The aircraft's preliminary design review (PDR) has been completed. The critical design review (CDR) was completed in February 2023.[7] The Cabinet Committee on Security's (CCS) approval is expected in early 2023. Metal cutting will start thereafter. "Once the project sanction is received, the first prototype can be rolled out in three years and the first flight in one to one and half years after that," said Dr AK Ghosh, project director of AMCA, during DefExpo in October 2022.[8] The aircraft is meant to replace the Jaguar, Mirage 2000, and MiG-29. Most parts of the airframe are to be made in India. The aero-engine will initially be imported and later made indigenously. Some avionics would be through joint ventures with friendly foreign companies.

Sixth-Generation Technologies

Sixth-generation technologies have moved from drawing boards to laboratories and manufacturing rigs. Several countries are developing them with targeted induction by the 2030s. The aircraft will have to cater for a highly contested battle space with very long-range combat engagements. Both the American and Russian designers are of the view that the concept of a networked family of fighters would have to emerge.[9] This would mean all specialisations and technologies would not have to be ported onto a single aircraft. Some aircraft can be laser weapons heavy while others could carry drone canisters and have oravionics heavy. The enhancement of air-to-air capabilities and survivability in the much higher anti-access/area-denial threat environment will be a requisite. The ground-strike ranges and precision would have to increase. A broad spectrum all-aspect stealth, and unified electronic warfare system would be a pre-requisite.[10] Inflight upgrades of software would be possible without affecting flight safety. Multi-spectral optical systems would operate in the laser, infrared, ultraviolet, and optical bands. There will be greater use of directed energy weapons (DEW). DEW on airborne platforms will require greater onboard power generation.

Close-combat dogfights are less likely, and well beyond visual range (BVR) aerial engagements will have to be possible in advanced electronic warfare (EW) and cyber-attack environments. One school of thought is that large-sized fighters would allow porting more technologies onboard, such as larger, longer-range radars, heavier weapons, a greater capacity DEW, and a more powerful EW suite. The penalty of larger aircraft could be compromised in stealth and higher costs. Next-generation stealth bombers would come in this category.

Surviving long-range air-to-air missile capability will be important. Optionally manned platforms will be the norm. Manned-unmanned teaming will require secure data links. High-speed data transfer and secure satellite communications would be crucial for a densely networked environment to support better 'data-to-decision' (D2D) capability. This will require AI and advanced digital capabilities, including high-capacity networking, and data fusion. Full glass cockpits with touch screens and helmet-visor displays would permit a 360° view and situational awareness. Variable-cycle engines will allow optimum performance in all phases of flight.

AI-supported smart structures and hybrid systems are already evolving. More efficient and easier-to-cool gallium nitride (GaN)[11] semiconductor material will be used in future radars. Made with advanced composite materials, Passive Aeroelastic Tailored (PAT)[12] wings and aero surfaces will be lighter and much more aerodynamically efficient. Nanomaterials will considerably reduce weight-for-equal-strength. 3D printing technology will allow greater design experimentation and spare parts on demand at short notice. The evolution of hypersonic aircraft would forever change the ability to respond to conflict. Survivable, long-range weapons combining both air-to-air and air-to-ground capabilities are being evolved. Most of these technologies are stand-alone works in progress. Future pilot support systems would include the On-board Oxygen Generating System (OBOGS).[13] Smart drugs and hybrid supplements for aircrews would increase their stamina, endurance, and alertness levels. It could also be a transdermal nutrient delivery system. Contact lenses displaying[14] directly into eyeballs, and bone-conducting technology[15] would allow next-generation helmets to emit vibrations to the skull, transmit sound directly into the head, and replace the current microphone-earpiece. Technologies will continue to evolve. Most of these would be in place by around 2025. Clearly, the pilot remains in the cockpit, though the aircraft could be optionally manned.

Sixth-Generation Programs

The US continues to take the lead in newer generation aircraft and makes huge investments. However, Japan was one of the first movers and showcased the sixth-generation jet fighter concept. The Mitsubishi

F-X sixth-generation project has been under development. However, on December 9, 2022, Japan joined the British-led, Italy-partnered tri-nation project Global Combat Air Program (GCAP).[16] The F-X program is now merged with BAE Systems' Tempest. Mitsubishi will remain the prime contractor for the Japanese variant. Each country would source its engine and avionics as appropriate to its requirements. France-based MBDA will be the armaments partner. Development and cost-sharing details are being deliberated. Production commencement is targeted for 2030, and service induction is around 2035. The aircraft would have a loyal wingman. The same is being evolved in a separate project with some American companies. This sixth-generation fighter would be designed to integrate with the defence programs of NATO countries and other partners. In a joint statement, the US supports this defence cooperation between like-minded countries.

The UK released its House of Commons Defence Select Committee report, 'Post-2030 Combat Aviation Force Structure' in July 2014.[17] It talked of the UK's next-generation fighter program to replace the Eurofighter Typhoon by 2030. The service life of Typhoons has now been extended to 2040. As mentioned before, the UK announced its combat air strategy and concept of a sixth-generation fighter, 'Tempest', in 2018. Sweden and Italy joined in 2019. Japan joined the project in 2022. India was also invited to join.

In November 2022, after intense negotiations, France, Germany and Spain agreed to start the next phase of development of their sixth-generation fighter, called 'SCAF', at an initial estimated cost of more than €100 billion.[18] The equally shared project will be led by France's Dassault. Airbus (Germany) and Indra (Spain) will be other partners. The first phase will cost about €3.5 billion. The aircraft will replace the French Rafale and German and Spanish Eurofighters from 2040. The program will include fighter aircraft, weapons, and drones, among others.

As Russia's fifth-generation aircraft, the PAK FA Sukhoi Su-57 'Felon', continues to evolve, Russia has launched the PAK DP development to replace the MiG-31[19] as the long-range interceptor by around 2028. The aircraft has been designated 'MiG-41' and is claimed to be a sixth-generation aircraft. The upgraded MiG-31BM will be in service till at least the early 2030s. Russia is also developing the single-engine Su-75 Checkmate, a light tactical stealth aircraft. The aircraft has a diverter-less inlet, a V-shaped tail, and internal weapons bays. This relatively low-cost fifth-generation aircraft will be available for export and compete with the Lockheed F-35. The first two of the four prototypes are already in production.[20] The first flight is likely in 2024.

Having produced over 200 J-20 aircraft, as per Dr Wang Haifeng, chief designer of the Chengdu Aerospace Corporation, China is already working on sixth-generation aircraft with the target to induct one by 2035. There are reports that the aircraft will make its first flight by 2026.[21] General Mark Kelly, the Chief of the US Air Combat Command (ACC), said in September 2022 that China's sixth-generation aircraft was on track.[22] The concept cross-section of the diamond-shaped wing and tail-less aircraft was displayed at the 2022 Zhuhai Air Show. An aircraft demonstrator or mock-up has also been spotted at the Chengdu plant. Experts expect a significant reduction in aircraft signatures and a leap forward in onboard processing power and sensor capabilities of the highly upgradable open system. The wing and tail shape would offer high lift, low drag, and high payload carriage. Planned thrust vectoring should compensate for the otherwise lower manoeuvrability of the wing-and-tail design. The WS-19 turbofan engine variant is expected to power the aircraft. The highly networked aircraft will team with unmanned aerial platforms.

India has not joined any global sixth-generation aircraft development program. The UK had pitched for India to join the Tempest program, but no call has been taken. Currently, India is on its own and is still at the stage of imbibing individual sixth-generation technologies. Some of these will get ported to the AMCA.

The US Next Generation Air Dominance (NGAD) program has many vendors competing. The US Air Force (USAF) and US Navy (USN) are pursuing separate programs. While the USAF wants a replacement for the F-22, the USN is looking at an aircraft to replace the F-18 Super Hornet and complement the F-35s. Lockheed Martin has made the most successful American fighters in recent years and showcased its latest design. Other airframe designers are Boeing and Northrop Grumman while companies like General Electric and Pratt & Whitney are working on the propulsion system. Lockheed's design is a stealthy, manned, diamond-shaped wing and tailless aircraft.[23] The design offers a higher level of stealth, high aerodynamic efficiency, and a large internal volume for weapons and fuel. The engines will have two-dimensional, diamond-shaped nozzles. With long-range combat engagements, manoeuvrability would have lower priority than stealth and sensor-weapon combinations hence a low-observable engine air-intake design is conceived. Aircraft are expected to have distributed aperture systems to provide very high situational awareness using advanced sensor fusion and networking. The USAF is reportedly looking at two separate aircraft variants, a long-range one for the Indo-Pacific theatre and a shorter-range one for Europe. Americans are working on a 'family of systems' approach. Aircraft-drone teaming would be an important part of the project. The status of the engineering, manufacturing, and development (EMD) phase of the NGAD is not very clear, but the target is to achieve operational capability by 2030.

In late 2021, the USN unveiled its latest vision for the F/A-XX. The aircraft should be equipped with a modern electronic warfare suite, be able to act as a command-and-control node, and have MUM-T capability to group with munitions-carrying unmanned aircraft. The initial design pictures released indicate a lambda-wing shape, canards, and a 'V' tail. The more recent concept offered by Boeing is closer to the Lockheed proposal for the USAF—a tailless aircraft with a diamond-shaped wing. While the USN still has to take a call, the requirements are gradually converging with the USAF. Longer range, higher speed, advanced sensors, and longer-range weapons (including hypersonic) have been specified. F/AXX would allow cutting-edge carrier-based power projection in futuristic threat environments.[24] The aircraft must have a longer range to allow the carrier to remain farther away from threatening enemy defences. The USN is separately looking at unmanned platforms for carrier operations that could have fixed or rotary wings and team with the carrier aircraft to lead in higher-risk missions. The unmanned members could carry suppression of enemy air defence (SEAD)-related loads for electronic warfare, support command and control, or even carry AAMs to clear the sky ahead. The USN has been actively supporting the MQ-25 tanker drone. The rest of the unmanned roles could be similar to those in the USAF. DARPA's swarm drones are part of the System of System Integration Technology and Experimentation (SoSITE) program[25] that is meant to maintain the US technology edge for future air dominance. The USN's Netted Emulation of Multi-Element Signature against Integrated Sensors (NEMESIS)[26] is essentially a drone swarm that would generate real-looking false signatures and decoys of surface, subsurface, and aerial platforms to confuse multiple adversary sensors simultaneously over a large geographical area.

Future of Combat

The future of combat and combat aircraft design and technologies are inextricably linked. Both drive each other. Most combat requirements find technological solutions. Sometimes technologies help change the way air combat evolves. For example, the autopilot relieved the pilot of certain basic flying tasks, giving him time for system management. Long-range sensors combined with onboard computation allowed the pilot to receive combat engagement solutions and guidance. Very long-range radars and weapons allowed combat engagements at much greater distances. IR sensors improved night vision and also allowed sneak attacks. Automated aeroengines increased efficiency and thrust weight and allowed carefree handling. EW equipment was a great tool for both defensive and offensive use. Shorter take-off and landing distances would mean operations even from bombed-out runways.

The future of combat is now intrinsically linked to evolving technologies and capabilities. Some of these will see how combat aircraft will engage in the air wars of the next 40-50 years. Clearly, the ability to integrate systems at the theatre-wide level will make a significant difference. This system-of-systems approach will allow MUM-T, permit sensor shooter mix across platforms, and allow combat information and data transfer from the ground, satellites, and other platforms. This would mean an automated selection of the primary sensor, the optimum combat solution, and the weapon/platform selection for the earliest engagement.

All this will require advanced communication and an unmatched capacity for uninterrupted onboard infostream processing.

AI will allow real-time data translation for high levels of situational awareness, reduced cockpit load, and optimum timely decision-making. EW and cyber advances and technologies will also contribute to aircraft security and combat safety. Combined with stealth, this should permit deeper penetration during counter-air missions and completing engagements before being detected or tracked.

Multi-spectral stealth, though still expensive to create and maintain and sometimes compromising, would have to be taken to new levels. First, it would have to become more affordable. Also, stealth would have to cater to larger aircraft. It is already evolving for bombers, and the next would have to be for FRA and AEW&C. Conversely, there will be a need to beat the stealth, as is being planned by Russia or China, by using low or very high-frequency radars.

DEW will have a game-changing impact on future combat. The requirement is lasers for low-power illumination and higher-powered weapons. Systems have now become small enough to be ported on fighter-class aircraft. Their power and range are increasing. The power sources onboard have become sufficient to meet the DEW requirements. DEW will give an unlimited inventory of weapons. Defence against them also has to evolve. Select future combat aircraft would also have to have the capability to neutralise threats in space.

Another area of action is next-generation human-machine interfacing. This will have to accommodate the system-of-systems approach, unprecedented situational awareness, and autonomous wingmen. Wide-screen Large Area Displays (LAD) and Adaptive Flight Displays (datasheet) will be used. Airborne equipment and networks would have to be cyber-hardened. Like smartphone, the software is the most important feature of the future fighter. Continuously updating the same will be important. For more frequent and flexible upgrades, a modular, open systems architecture would have to continue. There would be a need for reduced integration and certification time. AI enhancements and adaptive machine learning capabilities should allow agility and the ability to adapt to future technologies.

Any future platform must remain one step ahead of those of the adversary. A 'see first, shoot first, destroy first' capability is required. Handle much more than before and quicker than ever. Giving the right information to the pilot at the right time will be required. While AI will help the pilot or Weapon System Operator (WSO) with suggestions for weapon selection and tactical positioning for the kill while keeping outside the enemy weapon envelope, some of the functions of the manned aircraft will also be given autonomy. The AI could also take over if the pilot loses consciousness due to high gravitational force.

Any air force's ability to project power and at the same time support defence of friendly high-value assets will be crucial. The USAF has introduced Agile Combat Employment (ACE),[27] a proactive and reactive operational concept. The aim is to complicate and weaken adversaries' combat capabilities and increase their own flexibility. It will support anti-access and area denial operations. It will also shorten the observe, orient, decide, and act (OODA) cycle. ACE would also support joint all-domain operations (JADO) through convergence.

The maintainability of future aircraft should be easier, faster, and cheaper. The logistic footprint has to be reduced for a quicker turnaround through easy access hatches and with a minimal number of technicians. Aircraft engine or radar changes are already being done in less than 45 minutes. The ease of off-base operations and the possibility of operating from highway strips and short/battle-damaged runways must be inbuilt. Frontline maintenance activities must be performed through Built-in Test Equipment (BITE) and through handheld devices and app-based software, requiring minimal training.

The cost of modern fighters has always been an issue. A typical fighter flies around 8,000 hours in its lifetime. Each jet flying around 200 hours a year translates into around 40 years of operations. It also goes through around two upgrades. It is important for the platform to have the operational ability to justify the money spent. Managing aircraft project costs will be a challenge.[28] An increase in operational longevity would thus be an issue. Future fighters will operate in a 'combat cloud' along with future unmanned combat aircraft. Futuristic aircraft design, open architecture, and modularity would support this. Upgrades should be affordable and involve lesser downtime.

The IAF is looking for a cost-effective solution for its fighter jet requirement. The aircraft must have sixth-generation attributes but be low on operational cost. The aircraft would have to be built in India. India's R&D investment would have to increase for next-generation technologies. Dedicated task forces would have to be set up to drive individual technologies. Critical among these will be aeroengines, AI, stealth, advanced avionics, electronic warfare, cyber, hypersonic and DEW. Program management will be crucial for future combat aircraft. Joint ventures may be formed for crucial high-end technologies. Success in aircraft building is crucial for India to become a significant defence manufacturing nation. The time to act is now, lest we get left behind.

APPENDIX 1

J-20 China

First Flight: https://chinapower.csis.org/china-chengdu-j-20/

Service Entry: https://defence-blog.com/chinas-latest-j-20-stealth-fighter-has-been-officially-commissioned-into-military-service/

Numbers Built: https://engineerine.com/5th-generation-fighter/

External/Internal Points: https://www.thedrive.com/the-war-zone/24841/chinas-j-20-stealth-fighter-stuns-by-brandishing-full-load-ofmissiles-at-zhuhai-air-show

Payload:

Thrust Vectoring: https://www.militaryfactory.com/aircraft/detail.php?aircraft_id=860

Radar Range: https://eurasiantimes.com/edited-f-22-raptor-vs-j-20-might-dragon-will-speed-stealth-beat/

FC 31 China

First Flight: https://www.scmp.com/news/china/article/1074027/china-adds-new-fifth-generation-stealth-fighter-arsenal

Service Entry:

Numbers Built:

External/Internal Points: https://www.flightglobal.com/dubai-customer-sought-for-avics-new-stealth-fighter/118805.article

Payload: https://www.flightglobal.com/dubai-customer-sought-for-avics-new-stealth-fighter/118805.article

Thrust Vectoring:

Radar Range:

F-22 USA

First Flight: https://web.archive.org/web/20140705075752/http://lockheedmartin.com/us/100years/stories/f-22.html

Service Entry: https://www.militaryfactory.com/aircraft/detail.php?aircraft_id=20

Numbers Built: https://engineerine.com/5th-generation-fighter/

External/Internal Points: https://www.militaryfactory.com/aircraft/detail.php?aircraft_id=20

Payload:

Thrust Vectoring: https://www.militaryfactory.com/aircraft/detail.php?aircraft_id=20

Radar Range: https://web.archive.org/web/20150924005256/http://www.f22-raptor.com/media/documents/aviation_week_010807.pdf

F-35 USA

First Flight: https://news.lockheedmartin.com/2006-09-20-Mighty-F-35-Lightning-II-Engine-Roars-to-Life

Service Entry: https://www.militaryfactory.com/aircraft/detail.php?aircraft_id=23

Numbers Built: https://engineerine.com/5th-generation-fighter/

External/Internal Points: https://www.militaryfactory.com/aircraft/detail.php?aircraft_id=23

Payload: https://www.lockheedmartin.com/f35/news-and-features/everything-you-need-to-know-about-the-f-35c.html#:~:text=The%20F%2D35C%20can%20carry,combined%20internal%20and%20external%20weapons.

Thrust Vectoring: https://www.militaryfactory.com/aircraft/detail.php?aircraft_id=23

Radar Range: https://www.lockheedmartin.com/f35/about/5th-gen-capabilities.html

Su-57 Russia

First Flight: https://www.uacrussia.ru/en/aircraft/lineup/military/su-57/#:~:text=The%20maiden%20flight%20of%20Sukhoi,on%20all%20Su%2D57%20components

Service Entry: https://www.militaryfactory.com/aircraft/detail.php?aircraft_id=782

Numbers Built: https://engineerine.com/5th-generation-fighter/

External/Internal Points: https://www.militaryfactory.com/aircraft/detail.php?aircraft_id=782

Payload:

Thrust Vectoring: https://www.militaryfactory.com/aircraft/detail.php?aircraft_id=782

Radar Range: https://theaviationgeekclub.com/the-su-57-is-marketed-as-stealth-fighter-but-radars-have-between-6-to-10-times-greater-detection-range-against-the-felon-compared-to-f-22-f-35-heres-why/

Notes

1. "The USA is testing Its New 7th Generation Fighter Jet", YouTube Video, 11:17, posted by Daily Aviation, August 22, 2022, at https://www.youtube.com/watch?v=-mzyQln3Bes, accessed on December 25, 2022.
2. Gastón Dubois, "Sweden Commissions Saab to carry out Preparatory Study for post-Gripen Future", *Aviacionline*, January 6, 2022, at https://www.aviacionline.com/2022/06/sweden-commissions-saab-to-carry-out-preparatory-study-for-post-gripen-future/, accessed on December 29, 2022.
3. Ashish Dangwal, "Stunning Images Of Turkey's TF-X Fifth-Gen Combat Aircraft Prototype In Assembly Line Mesmerizes Netizens", *The Eurasian Times*, November 24, 2022, at https://eurasiantimes.com/stunning-images-of-turkeys-tf-x-fifth-gen-combat-aircraft-prototype/, accessed on December 28, 2022.

4. Aaron Mehta, "HASC Chairman: Turkey 'not coming back' to F-35 Program as NATO Trade", *Breaking Defense*, June 15, 2022, at https://breakingdefense.com/2022/06/hasc-chairman-turkey-not-coming-back-to-f-35-program-amid-sweden-protest/, accessed on December 28, 2022.

5. Oleg Danylov, "AI TF-X / MMU: a Turkish Fighter of the Fifth Generation", *Mezha Media*, November 25, 2022, at https://mezha.media/en/2022/11/25/tai-tf-x-mmu-a-turkish-fighter-of-the-fifth-generation/, accessed on December 28, 2022.

6. Franz-Stefan Gady, "Japan to Pursue Locally Developed Next Generation 'Future Fighter' Project", *The Diplomat*, February 5, 2019, at https://thediplomat.com/2019/02/japan-to-pursue-locally-developed-next-generation-future-fighter-project/, accessed on December 29, 2022.

7. Akhil Kadidal and Jaison Deepak. "Aero India 2023: AMCA Finishes Systems-level Critical Design Review", *Janes*, February 16, 2023, at https://www.janes.com/defence-news/news-detail/aero-india-2023-amca-finishes-systems-level-critical-design-review, accessed on February 27, 2023.

8. Dinakar Peri, "Fifth Gen fighter AMCA can be rolled out in Three Years after project Sanction: scientists," *The Hindu*, October 29, 2022, at https://www.thehindu.com/news/national/fifth-gen-fighter-amca-can-be-rolled-out-in-three-years-after-project-sanction-scientists/article66066386.ece, accessed on December 29, 2022.

9. Rajesh Uppal, "Countries Launch Family of Six-generation Fighters for Air-superiority in Future Anti-Access/Area-Denial Environment", International Defence, Security and Technology, November 12, 2020, at https://idstch.com/geopolitics/countries-launch-family-of-6th-generation-fighters-for-air-superiority-in-future-anti-access-area-denial-environment/, accessed on December 30, 2022.

10. Vijainder K Thakur, "Sixth-Generation Fighter Jet: How The Goalposts For Next-Gen Warplanes Are Ever-Changing", *The EurAsian Times*, October 17, 2022, at https://eurasiantimes.com/sixth-generation-fighter-jet-how-the-goalposts-for-next-gen-warplanes/, accessed on December 30, 2022.

11. "Silicon vs. Gallium Nitride (GaN): Properties & Applications in Semiconductors," *Arrow*, January 21, 2020, at https://www.arrow.com/en/research-and-events/articles/gan-vs-silicon-semiconductor-materials-compared, accessed on January 3, 2023.

12. Jay Levine, "Experimental Wing Proving New Design Methods", NASA, September 26, 2018, at https://www.nasa.gov/centers/armstrong/features/pat_wing.html, accessed on January 3, 2023.

13. Pearl Maria D'Souza, "LCA Tejas to Level up with on-board Oxygen System by early 2020, says DRDO", *The Indian Express*, September 20, 2019, at https://www.newindianexpress.com/nation/2019/sep/20/lca-tejas-to-level-up-with-on-board-oxygen-system-by-early-2020-says-drdo-2036300.html, accessed on January 3, 2023.

14. Emma Woollacott, "Could contact lenses be the ultimate computer screen?" BBC, May 20, 2022, at https://www.bbc.com/news/business-61318460, accessed on January 3, 2023.
15. Mark Sparrow, "Mojo2 Bone-Conducting Headset is the Ideal Solution for Exercising in the Rain", *Forbes*, October, 23, 2022, at https://www.forbes.com/sites/marksparrow/2022/10/23/mojo2-bone-conducting-headset-is-the-ideal-solution-for-exercising-in-the-rain/?sh=333f3db8356e, accessed on January 3, 2023.
16. Brad Lendon, "Japan, Britain and Italy Plan Sixth-generation Fighter Jet to Rival World's Most-Advanced Warplanes", CNN, December 9, 2022, at https://edition.cnn.com/2022/12/09/asia/japan-uk-italy-new-fighter-plane-deal-intl-hnk-ml/index.html, accessed on December 30, 2022.
17. Gareth Jennings, "UK sets out post-2030 Combat Aviation Force Structure", *IHS Janes 360*, July 29, 2014, at https://web.archive.org/web/20140820072232/http://www.janes.com/article/41309/uk-sets-out-post-2030-combat-aviation-force-structure, accessed on December 30, 2022.
18. Sabine Siebold and Michel Rose, "France, Germany, Spain agree on moving on with FCAS Warplane Development," Reuters, November 19, 2022, at https://www.reuters.com/business/autos-transportation/france-germany-spain-agree-next-phase-fighter-jet-development-source-2022-11-18/, accessed on December 30, 2022.
19. Gareth Jennings, "Russia Launches PAK DP Development to Replace MiG-31", *Janes*, January 25, 2021, at https://www.janes.com/defence-news/news-detail/russia-launches-pak-dp-development-to-replace-mig-31, accessed on December 30, 2022.
20. "UAC Plans to Build Four Checkmate Prototypes", *Tass*, August 16, 2022, at https://tass.ru/armiya-i-opk/15478749, accessed on December 30, 2022.
21. Tanmay Kadam, "China Unveils 'NGAD Rival' 6th-Gen Fighter Concept; Military Expert Says Maiden Flight Possible by 2026", *The EurAsian Times*, November 9, 2022, at https://eurasiantimes.com/china-unveils-ngad-rival-6th-gen-fighter-concept-military-expert/, accessed on December 30, 2022.
22. Ibid.
23. Thomas Newdick and Tyler Rogoway, "New Next Generation Air Dominance 'Fighter' Renderings From Lockheed", *The Drive*, October 26, 2022, at https://www.thedrive.com/the-war-zone/new-next-generation-air-dominance-fighter-renderings-from-lockheed, accessed on December 30, 2022.
24. Joseph Trevithick and Tyler Rogoway, "The Navy Just Released Its Vision for Its Future F/A-XX Next Generation Strike Fighter", *The Drive*, October 30, 2021, at https://www.thedrive.com/the-war-zone/42941/the-navy-just-released-its-vision-for-its-future-f-a-xx-next-generation-strike-fighter, accessed on December 30, 2022.

25. "System of Systems Integration Technology and Experimentation (SoSITE) (Archived)," *DARPA*, at https://www.darpa.mil/program/system-of-systems-integration-technology-and-experimentation, accessed on January 3, 2023.
26. Brett Tingley, "The Navy's Secretive And Revolutionary Program to Project False Fleets from Drone Swarms", *The Drive*, December 1, 2019, at https://www.thedrive.com/the-war-zone/29505/the-navys-secretive-nemesis-electronic-warfare-capability-will-change-naval-combat-forever, accessed on January 3, 2023.
27. "Air Force Doctrine Note 1-21, Agile Combat Employment", USAF, August 23, 2022, at https://www.doctrine.af.mil/Portals/61/documents/AFDN_1-21/AFDN%201-21%20ACE.pdf, accessed on January 4, 2023.
28. Stephen Losey, "Future NGAD Fighter Jets could Cost 'Hundreds of Millions' Apiece," Defense News, April 29, 2022, at https://www.defensenews.com/air/2022/04/28/future-ngad-fighter-jets-could-cost-hundreds-of-millions-apiece/, accessed on January 5, 2023.

7. Exploiting Air Power Beyond the Continent: Challenges and Opportunities

Swaim Prakash Singh

Introduction

Air power has become an essential component of a nation's military strength, offering strategic reach, flexibility in operations, and unparalleled lethality. It encompasses a wide range of assets, capabilities, and strategies that allow a nation to project force, defend its airspace, and shape the outcome of conflicts. The significance of air power extends beyond military strength, impacting geopolitical influence and overall security. To enhance air power, nations focus on technological advancements, operational versatility, collaboration, and interoperability with international partners. Adapting to the evolving global security landscape requires continuous prioritisation of Air Force development and modernisation to address the emerging threats and maintain a strategic advantage effectively.

Strategic considerations such as national security objectives, threat perceptions, and regional dynamics influence a nation's air power. Factors like territorial defence, power projection capabilities, alliances, and deterrence shape Air Forces' size, composition, and investment priorities, making them the primary contributors to a nation's comprehensive air power. Strategic considerations also guide international collaborations, defence partnerships, and procurement decisions, enabling nations to enhance their air power through cooperation and alignment with other countries. Possessing a strong Air Force serves as a strategic asset, influencing regional dynamics, strengthening diplomatic leverage, and contributing to the national security framework as a whole.

The operational capabilities of air power encompass a broad range of missions, from conducting deep offensive strikes to providing coordinated air support for ground forces. Its versatility allows for rapid deployment, intelligence gathering, precision strikes, aerial reconnaissance, airlift operations, humanitarian assistance and disaster relief (HADR) efforts. These diverse missions provide nations with operational flexibility and agility on the battlefield.

Technological advancements are a driving force in the evolution of air power, transforming the capabilities of modern Air Forces. Cutting-edge aircraft, advanced sensors, sophisticated weapons systems, and robust communication networks significantly enhance air power. Stealth technology, unmanned aerial vehicles (UAVs), advanced avionics, and precision-guided munitions increase effectiveness, range, and lethality. Continuous investment in research, development, and acquisition of advanced technologies is crucial to maintain a competitive edge in the rapidly changing global security landscape.

Air power enables nations to project force beyond their borders, extending their influence and safeguarding national interests. The ability to rapidly deploy aircraft, establish air superiority, and conduct precision strikes enhances a nation's force projection capabilities. This capability is especially critical in today's interconnected world, where emerging threats demand swift and decisive responses.

Turbulent Geopolitics

China has emerged as a strong partner for the islands and littoral nations of the Indian Ocean. Under Beijing's Belt and Road Initiative (BRI), the Maritime Silk Road Initiative has provided an additional avenue for economic and military cooperation among these nations.[1] China's potential to project military strength into the Indian Ocean Region (IOR) has been considerably enhanced by its military expansion programme over the long term. India is already significantly and steadily outmatched by its capabilities. China's naval presence has increased with the People's Liberation Army (PLA) Navy's (PLAN) antipiracy missions in the western Indian Ocean, which Beijing is making more permanent by constructing and operationalising logistical support facilities in Djibouti. In addition to the development of maritime infrastructure along the IOR, China's BRI programme also involves the construction of a vast maritime network.[2]

As part of the China-Pakistan Economic Corridor (CPEC), the Gwadar Port offers several significant benefits to both Pakistan and China. First, the Pakistani government views the port of Gwadar as a potential hedge against a future Indian blockade of Karachi, which now handles 90 per cent of Pakistan's seaborne trade. Second, Gwadar, which is barely 240 miles from the Strait of Hormuz, provides a critical strategic footing for the Chinese government, which has sponsored the majority of the US$ 1.2 billion project.[3] Third, Pakistan's collusive approach with China against India is a significant driver for strengthening India's air power over land and sea through quantitative and qualitative means. A fully functional military post in Djibouti, a naval facility at Gwadar Port in Karachi, Hambantota Port in Sri Lanka, and an outpost at Coco Island, north of Andaman and Nicobar Islands, are the immediate launch pads from where threats are required to be neutralised. In addition, India closely checks China's 'mission-based' deployments in the region,[4] and correctly utilising air power can be one of the most influential and decisive forces in its efforts.

As an important player in the emerging world order, India is part of almost all critical groups and international bodies. Due to its stature, India has also been a regular and consistent attendee in the G7 grouping. Closer to home, the strengthening bond and effectiveness of the Quad for the free and open Indo-Pacific is an example that needs monitoring and analysis. Though it has been officially stated that Quad is a non-military alliance, reviewing the objective in the future due to turbulent global geopolitics cannot be ruled out.

Air Power Tool for Political Signalling

In recent years, there have been many instances around the world where air power has been used as a tool for political signalling, resulting in the lowering of the guards and reducing the mounting tensions between the two countries. In the Indian context, the aerial strike on terror camps in Balakot, Pakistan, was a strong political signal to Pakistan and the world that India is capable of taking punitive actions if forced to.

China has used air power, citing it as part of a military exercise, to express its objections, hegemony, and supremacy on the Taiwan issue multiple times. China's military harassment of Taiwan has intensified in recent years, with planes or ships sent towards the island nearly daily, with the numbers rising in reaction to sensitive activities. Moreover, military activity has increased significantly since the then US Speaker Nancy Pelosi's visit in August 2022, with Chinese PLA Air Force (PLAAF) fighter jets regularly flying over the middle boundary line.

In April 2023, more than 200 Chinese warplanes carried out a three-day military exercise. It was officially quoted as the practice of hitting important targets on the island by "simulating the joint sealing off" of Taiwan through "waves of simulated strikes". Such military actions by China were in protest and political signalling against the visit of Taiwanese President Tsai Ing-wen to the United States.

The exercises were similar to the ones conducted by China in August 2022, when it launched missile strikes on targets in the seas around Taiwan in retaliation for Pelosi's visit. It also fired missiles over the island, which landed in Japan's exclusive economic zone, in a significant escalation. The live-fire exercises disrupted flights and shipping in one of the busiest shipping lanes of global trade.[5]

Such exercises serve as intimidation and an opportunity for Chinese troops to practice sealing off Taiwan by blocking sea and air traffic, an essential strategic option the Chinese military might pursue if it uses military force to take Taiwan.

IAF's Global and Regional Power Projection

The IAF plays a crucial role in maintaining the country's air defence and promoting national security. In addition to its primary role of defending India's airspace, the IAF also has the capability to project power globally and regionally, which allows the country to respond effectively to crises and protect its interests beyond its borders, if not engaged in any of the conventional military scenarios affecting its current holdings vis-à-vis its continental size.

One crucial factor is the size and composition of the IAF's fleet. The IAF has approximately 1,645 aircraft of different types,[6] including fighter jets, transport planes, and helicopters. In addition, the IAF has a mix of aircraft of each type, including modern and advanced aircraft such as the Su-30MKI, Dassault Rafale and M-2000, as well as older aircraft that have been in service for many years, such as the MiG-21 and the Jaguar. Another critical factor is the IAF's ability to meet the air defence needs of the country. The IAF is responsible for protecting Indian airspace and providing air defence capabilities to deter and destroy emerging external threats, if any. The IAF has an extensive network of radar and early warning systems in place, as well as a large number of surface-to-air missile (SAM) systems and air defence batteries, to protect the country's airspace.

Figure 7.1: Current IAF Inventory (as of August 18, 2022)

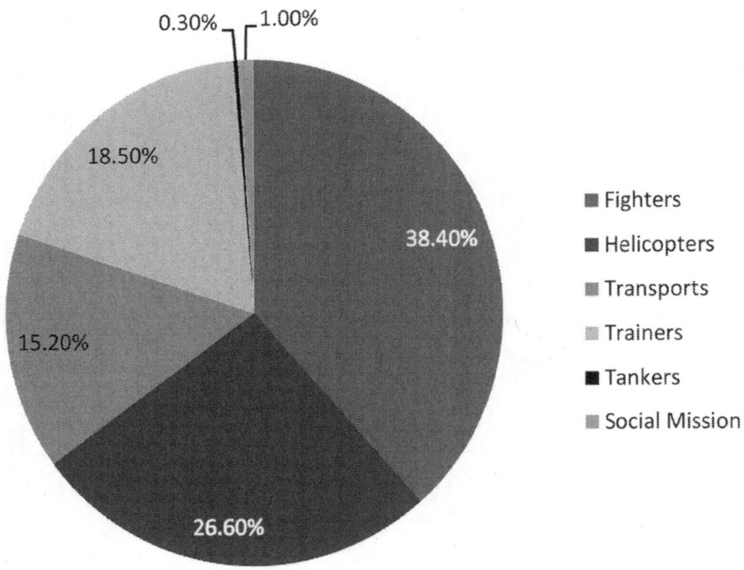

Source: WDMMA.org https://www.wdmma.org/indian-air-force.php.

The IAF projects its global and regional power through its ability to conduct long-range airlift operations. The IAF has a fleet of transport aircraft, such as the C-130J Super Hercules and the C-17 Globemaster, capable of carrying large quantities of personnel, equipment, and supplies over long distances. These aircraft transport troops, supplies, and equipment to various places globally and regionally, including HADR and United Nations Peacekeeping (UNPK) missions. The IAF can also conduct Air-to-Air Refuelling (AAR), allowing its aircraft to stay airborne longer and extend their range, enabling them to project power over greater distances. For this, the IAF operates several IL-78 refuelling aircraft that can refuel fighter jets and other aircraft mid-air, allowing the IAF to maintain air superiority over a larger area over a longer duration.

The IAF can also conduct reconnaissance and surveillance operations through aircraft, such as Airborne Warning and Control Systems (AWACS), Airborne Early Warning and Control (AEW&C), and Remotely Piloted Aircraft (RPA), which are equipped with advanced sensors and communications systems that allow them to gather intelligence and conduct surveillance over large areas. These aircraft play a critical role in providing the IAF with situational awareness, which is essential for effective power projection. In addition, the naval air arm also operates with aircraft, which adds to the air power capability of India in the IOR. The naval P-8I aircraft is one such fleet that adds teeth to the intelligence, surveillance, and reconnaissance (ISR) potential of the country.

IAF's Challenges in Power Projection

Despite these capabilities, the IAF faces certain challenges, partly due to its ageing fleet and the need to induct new aircraft. In addition, the IAF has been facing issues with aircraft availability and serviceability for some years, and the gap in fighter jets in the inventory has been increasing, which may affect their ability to meet all their commitments in case of hostilities. The IAF is also facing challenges regarding its ability to meet the demands for modernising and strengthening the armed forces. This may limit its ability to respond to crises and build its air power to operate beyond the continent in case of any political signalling or out-of-area contingency. Therefore, the IAF, in its centennial decade, needs to strengthen these aspects and aim to establish itself as a significant force to be a dependable aerospace force.

The IAF's current holdings are large, with specific gaps that need to be filled with newer and more advanced aircraft to meet the demands of the country's restructuring armed forces in the envisaged integrated environment. Additionally, investment in new technology and infrastructure is essential to providing the IAF with the ability to respond to crises and prove effective even beyond the continent in the coming years and decades. The IAF can project power globally and regionally through its ability to conduct long-range airlift operations, AAR, and its ISR capabilities.

This can be achieved if the Air Force can fulfil its shortfall of fighter aircraft, radars, and weapon systems through all possible routes of development and procurement, such as Buy-Indigenous Designed and Manufactured (IDDM), Innovations for Defence Excellence (iDEX), Buy and Make, Buy Global, or government-to-government agreements. This issue has received adequate attention in the political, military, and industry spheres, yet a long distance is to be covered to make it possible on the ground.

The ensuing ten years will be crucial in developing and producing indigenous fighter aircraft for the IAF. Hindustan Aeronautics Limited (HAL) has executed an order for the Light Combat Aircraft (LCA) Mk-1A, and the official reports indicate that the indigenous fighter programme is on track. The Aeronautical Development Agency (ADA) continues to work on the design and development of the LCA Mk-2 and Advanced Medium Combat Aircraft (AMCA). However, the number of these aircraft available in the final operational configuration by the planned time still needs to be seen. Similarly, the acquisition of AWACS and AEW&C aircraft, which are now prerequisites for air operations and also highlighted in the new doctrine of the IAF, is a challenge for the country. Experience indicates that the Indian research and development ecosystem of AEW&C is good as far as the production of individual systems of complex aircraft is concerned; however, integrating these subsystems for an effective operational deliverable still has a few more technological milestones to achieve.

The absence of adequate airfield infrastructure, when operating air power beyond the continent also reduces the proximity of bases and forces to potential conflict areas, impacting response times and the ability to reinforce or sustain operations. Projecting air power beyond the region often requires cooperation and support from host nations in the region. However, negotiating agreements, basing rights, and logistical support can be complex and influenced by diplomatic and political considerations. Balancing national interests, respecting host nation sovereignty, and addressing potential sensitivities or restrictions may pose challenges when seeking support for air operations.

Addressing these challenges requires comprehensive planning, investment in long-range capabilities, robust logistical support, technological advancements, and effective coordination with partner nations. By overcoming these obstacles, it becomes possible to project air power effectively beyond the Indian continent, extending the reach of military operations and safeguarding national security interests.

IAF's Opportunities for Power Projection

Since its inception, IAF has demonstrated its prowess as a crisis resolver in conflict and peacetime. The speed with which the IAF moved equipment, personnel, and National Disaster Relief Force (NDRF) teams in anticipation of Cyclone *Vayu* in June 2019 and earlier after earthquakes in Sikkim and Nepal or floods in Uttarakhand demonstrated its first responder capability on multiple occasions. India has come a long way regarding capability and response since the 1984 Bhopal gas leak tragedy, the 1999 Orissa cyclone, the 2001 Bhuj earthquake, and the December 2004 tsunami. The addition of the Boeing C-17 Globemaster III and the Lockheed Martin C-130-J to the Russian IL-76 and An-32 aircraft fleets has provided the IAF with global reach and heavy-lift capability. India is a major regional player in disaster management due to its large fleet of readily deployable helicopters.

Non-Comabt Evacuation Operations

The IAF has played a crucial role in evacuating Indian citizens and other foreigners from Afghanistan, Ukraine, Libya, etc., during conflicts and crises. The ability to quickly and efficiently transport people out of a war zone is vital to military operations. The IAF's airlift capability has been an essential tool in this regard. The IAF's ability to conduct operations in a challenging environment and the support they provide to Indian citizens and foreign nations in need have been key examples and are a testament to the IAF's readiness to support the nation in times of need.

In 2022, the IAF again played a crucial role in evacuating Indian citizens and other foreign nationals from Ukraine during the ongoing conflict between Russia and Ukraine. The IAF was tasked with the operation to evacuate the people in distress. Similar operations were carried out in Afghanistan in 2021 after the pullout of US forces from the country. Again, the IAF's fleet of transport aircraft, equipped with advanced navigation and communication systems, was able to operate in the challenging environment of Afghanistan, successfully flying in and out of airbases in the region, with the safety and security of the passengers being the topmost priority.

Vaccine Maitri

The IAF has been an effective instrument during India's COVID-19 *Vaccine Maitri* initiative. It played a crucial role in the Indian government's efforts to provide assistance and support to other countries in the fight against the COVID-19 pandemic. The IAF's airlift capability has been an essential tool in these efforts, which has been focused on the transportation and distribution of COVID-19 vaccines to other countries. The IAF's transport aircraft, including the IL-76 and C-17 Globemaster, were used to airlift vaccines and other medical supplies to countries in need. The IAF's airlift capability and ability to operate in challenging environments have made them an essential asset in this effort. It has ensured that the vaccines reach the countries in need quickly and efficiently. The Indian government's efforts to provide vaccines and other forms of assistance to other countries during the pandemic have been widely recognised as a demonstration of India's commitment to global health and its leadership in the international community. These efforts have not only helped other countries in their fight against the pandemic but have also helped boost India's diplomatic relationships with other countries.

HADR Operations

The IAF is the first responder during HADR operations. The IAF, with its vast fleet of transport aircraft and helicopters, is equipped to respond quickly and efficiently to natural disasters and other crises that require immediate humanitarian assistance. As a result, it plays a crucial role in disaster relief operations in India and other countries. The IAF's primary responsibility in the event of a disaster is to provide air transportation for relief workers and supplies, as well as to carry out aerial reconnaissance to assess the extent of the damage and identify areas in need of urgent assistance. Thus, the IAF plays a fundamental role in providing rapid response and assisting the civil administration in disaster management.

One of the key strengths of the IAF in HADR operations is its ability to deploy personnel and equipment to affected areas quickly. The IAF's transport aircraft, such as the C-130J Super Hercules and the C-17, can carry large amounts of humanitarian aid, including food, water, and medical supplies, as well as disaster response teams. The IAF's fleet of helicopters, including the Mi-17, is also well suited for HADR operations, as they can operate in challenging terrain, reach areas inaccessible by ground, and evacuate people affected by the disaster. In addition, the IAF's fleet is also equipped with medical facilities, including oxygen supplies and stretchers, to provide medical aid while in flight.

IAF: Exploiting Beyond the Continent

In 2022, the IAF surpassed the PLAAF and was declared third in the world ranking of air forces conducted by the World Directory of Modern Military Aircraft (WDMMA) based on operational capability. However, to exploit its prowess beyond the continent, the IAF would need to enhance its capabilities, reach, and influence in ways beyond its current capabilities.

The IOR is crucial for global trade, and air power can help safeguard maritime trade routes, sea lines of communication, and energy supply routes. Moreover, projecting air power beyond the Indian continent will enhance India's diplomatic influence by demonstrating its commitment to regional security and stability. Engaging with regional partners through joint exercises, HADR efforts will help build trust, strengthen relationships, and promote cooperation across various fields. Seizing these opportunities will require comprehensive planning, robust capabilities, effective coordination, and collaboration with partner nations. By doing so, cooperating countries can enhance their strategic capabilities, expand their sphere of influence, and contribute to regional security and stability by projecting air power beyond the continent. Following are a few ways the IAF can exploit itself to become an ever-ready responder to meet any challenges in the future.

Power Projection

Projecting air power beyond the continent presents several opportunities to enhance its strategic capabilities and contribute to regional security. It will allow India to extend its military capabilities and influence over larger geographic areas. Rapid response capabilities enable the projection of force and swift responses to emerging threats or crises in distant regions, bolstering a nation's credibility as a global power and fostering regional stability.

Developing Long-Range and Airlift Capabilities

The IAF should focus on developing its long-range capabilities. This could include investing in new aircraft, such as the indigenous projects of Tejas Mk I and II, AMCA, and greater numbers of C-17 and C-130 aircraft with the range and endurance to operate beyond the continent. It could also include training and exercises to prepare the IAF to operate in different environments and conditions and to develop tactics, techniques, and procedures to carry out long-range missions. In addition, the IAF will have to build its inventory by buying more long-range and higher airlift-capable aircraft.

Build up Force Enablers, Enhancers, Orchestrators, and Fighter Inventories

India as a nation and the IAF as a force in particular need to draw up a practical and result-driven roadmap to build their inventory to an optimum level. The inventory should be such that it caters to safeguarding national airspace and territorial integrity and manages escalating situations beyond boundaries. The current upgrade and modernisation plan indicates that the IAF will be a formidable force with adequate numbers of technologically advanced inventories by 2032, which coincides with 100 years of its existence. However, delays in meeting the deadlines and delivering equipment in the final operational configuration in mass numbers have been a concern in the past. Therefore, a firm focus on meeting the target is a must.

Additionally, India will have to review the procurement plan and route to acquire adequate AWACS, Flight Refuller, and ISTAR aircraft to operate effectively beyond its borders. This can be best related to the hypothetical situation of participating in a joint multinational coalition military action in the Indo-Pacific Ocean region in the future. In such a scenario, the IAF will require more fighters, AWACS, and Flight Refuelling Aircraft (FRA) fleets.

Building Sustained ISR Capability

Using the air power capability of the IAF and Indian Navy, India can utilise the opportunity to have a sustained round-the-clock ISR capability, especially during heightened situations. Advanced surveillance and reconnaissance systems provide valuable situational awareness, supporting timely decision-making and facilitating targeted operations. Operating air power in distant regions will also involve multinational cooperation and alliances, fostering interoperability and promoting regional security and cooperation, especially in the IOR.

Building Deterrence

The projected air power also serves as a powerful deterrent to potential adversaries. By demonstrating the ability and willingness to project force over long distances, India can dissuade aggression and promote stability in the region. The speed and flexibility of air power offer opportunities for rapid deployment and crisis response, enabling timely intervention and assistance in the face of emerging threats or humanitarian crises.

Building International Partnerships

The IAF should also focus on building international partnerships. This could include establishing joint training and exercise programmes, sharing intelligence and other information, and developing joint procurement, research, and development initiatives with different Air Forces. Building international partnerships will allow the IAF to benefit from the strengths and capabilities of other Air Forces and help promote stability and security in the region.

The IAF has decided on the theme 'Beyond the Boundaries' for joint conduct and participation in international exercises in 2023. It aims to engage with other Air Forces worldwide for mutual professional and diplomatic exchange. In addition, the IAF has decided to conduct or participate in nearly twelve international exercises this year, both in Indian skies and abroad. It also aims to engage with other Air Forces in trans-oceanic bilateral and multilateral formats, including with Quad countries.

Developing Joint Operations Capabilities

The IAF should also focus on developing its joint operations capabilities in an integrated scenario which needs to be practised more regularly. This could include the integration of air and missile defence, ISR, special operations forces, and other military assets. Carrying out joint training and exercises with the aviation assets of the IAF and Indian Navy (IN) will not only increase synergy but also increase the efficacy of operations manifold. In addition, the utilisation of AWACS, P-8I aircraft, ISR assets of both services and FRA overseas will further increase sustained operations.

Building a Strong Defence Industry

Building a strong defence industry would also be vital for India to achieve its goal of exploring beyond the continent. India must be able to create, repair, and maintain its military assets in-house and be less dependent on importing military hardware. This would enable the IAF to operate with greater flexibility and self-sufficiency, allowing it to operate more effectively in far-flung locations. The possibility of exploring Africa as the most potent defence market is the highest in the current expansion of the defence market and industry. Therefore, India must keenly direct all governmental efforts towards this continent.

Focus on UNPK

India has actively participated in UNPK missions, providing troops and air support. Therefore, this can allow the IAF to gain operational experience and build relationships with other Air Forces in peacekeeping operations. Contributing to a more significant number of UN missions with aerial diplomacy as its core contributory factor apart from the peacekeepers will keep India ahead in establishing the air power infrastructure and capacity building beyond its boundaries.

Aerial Diplomacy

Air power has the potential to play a significant role in global diplomacy through the generic concept of 'aerial diplomacy'. However, this facet can be further divided into various categories, which can be highly beneficial in inducting newer technologies and ideas into the IAF. Apart from 'flight suite diplomacy', which has seen its beginning in 2023, the IAF may look into 'AWACS diplomacy', 'Battle Management System diplomacy' and 'Multi-domain diplomacy' as well. Countries such as the US, Australia, Japan, Russia and France could be ideal countries to start with.

Importantly, exploitation beyond the continent would be a long-term goal, requiring sustained engagement and commitment from the IAF. It would also require careful planning and coordination with other regional actors and strategic partners, as well as developing the necessary capabilities and resources to operate effectively in new and challenging environments.

Conclusion

The IAF is responsible for maintaining the country's air defence and promoting national security. As the world becomes increasingly interconnected, the IAF's airlift capability will play an increasingly important role in the country's ability to project power and respond to crises beyond its borders. A critical aspect of a futuristic airlift capability for the IAF would be the ability to move large quantities of personnel, equipment, and supplies over long distances quickly and efficiently. To achieve this, the IAF requires a fleet of modern and advanced aircraft, such as wide-body transport planes like the C-17 Globemaster or aircraft of a newer generation like the A-330 MRTT or the C-130J Super Hercules. These aircraft have the range and capacity to support long-distance airlift operations. They can also be used for other missions, such as para trooping, air-dropping, aerial refuelling and medical evacuation.

The IAF's futuristic airlift capability would operate in a challenging and remote environment. This would likely involve acquiring aircraft specifically designed for short take-off and landing (STOL) operations, such as the C-27J Spartan or the Embraer KC-390. Such aircraft would also need to be equipped with advanced navigation and communications systems and defensive systems to ensure their safety in hostile environments. In addition, it could integrate and coordinate its airlift operations with other military and civilian agencies.

In addition to aircraft, the IAF would also need to invest in supporting infrastructure and logistics to ensure its airlift capability can operate effectively beyond the continent. This would include constructing and maintaining airfields and logistics hubs in strategically important locations for the IAF's operations, as well as developing ground support equipment and air traffic control capabilities.

In addition, the IAF could procure or lease civilian or cargo planes to improve its airlift capability. The IAF will also have to review its procurement plans for fighter aircraft and force enablers and orchestrators to maintain a powerful aircraft inventory for its territorial boundaries and beyond. As part of the whole-of-government and nation approach, 2030 could be set as a target for making the aircraft inventory good for the IAF so that it celebrates 100 years of its existence in 2032 as a truly formidable, potent Air Force capable of meeting any commitment over its airspace and anywhere on the globe.

Notes

1. Darshana M Baruah, "What Is Happening in the Indian Ocean?", Carnegie Endowment for International Peace, March 3, 2021, at https://carnegieendowment.org/2021/03/03/what-is-happening-in-indian-ocean-pub-83948. https://carnegieendowment.org/2021/03/03/what-is-happening-in-indian-ocean-pub-83948, accessed on September 24, 2022.
2. David Brewster, "India and China at Sea: A Contest of Status and Legitimacy in the Indian Ocean", *Asia Policy*, No. 22 (2016), pp. 4-10, at https://www.jstor.org/stable/24905133, accessed on September 24, 2022.
3. Alex Vines Obe, "Piracy, not China, is the real issue in the Indian Ocean", Chatham House, February 3, 2012, at https://www.chathamhouse.org/publications/the-world-today/2012-02/piracy-not-china-real-issue-indian-ocean, accessed on October 18, 2022.
4. "Why India is placing Su-30 fighter jets in South India", *The Economic Times*, January 20, 2020, at https://economictimes.indiatimes.com/news/defence/why-india-is-placing-sukhoi-jets-in-south-india/printarticle/73431727.cms, accessed on September 30, 2022.
5. Huizhong Wu, "China military 'ready to fight' after drills near Taiwan", AP News, April 11, 2023, at https://apnews.com/article/china-military-taiwan-us-7549c646a377f1f199d2cda983573279, accessed on May 24, 2023.
6. "Indian Air Force (2023) Current Active Inventory: 1,645 Aircraft," *WDMMA*, August 18, 2022.

8. Future Integrated Air Battle Management

Amit Dev

"If we lose the war in the air, we lose the war and we lose it quickly."
—Field Marshal Bernard Montgomery

Introduction

To deal with emerging threats, the armed forces must develop the capabilities to fight and win wars. The national leadership should understand the complexities of warfare and provide the necessary support. A visionary military commander must strive for the best equipment, workforce, logistics, and infrastructure because losing a war has grave consequences for the state. However, operational plans should consider the existing capabilities. The induction of new technologies and the systematic upgrade of existing systems are necessary to deter the adversary and build capability for the future.

For centuries, enlightened leaders have transformed the ways and means of prosecuting wars. However, every capability has a shelf life. Archers, cavalry, chariots, and elephants were once prized possessions of commanders in battle but are no longer relevant in today's warfare. The days of close-combat aerial dogfights are over. Future air-to-air engagements will take place well beyond visual ranges with enhanced automation and battlefield transparency. Improved ranges, accuracy, and lethality of weapons have increased the complexity of modern warfare. Air battle management will thus require foresight and planning.

Threat Perception and Capability Building

Capability development for war depends on the perceived threat and the nation's willingness and capacity to address it. India has adversarial relations with two of its neighbours, China and Pakistan. Sino-Indian relations have witnessed border clashes, that have increased in intensity and frequency. The standoffs in Doklam, Galwan and Yangtse indicate China's intent. The construction of warfighting infrastructure in Tibet is a significant shift in China's policy towards India. A border confrontation with belligerent and aggressive China appears to be a real possibility.

On the other hand, anti-India sentiment is the glue that binds Pakistan. Pakistan's economy may not give them an appetite for a full-scale war with India. They will, however, continue with the low-cost option of breeding terrorists and pushing them across the border. The situation may aggravate a short and swift war. In such an event, air power will have a significant role in the nation's response strategy. The speed of retaliation will be crucial. The government must plan appropriate responses and build capabilities for the entire spectrum of conflict.

In addition, the strategic competition in the Indo-Pacific casts its shadow on the Indian subcontinent. India should be aware of future regional and global geopolitical developments and formulate its response. Partnerships and alliances may be necessary to protect national interests to effectively counter such threats. Like-minded countries will have to come together and fight for the global commons. There would be a need for a potent and responsive armed force that could quickly deploy and be ready for operations. Capability building and achieving the desired level of interoperability take time. Therefore, training with partners during peacetime would be necessary to refine the processes and procedures.

Challenges for Future Air Wars

From its humble beginning, air power's evolution has changed the very nature of warfare. Future wars cannot be imagined, without the application of air power, in one form or another. Air power today is a dominant combat power and has become the ultimate tool in a nation's deterrence and response strategy. The development of air power capabilities will be necessary to avoid adverse fallout during future conflicts. The time has come to shift from 'technology-driven doctrine' to 'doctrine-driven technology.' It is essential to achieve '*Aatmanirbharta*', or self-reliance, in defence manufacturing. No nation can aspire for greatness based on borrowed technology because dependence may lead to compromises.

Preparation for air wars is challenging because technologies associated with aerial platforms and weapon systems reach obsolescence faster. In addition, they are upgraded many times due to the rapid increase in the rate of technological changes. In such an environment, the speed of decision-making is critical. The need for speed in planning, procurement, preparation, and operations is more relevant today than ever due to growing threats.

Technological Advancement

Air Forces are inherently technology-intensive and sensitive forces. A small technological development may have a significant impact on the battle. For example, a better radar or a more capable missile could make all the difference in achieving a favourable air situation. It was visible during the Kargil war when Pakistan Air Force (PAF) fighters refused to engage in combat due to the 'beyond visual range' (BVR) advantage enjoyed by the Indian Air Force. Therefore, it is essential to implement timely changes to handle present and future threats. Delayed procurement decisions could result in substantial capability gaps, detrimental to national interests.

Success in future wars will also depend on the ability to shift through large amounts of data and arrive at optimal solutions. It is essential to harness cyber, space and information technology to integrate various platforms, sensors, and command and control centres. Artificial intelligence, machine learning, quantum computing, and networked data centres will enhance the processing speed and reduce the decision cycle. Software upgrades and automation will improve decision-making, further shortening the observe, orient, decide, act (OODA) loop.

Weapon Systems

The induction of long-range surface-to-air missiles (SAMs) has significantly strengthened the air defence capability of nations. The survival of aerial platforms has become an area of concern. Their employment in future battles would require careful consideration. It is especially true for slow movers because they provide a longer reaction time to the enemy's air defence. Suitable countermeasures will be necessary for safe operations in a hostile battle space. From the early stages of the war, the suppression/destruction of the enemy air defence (SEAD/DEAD) will be imperative for creating safe corridors for air operations.

India's northern borders have very high mountain ranges, which adversely impact the networking of radars and communication equipment. Extreme temperatures in winter, high altitude, poor communication, and a lack of infrastructure prohibit optimal deployment and integration of radars. Deployment of Airborne Warning and Control Systems (AWACS) would be essential for assured detection and timely engagement of hostile tracks. These platforms not only overcome physical barriers but also provide flexibility in deployment, increasing the probability of their survival.

Climatology

The effect of adverse weather on aviation is a well-known phenomenon. Its ramifications in the case of helicopter and transport operations in the valleys are grave. The combination of high altitude, poor visibility, and cloudy weather has resulted in numerous air accidents in the past. The pilot's familiarity with the terrain and experience are invaluable in avoiding such accidents and ensuring the success of the missions. A timely weather update to the crew is also essential for error-free decision-making. The launch criteria for inclement weather should be stringent to ensure safe operations in hilly terrain.

Unmanned Aerial Systems

The induction of unmanned combat aerial vehicles (UCAVs), swarm drones, and low radar cross section (RCS) aerial platforms permits tasking with reduced risk and cost. Absorbing these technologies and operationalising them would require a seamless transition. Thus, finding the right balance between manned and unmanned aerial platforms will be essential in the future. Picking up low RCS platforms with existing air defence radars has become difficult and would need to be addressed. Sometimes old time-tested equipment, skills and processes may no longer be relevant to counter new threats.

Today's fighter aircraft are far more capable. The distinction between a pure strike aircraft and an air defence fighter has blurred, which provides flexibility in deployment, employment, and exploitation. A multi-role aircraft on a ground attack mission can swing roles and take on air defence tasking instantly. This ability to switch roles demands unity of control. An attempt to split assets and distribute them in penny pockets will be counterproductive and undesirable.

Air power is inherently offensive. Its effectiveness depends on knowing what to strike and when to strike. The stand-off precision weapons may be inherently capable, but they will hit the desired mean point of impact only if the coordinates are accurate. For weapons with electro-optical terminal guidance, the imagery of desired resolution and format are essential. Factors like target location, the potential for collateral damage and the likelihood of mission success are analysed based on the gathered intelligence. A thorough analysis of the target system is a prerequisite for selecting aim points for the desired effect. The target study would involve functional and vulnerability analysis before undertaking 'target-to-weapon' and 'weapon-to-platform' matching.

Information Gathering and Assimilation

Another important aspect would be integrating the available information across domains. This will be essential for future air battle management. Information gathered through intelligence surveillance reconnaissance (ISR) assets, human intelligence (HUMINT), electronic intelligence (ELINT), communication intelligence (COMINT), and offensive cyber have to be connected for the picture to emerge. Accurate intelligence is the fundamental requirement for informed decision-making and targeting. Integrating various intelligence agencies will be essential for deriving the optimal value of the information received. Quick and easy access to data is vital for in-depth analysis and effective targeting. Withholding information, deliberately or due to ignorance, is not an option. Targeting opportunities in the air should be acted upon swiftly to achieve a quick kill. During the heat of the battle, any delay in receiving or processing information is a luxury one cannot afford. For timely access to information, a robust wartime structure and a vibrant intelligence grid are considered an absolute necessity.

In a network-enabled environment, combat aircraft hunt in packs, exchanging information through real-time secure data links, which significantly reduces reaction time to engage targets. In addition, connecting all operating platforms through a common operational link will provide better situational awareness to the crew. In the future, we may witness manned and unmanned aircraft sharing vital target information seamlessly. Utilising these capabilities for dynamic and time-sensitive targeting will help in the timely engagement of hostile tracks.

A networked environment and secure communication are the backbones of air operations. Networks are one's greatest assets and also their most critical vulnerability. Its security from physical or cyber-attacks will be imperative. Multiple redundancies will be essential for unhindered operations. A secure networked environment will become a prerequisite for future air operations.

Electronic Warfare

Electronic warfare (EW) has been effectively utilised in the past to degrade, deceive, deny, and disrupt the use of the electromagnetic spectrum. It will continue to play a significant role. The control of the electromagnetic spectrum is essential for unhampered air operation. The information from various ELINT systems needs to be collated, analysed, and disseminated for updating the threat library. Sharing information between the aircraft will increase the probability of survival in a contested battle space. With the development of electromagnetic pulse (EMP) weapons, the means of fighting the war will change drastically. Hardening critical infrastructure and assets against EMP weapons will be necessary for the future.

Space Assets

Armed forces depend on space-based assets for communication, navigation, surveillance, intelligence, and targeting. The dependence will increase with time. The near-space is likely to be used for real-time surveillance. The Low Earth Orbit (LEO) satellites have increased battlefield transparency. The improved resolution and faster updates have become vital for analysis and targeting. The weaponisation of space and space warfare is gradually coming under the realm of reality. Nations have already acquired and demonstrated anti-satellite capabilities. It would be prudent to assume that rogue nations will attempt to deny and disrupt the use of space-based assets.

The seamless integration of air and space will increase operational efficiency and effectiveness. Unity of control will create a favourable aerospace environment for the prosecution of the war. On the other hand, cyber and space are fast emerging as separate domains for warfighting, which needs to be acknowledged and prepared for in the years ahead.

Joint Operations

Integration is essential to synergise the effects of individual services. The 1971 Indo-Pak war is the finest example of the synergised application of air power in all its classical roles. Air superiority in the Eastern sector allowed the surface forces to operate without opposition from enemy air. Air operations like the *Tangail* airdrop and *Meghna* heli-lift were possible due to prevailing air superiority. The 1971 rocket attack on the Governor's house in Dhaka had an immense psychological impact on the Pakistani leadership. It resulted in hastening the process of surrender, despite the availability of more than 90,000 Pakistani soldiers on the ground. The air strike was the proverbial last nail in the coffin. It achieved what John Warden later referred to as 'strategic paralysis' caused by attacking the leadership, the innermost ring of Warden's five-ring model. The capability of aircraft and missiles to cross physical barriers and strike at the heart of the enemy's target system set air forces apart from other forms of combat power. The air assets can simultaneously attack targets at strategic, operational, and tactical levels, unlike the Army, which progresses sequentially.

A joint approach to procurement is necessary for the commonality of equipment between the services. Wherever commonality of equipment exists, joint training helps in facilitating interoperability. At times, platforms and weapon systems procured from the same vendor are not interoperable because of minor differences in the configuration. Resolution through consultation at the time of formulation of Qualifying Requirements (QRs) would be a more prudent approach. Lack of integration creates hurdles in the smooth conduct of operations and the efficient execution of tasks.

Control of the air is the central philosophy around which Air Forces plan their operations. It has been an area of concern for the Army because it is perceived as a distant war, not directly connected to ground operations. Armies may want the air power to be tethered, like artillery. Perhaps the army leadership is used to having all elements of combat power under its command. It is understandable from the Army's viewpoint. However, it would be sub-optimal exploitation of air assets. Operational flexibility is desirable to achieve optimum exploitation of available air assets.

As far as the Navy is concerned, the enhanced radius of action of shore-based aircraft and the availability of aerial refuellers have increased the vulnerability of surface vessels at sea. Navies across the globe have procured potent air defence systems. The aircraft carriers further strengthen the defensive posture of the fleet. When operating away from the umbrella of shore-based aircraft, aircraft carriers are necessary for fleet defence. It is challenging to locate and identify aircraft and surface vessels operating at sea because of limited resources for surveillance covering a large area. Real-time surveillance needs strengthening for effective targeting in the maritime domain. Forward positioning of shipborne surveillance radars and integrating them with the IAF's air defence network would enhance early warning in the coastal belt. Integration of AWACS and AEW&C aircraft with the fleet air defence will help augment the detection of hostile tracks in the vicinity of the fleet. The existing joint organisation needs further strengthening and empowerment for greater efficiency.

Air Land Battle

Air power, with its inherent characteristics of speed, flexibility, manoeuvrability, precision, and reach, has become a vital tool in the armoury of war planners. The vulnerability of surface forces to aerial attack limits the options for surface force commanders. Aircraft are critical assets to be employed in support of offensive and defensive ground operations. The effective employment of air power ensures little or no interference from the enemy's air and reduces friction on the ground.

Joint planning is essential for the efficient application of combat power. The stitching of individual service plans later has many pitfalls and must be avoided. The basis of the Army's utilisation of firepower is the level of degradation of the opposing force, while the IAF resorts to effect-based operations (EBO). EBO involves precise targeting of the critical element in the target system. The debate over degradation versus neutralisation needs resolution through procedural changes in the planning process. The formalised joint planning process (JPP) is considered crucial for an integrated targeting plan. Perhaps the time is ripe to shift from target-based planning to effect-based targeting and for the joint target list to evolve into a joint targeting plan. The plan should be coherent and in consonance with the desired end state.

With ever-increasing battlefield transparency, camouflage, concealment, and deception (CCD) deserve renewed focus to enhance survivability. Infrastructure development in forward-looking areas must incorporate the CCD during construction. During mobilisation and deployment, the forces must be conscious of the threat and plan accordingly because no air defence can be assured to be impregnable. There will always be leakers causing unacceptable damage. Therefore, the forward-deployed forces should embrace CCD like a chameleon because their survival depends on the anonymity of deployment. The CCD measures for in-depth targets have also become necessary because of the increased reach of platforms and the enhanced ranges, accuracy, and lethality of air-launched weapons.

The airspace is progressively getting crowded due to increased dependence on aerial platforms for warfighting. Meticulous planning, close monitoring, and efficient execution will be crucial for the deconfliction of traffic and efficient utilisation of congested air space. The radar controllers and real-time Air Battle Managers (ABM) will have an enhanced role in any future conflict. The chances of fratricide have also increased because of the higher air defence density and lethality of weapons. In a contested aerial engagement, it may become difficult to differentiate friend from foe, leading to misidentification. The automation of the identification process will minimise the chances of fratricide. Regular joint training will help in achieving interoperability and proficiency.

The joint operations centres are the nerve centres for the conduct of the air-land battle. The personnel must be integrated into the existing air defence network and be ready to undertake operations at short notice. With increasing dependence on the medium of air, there has been a quantum jump in air traffic. Artillery shells, cruise and ballistic missiles, SSMs, and SAMs are also competing for the same airspace with manned and unmanned platforms. Centralised control and decentralised execution are the way forward for future air battle management in the Tactical Battle Area (TBA). Detection, identification, engagement, and destruction of targets will become increasingly challenging because of the increase in the ranges of modern-day SAMs and BVR missiles. The shift from point defence to area defence has necessitated organisational changes, that have to cater to the changed operating environment. The next generation of ABM would require to be equipped to handle the increased volume of traffic and expanded role.

There have been intense debates in the past about the benefits of 'Battlefield Air Interdiction' (BAI) versus 'Close Support.' At times, the viewpoint is coloured based on the colour of the uniform. The olive green sees air support as the means of survival of troops in a defensive battle and for the survival of ground force commanders' offensive plans. There can be no doubt about the argument. In both contingencies, air assets have to be deployed in support of the surface force. These operations will fall under the purview of a response to an unexpected situation rather than the planned employment of air power. To the men in blue, the targets within range of the integral weapons of the Army must be engaged by them. The air assets should be tasked to engage targets a little deeper, thus synergising the efforts of the individual services. The demand for allocation of air assets ab-initio to various formations may deny their flexible employability and result in suboptimal exploitation. However, air power may be part of offensive plans if its application is considered necessary for successful mission accomplishment. The two principles of war, i.e., 'economy of effort' and 'concentration of force,' should be kept in mind while employing air assets in support of surface forces. Engaging targets in a dynamic, fast-moving battle in the proximity of friendly forces has its own perils.

Restrictions have to be imposed on strike aircraft to avoid fratricide, thus reducing their effectiveness. Considering the changes in the operating environment in the TBA, the role of the Forward Air Controller (FAC) also requires a rethink. Engaging targets a little deeper provides full freedom of engagement and is, therefore, likely to be less restrictive and more effective. The increased availability of stand-off precision weapons will ensure the safety of aircraft and their availability for the next mission. Engaging suitable targets in depth also has its effect at multiple forward locations simultaneously. An analogy of taking a tree as a target best explains this point of view. The BAI is like hitting the trunk of the tree, which will affect all branches and leaves and, therefore, be more efficient than engaging each branch and leaf independently.

The conduct of large-scale airborne operations may have been planned in the past with resounding success. However, today it is not desirable because the attendant risks may not be acceptable to the planners. Some even consider it suicidal because of the potent air defence deployment in the TBA. These missions may be undertaken in a benign operating environment with little or no opposition from air or ground. However, small-team insertion and extraction missions will continue to be planned after assessing the risks and rewards. The airlift of troops by both rotary and fixed-wing aircraft would be extensively employed for a quick build-up of troops. Helicopters will have a significant role in inter-valley troop transfer, forward deployment, and resupply of troops, especially in hilly terrain. However, large-scale operations in mountainous terrain would require an upgrade of infrastructure in the intended area of operation.

The recent induction of attack helicopters in the IAF has enhanced the offensive capability, which would prove decisive in the air-land battle, especially in a target-rich environment. The use of these assets against UAVs will require further validation to assess their efficacy in combat. The integration of air-to-air missiles (AAM) on armed and attack helicopters will open a new chapter in aerial warfare. The effectiveness of attack and armed helicopters will depend on the upgraded electronic warfare suit and weapon configuration.

Conclusion

The future of air power will continue to focus on using manned and unmanned aerial platforms and developing new weapon systems. The weaponisation of UAV, the development of swarm drone technology, and the deployment of advanced weapons will change the nature of future wars. The network-centric operations will be more prevalent, and the induction of long-range SAMs, drones and low RCS platforms will challenge the planners. The technological advancements will be critical for bridging the capability gaps. The stand-off ranges and lethality of new-age weapons will provide targeting options well inside enemy territory. The ability to look deeper and shoot further will provide options for strategic strikes.

Cyber and space warfare will become more important in future conflicts, as these domains will no longer be in a supporting role but rather be integrated into the main aspects of warfare. Older platforms will be challenging for future commanders, and innovative equipment utilisation will be necessary to maintain the numerical advantage in warfare. In addition, the nature of warfare will see transformative changes in the coming decades, and there is a need for integrated air battle management to synergise the effect of air power.

9. Air Defence is not Defensive

Diptendu Choudhury

"Air Defence is everywhere"[1]

The arrival of air power into warfare brought about a unique paradigm shift with the use of the vertical dimension of the aerial domain, for attacking the enemy from above. It enabled carrying the offensive well behind the enemy lines and also deep into the enemy's heartland, unfettered by friction of terrain, and geographic challenges historically faced by the surface forces. The earliest known use of weapons specifically for the anti-aircraft role occurred during the Franco-Prussian War of 1870, in order to shoot down manned balloons. As aircraft ventured into enemy airspaces to recce, strafe and bomb, it inevitably led to the development of anti-aircraft weapons, ranging from machine guns to cannons, prior to the First World War. The speed and altitude of the aircraft necessitated high rates of fire, long-range capability, and reliable sighting systems, but were clearly not enough as they couldn't prevent them from dropping bombs. This led to the development of the interceptor aircraft, whose task was to engage the Zeppelins and long-range bombers which emerged during the war. Between the two wars, air defence expanded apace with the improvement in the performance of bombers and fighters, and by the Second World War, air defence had developed rapidly for the defence of cities, industrial infrastructure, and military assets from air attacks. The Cold War period saw the rapid development of surface-to-air missiles to engage the nuclear weapon-carrying long-range strategic bombers. Airborne interception (AI) radars, air-air missiles, improved sighting systems, ground radars for detection and ground-controlled interceptions, surface-to-air missiles and anti-aircraft weapons, etc., improved rapidly along with improvements in technology. However, it was the significant improvements in the technology and the performance of AI radars, and the capability of the air-to-air missiles (AAM) of the fighter aircraft, which brought about a new dimension to air defence. Now for the first time, the enemy aerial threat could be detected and shot down well before it reached the target area. From the original infra-red missiles which had to be fired in the rear quarters of the enemy at relatively close ranges, to the semi-active and active radar-guided missiles which could be fired from large beyond visual ranges (BVR), the air defence fighter became an offensive platform. It could now seek out and shoot the enemy down offensively at large ranges, over the adversary's own airspace well before it even crossed the borders. This offensive capability also enabled dedicated air defence aircraft to fly as fighter escorts to friendly strike or bombing missions deep into enemy territory, and keep them safe from enemy interceptors. The term air defence has since become somewhat limiting in its terminology, as this long-range capability allows air defence fighters to literally 'carry the fight into the enemy camp' deep into adversarial air spaces offensively.[2]

A Wider Responsibility

A Broader Concept Jasjit Singh, the doyen of Indian air power, explains that when the role of the Indian Air Force (IAF) shifted "to a broader concept of 'air defence,' in conceptual terms, it stopped short of its logical niche and ultimate effect it had to achieve: the defence of India and protection of its interests and values in the context of its attributes and capabilities, though in practice it kept performing that role."[3] While the IAF had grappled with the conceptual dilemma of the scope of its air defence role for many years in the past, today it has a clear understanding, knowledge, capability, and commitment, to the much larger role it plays in the wider construct of India's national security and her interests. For it, air power is doctrinally the total ability of the nation to assert its will through the medium of air. Unfortunately, in the absence of this clarity in the national security establishment in India, the IAF even today tends to be seen primarily as merely the keeper of air defence of the nation, thereby marginalising its offensive role, which is the very essence of air power. According to the current Chief of Air Staff, "The IAF has over the years transformed into a modern aerospace power that is capable of controlling and exploiting air and space environments in order to achieve India's national and security interests".[4] It is this wider doctrinal discourse, which has been articulated in the latest basic doctrine of the IAF, that needs to reach the policymakers security establishment, strategic and academic community, the media and especially the aware citizens. In this wider construct of the roles and responsibilities of air power in India's security, air defence forms a large and ubiquitous component, whether it be safeguarding sovereignty and strengthening deterrence, in peace; external and internal security and shaping operations, in no-war-no-peace (NWNP) conditions; to the command and control of air and the equally significant offensive air operations, in war. Air power and certainly air defence, whether employed singly or jointly, thus are a significant constituent of the nation's combat power and have a broader engagement in its security and interests.

In Peace The IAF's air defence plays a vast role which practically covers the entire Indian sovereign airspace, to closely monitor each and every air movement, identify it and keep track of it. Most in the nation do not realise that this operational air defence activity is carried out round-the-clock, day and night, through the year, year after year. Close surveillance, control and reporting of both our own and the adversary's airspace, is the very backbone of air defence. Equally, few are probably aware that India's sovereign airspace is composed of military and civil airspaces, which during peacetime are utilised by both the military and civil aviation synergistically, due to the close coordination and real-time mutual communication made possible by a 'flexi-use of airspace' policy.[5] However, during hostile situations or war, the sole responsibility of the nation's total airspace management rests with the IAF. This is a humongous task which it performs efficiently and creditably. Not far back during the entire period during and after the Balakot air strike, IAF's air defence managed the national airspace with an almost negligible disruption of civil air traffic. In comparison to the total airspace closure by the PAF over Pakistan, the continuation of civil flights in India while the operations were on and under the highest level of air defence alert status, is a testimony to the IAF's professionalism. During peacetime, there is continuous radar surveillance being carried out over our own and hostile airspaces, along with the continuous air defence alert maintained by armed IAF fighters on Operational Readiness Platforms (ORP). This round-the-clock air defence watch that is maintained, has led to countless live scrambles and interceptions by fighters and even helicopters, against all types of unidentified aerial intrusions or air movements, whether it be military or civil aircraft, drones, or even stray balloons which have drifted across the borders due to strong winds.[6] In peacetime, in any hostile situation or even the mere likelihood of one, the first action by the IAF is raising of the air defence alert status in a specified sector or across the nation. This immediately leads to the swift redeployment of all its air defence assets which include radars, mobile communication systems, Surface to Air Guided Weapon (SAGW) systems, and fighters, to their operational locations within hours. Simultaneously, all air defence sensors and SAGW systems are put on high alert to maintain a 24 x 7 enhanced surveillance watch. Each and every air defence element, kinetic or non-kinetic, are integrated in real-time at the specialised air defence nodes of the IAF. These nodes which are the nerve centres of IAF's air defence, have direct control over all the combat assets in their sector. They exercise functional control over the armed fighters on the ORPs in order to scramble them in minutes, and also over the SAGW systems to launch them if required. Another interesting less-known fact are the numerous special peace-time air defence readiness alerts which are temporarily conducted over vital areas or installations of the nation, on occasions of national importance like Republic and Independence days. On these occasions, the IAF takes over total control of a designated volume of airspace, in which armed air defence fighters and armed helicopters carry out Combat Air Patrol (CAP) missions against any possible aerial threats. Thus, 'air defence is not only everywhere, but it is also on round the clock through the year, year after year.'[7]

No-Peace-No-War India's threat scenario not only includes the long continuing state-sponsored terror by Pakistan, it also includes China's unique strategic grey zone threat, which is a 'method of warfare "beyond-limits" through the employment of ten thousand methods combined as one: combinations that transcend boundaries.'[8] The NWNP condition which exists in the interregnum between war and peace in India's national security construct, has justifiably become a part of the IAF's air strategy. Under the overarching umbrella of information dominance, the strategy includes shaping operations as well as external and internal security operations, which aims to avoid war and foster the transit towards peacetime conditions. Today, there is an ever-increasing exploitation of the third dimension by state and non-state actors in peacetime. This ranges from the use of drones to push in drugs, weapons, and fake currency in Punjab,[9] to the increasing possibilities of kinetic action like the drone strikes on the oil refineries in Saudi Arabia.[10] Air defence is therefore a golden thread which runs through a wide range of operations, whether it is deterrence through posturing, influencing operations, offensive air defence, punitive strikes, special operations, surveillance and interception, or countering unmanned aerial systems. The rapid air defence deployment and patrol missions in Eastern Ladakh and Arunachal by IAF fighters for asymmetric deterrence, punitive air strikes, regular ISR missions for border management, a variety of missions undertaken for counter-insurgency/counter-terror and Left Wing Extremism, air defence alerts in special contingencies, etc., are all a part of NWNP roles that the IAF routinely engages in.

During War The wartime air strategy of the IAF has significantly changed from that of the past decades. Given the 'Two-Adversary-Multi-Front' threat that India faces from the West, through the North and to the North East, and the fact that both adversaries have strong Air Forces, the command and control of air is a vital imperative for any conflict/war scenario in the future. The ongoing Russo-Ukraine war has emphatically underscored the salience of the control of air. In the Indian context, considering the fact that all its battlespaces will be highly contested, Counter Air operations, which comprises in equal parts Offensive Counter Air (OCA) and air defence operations, are both critical for the application of India's combat power. The efficacy of command and control of air operations, and indeed all military operations of the future, will be increasingly dictated by the shortening of two vital chains—the data-to-decision C2 chain, and the sensor-to-shooter Kill chain. Air defence, whether kinetic or non-kinetic, underpins all air operations and directly impacts all surface operations in war. OCA sets the stage for all applications of military power which includes coordinated air operations undertaken jointly with the other Services in the frontal and intermediate depth battlespaces, and those undertaken independently by the IAF by way of strategic air operations deep into the adversarial heartland. To enable this, OCA includes Suppression/Destruction of enemy air defence (SEAD/DEAD), airfield attacks, fighter sweeps, and escort missions to all key strike missions, all of which are undertaken by air defence aircraft in an offensive avatar. On the other hand, air defence operations which is the other constituent of counter air operations, is vital for some degree of control of air. As Kapil Kak explains,

> "Command of the air or air superiority, the raison d'être of the counter-air campaign has often not only generated inter-service controversy but as a key doctrinal component remained little appreciated. The overall strategy is to seize the initiative, carry the war into enemy territory, neutralise air power, and establish control of the air to provide freedom of action for our surface forces. Such an air offensive is aimed not only to further land, maritime and other operations, but also for the very successful pursuit of overall war aims and defence strategy."[11]

However, in the Indian context, considering the highly contested airspaces and battlespaces, air superiority in its true sense is an ideal but an unrealistic expectation. Therefore, the much-needed control of the air necessary for joint operations, will essentially be in time and space, and will vary greatly depending on the scenario, mission objectives, and phase of the conflict. According to Kainikara, "control of the air is a comparative state which depends on the air power capability outcomes of the two sides, and which ranges from the highest state to the lowest state of ownership of air-air supremacy, air superiority, favourable air situation, tolerable air situation, and finally to air parity when neither side is able to gain control."[12] Though air superiority is the ideal desired end state of CAO, in India's future wars, a Favourable Air Situation (FAS) is the most likely degree of control which can be achieved due to the high likelihood of contested airspaces against a near-peer (PAF) and a stronger (PLAAF) Air Force.[13] The enemy air will definitely exploit its offensive air power capability towards the fielded military, and the strategic targets in Indian territory, as would the IAF against it. Hence, air defence operations synergised holistically by an integrated air defence system which is a combination of ground-based and airborne sensors, air defence fighters and SAGW systems, will be a future warfighting imperative.

The Broader Concept

Integrated Architecture Air defence concepts have evolved from the older point defence construct in which high-value assets, infrastructure, or defined areas, were defended with anti-aircraft guns, into the present-day extended integrated area defence (EIAD) concept which covers a large volume of airspace over a large swath of geographical area. This large space is defended by a variety of sensors, surface-to-air, and air-to-air weapons, that are seamlessly integrated together by data and communication networks. It comprises several SAGW systems with different capabilities, engagement altitudes and ranges, integrated and arranged in tiers, thus enabling a much larger area and airspace volume of air defence coverage. The air defence surveillance coverage of this much-expanded volume is made possible with a mix of advanced three-dimensional radars, radars that track very slow-moving targets at very low altitudes, radars capable of tracking free fall and guided bombs, high-speed cruise missiles, and ballistic missiles. The kinetic element of EIAD comprises SAMs with varied ranges of kill envelopes, and air defence interceptors which are dynamic weapon platforms that operate across all the tiers of the EIAD. All these individual systems are integrated seamlessly to form a larger 'system of systems.' Tier one of the multi-tiered air defence system is the outermost layer with a surveillance reach and volume that extends well into the enemy territory, and is tasked with searching, detecting, identifying and tracking threats. Next is tier two, which comprises of long-range SAMs, the lethal envelope of which also extends hundreds of kilometres deep inside the enemy territory. Tier three is made up of the medium range SAM systems, and covers the intermediate spaces of less than a hundred kilometres. The penultimate tier fourth layer is the domain of low-level quick reaction short-range SAMs with lethal ranges in tens of kilometres. Tier five is the innermost core and is actually the vital asset itself that is being defended, and is covered by terminal defence weapons. It consists of a close-in weapon system (CIWS) that typically comprises of quick reaction missiles, or high calibre guns with extremely high rates of fire, or a combination of both. These are also capable of engaging and destroying small precision or free-fall bombs and missiles.

The kinetic shooters that include air defence interceptors and SAGW systems, are totally integrated and interconnected with the non-kinetic sensors consisting of a surface and airborne surveillance systems via high-speed integrated and secure networks, are all holistically fused with advanced command and control systems, to form the integrated 'Kill Chain'.[14] The real core of the IAF's integrated architecture is the extremely successful Integrated Air Command and Control System (IACCS), which weaves all the sensors and shooters together, and allows all the air defence activity to be closely monitored and controlled by IAF's highly specialised air defence fighter controllers. The system's multi-layered transparency permits every individual air movement or mission within the entire networked airspace, civil or military, friendly or hostile, to be monitored and tracked in real-time, and provides an integrated air situation picture that is directly connected to the shooters by data links of the air defence nodes. The robust and combat-proven integrated architecture is a war-winning critical combat enabler, which will in the future extend to include India's island territories as well.

Expanding Air Defence Umbrella The expanded capabilities of contemporary air defence has brought about significant conceptual changes from the legacy concepts which were limited to the coverage of specific areas of responsibility. The extended depth, altitude and volume of airspace coverage that are possible today are due to the synergistic combination of a variety of surface and airborne-based sensors, and multiple forms of kinetic capabilities ranging from the fighters armed with a variety of air-to-air missiles, and a wider range of surface to air weapon systems. The air defence surveillance coverage of sovereign airspaces today is no longer restricted to the mainland and covers India's Island territories as well. The number of civilian facilities on the mainland which require air defence cover have grown exponentially over the years apace with India's economic growth. These include strategic assets like major industries, shipping and major transportation and communication hubs, vital data, network, and communication hubs, petroleum and hydrocarbon processing and storage facilities, power sector assets and infrastructure, transportation facilities like airports, ports, container terminals, etc. Given India's sustained economic growth and development trajectory, the list of such facilities is an ever-growing one.[15]

Air defence protection of friendly surface forces in the tactical battlespaces are a part of IAF's coordinated operations, and forms only a limited portion of the much larger area over which it conducts a wide range of air operations.[16] Air defence is equally an integral part of IAF's offensive operations that target the high-value strategic centres of gravity deep in the enemy heartland. Air Interdiction (AI) missions against the vast array of vital enemy infrastructure, logistics and communications, military and non-military targets in the intermediate spaces up to around 100 km in-depth, are critical for isolating, shaping the tactical battle areas (TBA) and therefore are critical to the surface battle. The large volume of AI missions flown towards coordinated air operations and indirect assistance of the surface war, comprises of almost 80 per cent of the Air Forces target list and have to be provided air defence coverage. Therefore, IAF's air defence responsibilities are no longer limited to the Army's deployed forces in the TBA, but extend into the larger battlespaces much deeper into enemy territory. All TBAs of the Army thus come under the battlespace coverage of the IAF's EIAD envelope, bolstering their air defence significantly. This is a fact often missed by those who look at air defence from their limited Service-centric points of view, and seek independent tactical control of Service specific air defence or an integrated air defence Command, missing the larger benefits to them from an EIAD structure. Today, while there is some understanding of the inevitable need to plug into IAF's EIADS, and yet the inability to see the future air threats beyond their Service-specific tactical needs, continues to persist.[17,18] The fact is the IAF looks at the nations' future aerospace defence responsibility in a holistic manner, and has systematically over the years invested heavily in terms of assets, manpower, training and operations. Given the large volume of airspace to be managed, the IAF's air defence has with considerable foresight anticipated India's future aerospace defence requirements against ballistic and cruise missiles, stand-off weapon threats, etc., has today become a future-ready system of systems, operated by a team of teams.[19] Considering the humongous volume of peacetime surveillance that is solely the IAF's responsibility, it has over the years painstakingly and prudently apportioned its Service budget to balance the air defence imperatives with its other inventory needs. A cost-benefit analysis of the peacetime utilisation of IAF's air defence assets—fighter aircraft, airborne sensors, radars, SAGW systems and manpower, vis-à-vis those of the other Services, will unambiguously underscore this fact.

IAF's air defence is under centralised control only for the sensor tasks of surveillance and data fusion. While all the air defence sensors are networked centrally through the IACCS to provide a common air picture, the shooter elements of air defence fighters and SAGW units, operate in a decentralised manner under the air defence Commander, within each Air Command's defined area of responsibility. The key aspect here is that while surveillance can be centrally controlled at the national level, the size of our country necessitates air defence operations to be decentralised to the Air Commands.[20] Very importantly, all offensive operations and air defence operations of each of these Air Commands are seamlessly interfaced with each other, to ensure common use of resources for sharing targets and air defence responsibilities that overlap all the Army's Commands. Future national security imperatives necessitate that all air defence assets contribute in peacetime to ensure their cost-effective utilisation and be available to deploy rapidly to plug and play at very short notice into the larger national air defence mainframe that the EIADs provide. Without any disrespect to the limited air defence needs of other Services, the IAF is conceptually, doctrinally, operationally and technologically way ahead, because of its holistic approach that is totally invested in the nation's aerospace defence. These are also the reasons why conceptually, an air defence Command is a retrograde step for national security. Its proponents will do well to examine why the massive erstwhile PVO Strany, USSR's independent air defence forces, was dismantled and merged with its Air Force,[21,22] and also why the Aerospace Defense Command of the US which was responsible for continental air defence was disbanded in 1980, and why only the North American Aerospace Defense Command (NORAD), which conducts aerospace warning, aerospace control and maritime warning in the defence of North America and Canada combined, remains.

No Longer Defensive

The word 'defence' limits the understanding of the role air defence plays in air power today. The term 'Air Defence' itself has expanded beyond its past relevance—from a purely legacy defensive perspective to a more comprehensive offensive approach of today. Why is this so? Is air defence a limited defensive operation where it engages the adversary only in our sovereign airspace? Can air defence operations which include OCA missions, fighter sweeps, escort missions and SEAD/DEAD missions, which penetrate deep into the enemy's air defence system to destroy it in the air and on the ground offensively, be continued to be seen from a purely defensive construct? Understandably some air power theorists will resist this approach with the argument that air defence is fundamentally about the defence of a nation from adversarial air threats, and that the air power community world over understands it as so. But it is this very dogmatic approach which conceptually limits air defence to a purely defensive construct. If air power is considered to be intrinsically offensive in nature, then arguably is air 'defence' conceptually limiting? While it may be considered to be a role where offensive actions are carried out in defence of the nations' airspaces, how does one explain when the reach of such actions extends deep into the adversary's air space?

The US doctrine on Counterair Operations explains OCA as—attack operations intended to destroy, disrupt, or degrade counterair targets on the ground and may be accomplished through kinetic or non-kinetic actions. Their main goal is to prevent enemy employment of air and missile capabilities; and SEAD as an activity to neutralise, destroy, or degrade enemy surface-based air defences by destructive or disruptive means. It also includes fighter escorts and fighter sweeps which target the enemy's airborne air defence elements. All aerial offensive actions against the adversaries' air power have been clubbed under counterair operations, which is explained as, "The counterair mission integrates offensive and defensive operations to attain and maintain a desired degree of control of the air and of protection by neutralizing or destroying enemy aircraft and missiles, along with threats to air operations from other domains." The doctrine also differentiates it from Defensive Counter Air (DCA), which includes, "Active Air and Missile Defence (AMD) and Passive AMD. Active AMD is direct defensive action taken to destroy, nullify, or reduce the effectiveness of hostile air and ballistic missile threats against friendly forces and assets. It includes actions to counter enemy manned and unmanned aircraft, aerodynamic missiles (cruise, air-to-surface, and air-to-air), and ballistic missiles." It is further broken down to 'Air Defence' which are, "Defensive measures designed to destroy attacking aircraft and aerodynamic missiles, or to nullify or reduce the effectiveness of such attack. It includes the use of aircraft, surface-to-air missiles, anti-aircraft artillery, electromagnetic warfare (including directed energy), multiple sensors, and other available weapons or capabilities," and—'Ballistic Missile Defense' which is self-explanatory. Passive AMD on the other hand—"includes all measures, other than active AMD, taken to minimize the effectiveness of hostile air and missile threats against friendly forces and assets." The doctrine also includes Integrated Air and Missile Defence (IAMD) which it explains as, "the integration of capabilities and overlapping operations to defend the homeland and United States national interests, protect the joint force, and enable freedom of action by negating an adversary's ability to create adverse effects from their air and missile capabilities. IAMD is an approach to counter some but not all air and missile threats."[23]

As far as the IAF is concerned there are some contextual challenges when compared with the USAF doctrine. The first is that in the USAF doctrine, the OCA and DCA are missions exclusively for the control of the air. It is only DCA in which active and passive AMD constitute the air defence part. But for the USAF counterair is the foundational framework at the theatre level',[24] whereas, the air defence of mainland USA, which does not have adversaries sharing its borders, is executed under IAMD. It is distinctly separated from the theatre-level air defence, which comes into play in the overseas military operations and deployed assets of the US, where its adversaries lie directly across or are in close proximity. It must also be considered that post World War II the US has very rarely fought an enemy with strong Air Forces, which was capable of offensive air strikes against their deployed forces or overseas operating bases. In the Korean and Vietnam wars, except for a notional air threat, the US never really faced any serious air threat from its adversarial Air Forces, and in fact, all its offensive air operations were conducted against Air Forces who were defending their homeland and fielded forces. In all its contemporary wars since, the US has fought against practically nil air opposition, and hence its doctrinal preponderance is on CAO, and control of air which is predicated on air superiority.

In the case of the IAF, since India's adversaries are directly across its borders and have strong Air Forces, the OCA and air defence operations are combined under CAO, for the control of the air. **That is also why there are no DCA operations in the IAF doctrine, simply because all defensive air defence operations will take place directly in Indian sovereign airspace and not in a theatre outside our boundaries.** Therefore, in the case of the IAF since its sensors cover, and the SAGW combat envelopes of the first, second and third tiers of its EIADS actually extend significantly into enemy territory, and the IAF's concept of air defence operations is to engage and shoot down the adversary inside its territory, air defence operations are actually offensive. It is only when the adversary has managed to penetrate the first three tiers, the air defence operations to shoot down the ingressing aircraft with the short-range SAMs and the CIWS are purely defensive. In the Indian context, with the induction of the S-400 Triumf Long Range SAMs the IAF's air defence actually takes on an offensive connotation—"The S-400 is believed to be a game changer by the Indian Air Force which has strengthened itself in terms of the air defence capabilities in a big way in the last few years with the arrival of the indigenous MR-SAM and Akash missile systems along with the Israeli Spyder quick reactions surface to air missile systems."[25] Given the capability to destroy aircraft, cruise and ballistic missiles, at ranges from 400 km and lesser depending on the target cross-section, and at altitudes up to 30 km, it provides an enormous air defence coverage that extends well into the adversary's territory on our West, and covers forward enemy air bases as well. In the past, the IAF air defence was focused on defending its forward air bases and vital military and national assets in small independent pockets. Today, its wide range of sensors, its multiple combinations of forward-deployed SAGW systems and its fourth generation of fighters are closely integrated and capable of offensively threatening the adversary's Air Force well inside its own territory. This makes the IAF's air defence offensively capable, which aims at seeking out and engaging the enemy over its airspaces, rather than the erstwhile approach of defending against it inside the Indian airspace. In the North however, given the terrain challenges of the Himalayas, the coverage of sensors and SAGW systems preclude the possibility of such depth coverage, but is still possible to a lesser extent in certain areas depending on geography, and operational imperatives.

Future Impact on Joint Operations

Though the capability of the air defence is certainly offensive, a lot will depend on the adversaries air defence capabilities and concept of operations. Doctrinally, the IAF's air defence is conjoined with its offensive capability since all its offensive operations will take place over highly contested to contested air spaces. This means the IAF will not only have to fight the enemy in the air to gain FAS, but also target the enemy's air defence radars, SAGW systems, airfields and air assets on ground, in order to reduce the combat potential of its Air Force. Unless it does so, the Indian Army's fielded forces will be on the receiving end of a serious threat from the adversary's air in the continental domain, something it faced to a very limited extent in the 1965 and 1971 wars. The IA is well aware of this, and hence whilst to an extent its concern about strengthening its tactical air defence is understandable, it is conceptually and operationally flawed. This is primarily because the IA does not factor in IAF's fairly potent offensive air defence capability into its operational air defence matrix. It, therefore, seeks to independently defend itself against the enemy air, and also seeks a greater decentralised and independent air defence operational capability. This leads to serious concerns, not only at the operational level for warfighting, but also at the strategic level for national security, given the threat to the civilian populace and the vulnerability of India's strategic assets and infrastructure in the homeland. Thus, the IA's approach to an independent air defence has three serious issues.

Firstly, by continuing to pursue independence of its air defence operations, it is conceptually and operationally contradicting the joint approach and the very ethos of fighting future wars together. Its argument for command and control over all tactical air defence assets comes from the intrinsic need to have all forces under its command, which is fundamentally different from the IAF in which air power is one entity and is operationally employed as a whole against the adversary, irrespective of where the assets are based, or which IAF Command they come under. This is not so for the IA and this possibly plays a significant role in its operational approach to air defence. The Russo-Ukraine war has clearly shown how the offensive capability of an Army gets impacted if not integrated with its own air defence and air power. Poor integration and leveraging of Russia's air defence and offensive air power with the Russian Army's land campaign has seriously impacted the performance of its military as a whole, resulted in a mission creep, and shifted goalposts in its larger national strategy.

Secondly, by not plugging in to the IAF's EIAD mainframe architecture, the IA not only denies itself an extended air defence cover to its fielded and in-depth forces, but it also leads to serious airspace management issues. It has a misconstrued perception that the IAF's controls airspace for its individual service requirements, and inhibits air movements of other services and civilian users. This is inherently incorrect as all air operations, whether in peace or war, are strictly governed by airspace management norms to ensure optimal freedom of all air movements, as is done the world over. IAF's coordinated air operations, Intelligence Surveillance & Reconnaissance (ISR) missions, its offensive air operations that are integrated with the AWACS/AEWC aircraft and surface radar coverages and are also closely coordinated with all friendly air defence CAP and SAGW elements, transport and helicopter movements, all use this airspace extensively, and often simultaneously. It is the same airspace volume through which Army's aviation also operates, and its artillery fire and long-range weapons transit through. The enemy air which aims to support its forces and attack our ground forces, will also attempt to exploit this airspace. Thus, it is neither rocket science nor a selfish service whim, that usage of this high-density volume of airspace, "*needs definite close control, to ensure we are able to detect, identify and engage each and every air threat, and permit full freedom of operations for our own. Over and above these, each and every air movement is intricately coordinated and de-conflicted to ensure safe routing through the enemy's radar gaps, provided protection by our own AD ac and SAGW systems, and kept safe from IA's weapon systems and firepower in the TBAs. Army aviation which often feels tied down by the airspace management norms in the TBA, need to appreciate that it actually maximises their air operations, while ensuring air defence coverage from enemy air, de-confliction with artillery fire, fratricide avoidance, de-conflicting friendly air traffic, collision avoidance, and finally enable combat search and rescue.*"[26]

Thirdly, it is given that the future of India's national security approach is predominantly focused on protecting its territorial integrity,[27] and that the Army's offensives are only possible in the West and that also too shallow depths, IAF's offensive air defence will amply cover these battlespaces. It will also cover a significant intermediate space where air interdiction will play a major role to '*shape* and *impact*' the Army's tactical battle areas by targeting the enemy's military infrastructure in-depth, destroying degrading and delaying the 'enemy's reinforcements, supplies, or strategic military potential before it is effectively brought to bear in the battlefield.'[28] Offensive air defence also provides the first tier of protection over and above the dedicated air defence which the IAF commits to the Army's TBAs. It also provides the IA's defensive formations, depth assets and infrastructure with a multi-tiered air defence. Thus instead of an independent air defence, plugging into a larger integrated air defence construct makes more operational sense. It will also serve to fill gaps, provides redundancy and bolsters the overall air defence of the nation.

The Army will do well to ensure that their future SAGW system accretions are integrated into a joint dynamic deployment plan, to bolster the area air defence at short notice. This will enable the flexibility to keep the air defence deployments agile and flexible, to not only keep the enemy guessing but also make it difficult for the enemy air power to conduct SEAD. For a truly joint approach, Army's offensive elements must plug in their long-range resources to bolster the multi-layered offensive EIAD coverage, extending well into hostile air space given the extant no-peace-no-war conditions, and only retain highly mobile SAGW systems for their terminal air defence. An interoperable capability of the Army's mobile air defence systems which can plug into the IAF's EIAD mainframe wherever they deploy, is truly the joint way ahead.[29] While the integration of air defence operations is a future necessity, any future thought on an air defence Command with an operational role needs serious reconsideration. This is because air defence "comprises the largest role and more than half the assets (ac, sensors, and weapon systems), infrastructure and manpower of the IAF,"[30] and has multiple roles in other air operations of the IAF. On the other hand, the air defence elements in terms of assets and manpower and their role, form only a very small portion of the operational repertoire of the IA and IN. "A back-of-the-envelope calculation of IAF's open source inventory reveals 80% of the fighter ac are AD capable, and more than half the combat squadrons are dedicated to the AD role. Once all the radars, SAGW systems, networking assets and their total regular running costs are added, the inventory is massive."[31] An equally critical fact from an operational perspective is that all fighters of the IAF are strike capable and have an offensive role as well. "*This is the single most important argument as to why AD operations of the IAF cannot be pushed under a single Command.*"[32] It would be prudent to consider that leading military powers have done away with such a structure for very good reasons.

Air defence in the Indian Navy (IN) is only a warfighting function limited to its assets while at sea, and is a subset of the protection of its ships or fleet. Hence it prefers to keep its air defence independent, while at sea. In view of the 'never enough' resources for air defence of the vast Indian sub-continent, the Navy's incidental contribution to any advance warning while deployed at sea will contribute significantly. "This is especially so since advance warning of any enemy air threat to national assets, which includes naval ports and bases, is invaluable for air defence from a national standpoint. A push system, where the IN passes any relevant information into the air defence mainframe whenever national assets are likely to be threatened, is the joint way ahead." [33]

Some End Thoughts

Air defence is an extremely complex warfighting art which has broken out of its erstwhile limited defensive construct. It is a 24×7×365 responsibility of the IAF and is a critical warfighting necessity in the entire spectrum of national security, ranging from peace to war. While it remains only an operational necessity limited to the deployed or fielded forces or assets of the other services, for the IAF air defence is the conjoined twin of offensive air power and underpins all air operations. It is precise because of the 'all pervasiveness and 24x7x365 operational construct' of IAF's extensive air defence architecture, the vast underpinning of air defence in its operational strategy and warfighting tactics, and the time-tested and future relevant operational muscle memory of its combat personnel, any short-sighted changes will have serious implications on national security. Therefore, any attempts at integration of air defence into a joint command and control function by simplistically misperceiving it as a 'low hanging fruit', without considering the overarching operational ideology, roles, responsibilities and warfighting norms of service, would be imprudent. The real challenge to the much-needed operational network integration is that the architecture of the other Services are limited in their scope and primary applications. The IA's 'Akashteer' is primarily for tactical SAGW fire control integration, and the Navy's 'Trigun' is essentially for greater maritime domain awareness. But if air defence is to be systemically integrated from a joint operations perspective, then both the IA and the IN need to invest in adapting their networks with a 'plug and play' concept into the heavily invested, robust and combat-proven IAF's air defence mainframe IACCS architecture,[34] without diluting or compromising its primary purpose. Investment in future capacity building of EIAD capabilities especially in the North, and North East are much-needed, and air defence of our islands in the Indian Ocean Region (IOR) are vital for bolstering national security. Another significant change is to bring about a total sensor fusion in the entire peacetime aerospace and maritime air surveillance, control and reporting (C&R) functions amongst the military and civil aviation to establish a National Aerospace Monitoring Centre. This would bring about real-time monitoring capability of the air and space continuum, with multi-agency peace time air defence integration protocols and policies, amongst the military and civil organisations.[35] This will also enable a swift and smooth transition towards India's future aerospace defence requirements.

India's extant and future threats from vertical dimensions of the air, space and cyber domains have already impacted both continental and maritime domains to the 'point of no return' wherein it will be impossible to carry out operations in the surface domains without the inclusion of the vertical. A multi-domain security approach is a way ahead for India's larger national interests and security, and aerospace defence, therefore, is an undeniable necessity of the future. Offensive air defence capacity of advanced multi-domain sensors, fifth-sixth generation combat platforms, and advanced long-range aerial, SAGW and BMD capable weapon systems would be continuing requirements of the future. Indigenous research development and investment would therefore truly be the strategic way forward. The PM's remark in the Shangri La Dialogue "We will work with others to keep our seas, space and airways free and open,"[36] is a prescient future signpost for the years to come.

Notes

1. Diptendu Choudhury, "Air Defence is Everywhere", VIF Publication, July 24, 2020, at https://www.vifindia.org/article/2020/july/24/air-defence-is-everywhere.
2. Ibid.
3. Jasjit Singh, *Defence from the Skies* (KW publishers, New Delhi, 2013), p. xx.
4. Doctrine of the Indian Air Force, IAP 2000-22, Air Headquarters, New Delhi, 2022, p. v.
5. "Manual of Flexible Use of Airspace in India", Issued by Ministry of Civil Aviation, Government of India, 2014, at https://aim-india.aai.aero/sites/default/files/ais_docs/FUA%20Manual%20ver%201.0.pdf.
6. Diptendu Choudhury, "Transformation of Aerospace Power: A Structural Appraisal", *Air Power Journal*, Vol. 17, No. 2, Summer 2022, p. 35.
7. Choudhury, n. 1.

8. Qiao Liang and Wang Xiangsui, *Unrestricted Warfare* (PLA Literature and Arts Publishing House, Beijing, 1999), pp. 179-199. The book by two PLA Air Force Colonels summarises in the end -Although the boundaries between soldiers and non-soldiers have now been broken down, and the chasm between warfare and non-warfare nearly filled up, globalisation has made all the tough problems interconnected and interlocking, and we must find a key for that. The key should be able to open all the locks, if these locks are on the front door of war. And this key must be suited to all the levels and dimensions, from war policy, strategy, and operational techniques to tactics; and it must also fit the hands of individuals, from politicians and generals to the common soldiers. We can think of no other more appropriate key than "unrestricted warfare".
9. "BSF Thwarts Pakistani Drone's Arms Drop Attempt in Punjab", *Times of India*, January 15, 2023, at https://timesofindia.indiatimes.com/india/bsf-thwarts-pakistani-drones-arms-drop-attempt-in-punjab/articleshow/97010468.cms.
10. "Yemen's Houthis claim drone attack on refinery in Saudi capital", Reuters, March 11, 2022, at https://www.reuters.com/world/middle-east/attack-refinery-riyadh-did-not-affect-petroleum-supplies-spa-2022-03-10/.
11. Kapil Kak, "A Century of Air Power: Lessons and Pointers", *Strategic Analysis*, March 2001, Vol. XXIV, No. 12.
12. Sanu Kainikara, *A Fresh Look at Air Power Doctrine* (Air Power Development Centre, Canberra, Australia, 2008), p. 53.
13. Choudhury, n. 1.
14. Choudhury, n. 1.
15. EIAD is Extended Integrated Air Defence, an acronym coined by the author to illustrate the offensive capability afforded by the long range SAM to the IAF's AD concept. The word 'extended' added to the acronym IAD illustrates the offensive coverage of the system well into adversarial airspaces. First used in the article "Air Defence is Everywhere", VIF Publication, July 24, 2020, at https://www.vifindia.org/article/2020/july/24/air-defence-is-everywhere.
16. Coordinated Air Operations are what was earlier Counter Surface Force Operations, and includes Air Land Operations and maritime Air Operations. Doctrinally, they are covered by AD Operations of the Air Force which comes under areas where it will establish Favourable Air Situations as a part of the Control of Air over the designated battlespaces.
17. V K Saxena, "The Future of Ground Based Air Defence", VIF, at https://www.vifindia.org/article/2022/october/17/the-future-of-ground-based-air-defence.
18. V K Saxena, "Air Defence Command—Some Salient Points and Imperatives", VIF, at https://www.vifindia.org/article/2021/february/02/air-defence-command-some-salient-points-and-imperatives.
19. Choudhury, n. 1.
20. Ibid.
21. https://nuke.fas.org/guide/russia/agency/pvo.htm

22. Diptendu Choudhury, "Russia's Military Understanding of Air Power: Structural & Doctrinal Aspects", VIF, May 23, 2022, at https://www.vifindia.org/article/2022/may/23/russia-s-military-understanding-of-air-power.
23. "Counter Air Operations", Air Force Doctrine Publication (AFDP), March 2021, pp. 7-11, at https://www.doctrine.af.mil/Portals/61/documents/AFDP_3-01/3-01-AFDP-COUNTERAIR.pdf.
24. Ibid.
25. Manjeet Negi, "Russia to supply third S-400 air defence missile system to India by Feb 2023", *India Today*, December 24, 2022, at https://www.indiatoday.in/india/story/india-third-s-400-air-defence-missile-system-russia-supply-feb-2023-2313139-2022-12-24.
26. Choudhury, n. 1.
27. AIR News, December 13 2022, at https://newsonair.com/2022/12/13/defence-minister-makes-statement-in-parliament-on-india-china-face-off-in-tawang-says-armed-forces-are-committed-to-protect-territorial-integrity-of-our-country/.
28. IAF Doctrine, n. 4, pp. 53-57.
29. Choudhury, n. 1.
30. Ibid.
31. Ibid.
32. Ibid.
33. Ibid.
34. Ibid.
35. Ibid.
36. https://www.narendramodi.in/pm-%20modi-%20to%20-deliver%20-keynote-%20address%20-at%20-shangri-la-%20dialouge-%20in%20-singapore-540324.

10. Helicopter Operations in Contested Battlespace

Rajesh Varma

> "Victory smiles upon those who anticipate the changes in the character of war, not on those who wait to adapt themselves after the changes occur."
>
> —Guilio Douhet

Introduction

The first generation of warfare dates its origin to 1648[1] and while it survived for centuries, the last hundred-odd years has witnessed warfare metamorphosing through four generations in rapid succession. Theorists are propounding the evolution of sixth, seventh and eighth generation of warfare in future which advocates logical progress in non-contact, non-kinetic engagements between the adversaries. The Gerasimov Doctrine, enunciated by Russia in 2013, scripted the background for Grey Zone warfare and exemplifies the ambiguous and convoluted nature of future conflicts where disinformation, political influence and economic coercion would be the primary non-military means to achieve security goals.[2] Therefore, at the operational and tactical level, these changes in the character of warfare, coupled with rapid growth in technology, is likely to usher in a new era of warfighting.

The employment of helicopters, as a practical aircraft for military operations, dates to the Second World War with the Allied and Axis forces deploying rudimentary helicopters for light aviation tasks and rescue missions in denied or austere locations.[3] From this humble beginning, helicopter operations have witnessed a colossal growth in the military domain as their ubiquitous capabilities enabled them to undertake diverse tasks in testing conditions. Evacuation of critical patients injured in the battle zone and rescue missions of downed aircrew during the Korean and Vietnam wars, aptly glorified by the media, gave the helicopters recognition in the benign role while their subtle contribution in covert and overt Special Operations missions showcased them as a dependable and an inescapable asset for future conflicts. The success of Attack Helicopter (AH) missions during Operation Desert Storm and some audacious operations executed by the Israeli Air Force (IsAF), against the Hamas leaders, propelled AH operations into prominence with rave reviews and optimistic predictions on their future employment.

The evolving dynamics of warfare, obdurate developments in technology and the emergence of multiple contestants on the battlefield would test and challenge operations by a slow-paced aircraft in a congested bubble with myriad complexities. The success of previous helicopter operations would thus need to be evaluated prudently and dispassionately before being emulated, a lesson which the Russians are coming to terms with in their ongoing conflict with Ukraine. The modern battlefield and contested airspace have brought to the fore, yet again, the inherent vulnerability of the helicopter and its ability to fly 'low and slow' is glaringly emerging as more of a bane. This chapter analyses and evaluates the employment of military helicopters in a contested battlefield of the future and the technological advancements that would need to be leveraged to enhance the resilience and survivability of these machines.

Helicopter Operations in Battlefield: A Historical Perspective

The first rotary-wing aircraft got airborne in the year 1907,[4] three years after their fixed-wing counterpart. Subsequently, they were first used in the battlefield during the First World War by the Austro-Hungarian Empire for artillery observation missions. During the Second World War, the Germans utilised the FI-282 Colibri helicopters for executing artillery fire correction[5] but it was the French who revolutionised the employment of helicopters in combat and during the Vietnam conflict in 1954, they carried out the first infiltration and exfiltration of a troop detachment by helicopters.[6] The use of helicopters by the US Army during the Vietnam conflict was to change forever the American doctrine of tactical warfare. Helicopters proved to be multidimensional and performed tactical airmobile missions, including insertion and extraction of ground forces, the rescue of downed aviators, close air support with helicopter gunships, aerial reconnaissance and medical evacuation missions under adverse conditions.[7] In total, about 12,000 helicopters were used in Vietnam, of which nearly 5,000 were lost because of their vulnerability.[8] After the Vietnam war, the Soviet took the lead in production of transport and attack helicopters.

Over the next decades, many helicopter operations were executed to transport men and material into the combat hotspots by exploiting the dexterity and flexibility offered by these aircraft. Operation Eagle Claw was an overambitious operation involving multiple aircraft, including eight United States Navy RH-53D Sea Stallion helicopters, to undertake the rescue of 66 American hostages held in the US Embassy in Tehran in 1980.[9] Operation Gothic Serpent was a mission to capture warlord Mohamed Farrah Aidid in Somalia and involved extensive use of helicopters in reconnaissance and combat roles. Both these missions failed to achieve their aim due to diverse reasons, the limitations in capabilities and vulnerability of the helicopter being the noteworthy ones. The significant losses of helicopters in the Soviet invasion of Afghanistan and Operation Just Cause in Panama further highlighted the susceptibility of a slow-moving platform as adversaries gained proficiency in the fields of detection and engagement of aerial targets. It also highlighted the consequences of flawed employment philosophies and the need to avoid predictable patterns of operation. However, despite these shortcomings, helicopter design and production in the military domain continued unabated which endorses two fundamental theories for helicopter operations in future. First, in comparison to the fixed-wing aircraft, the helicopter is much more vulnerable and would be increasingly susceptible to retributory action in enemy territory. Second, the fundamental capabilities offered by helicopters towards expeditious attainment of the intended aim would many a time outweigh the stated limitations and disadvantages. Therefore, despite the pervasive chinks in the armour, helicopter operations will continue to emerge as a military option which would be difficult to ignore or avoid.

Understanding Dynamics of Future Wars

As per Clausewitz, war is 'a deliberate and coercive act applied against an adversary to compel our enemy to do our will'.[10] The various activities involved in fighting the war at the strategic, operational and tactical levels are within the realms of warfare. The theory of warfare determines the practical aspects of warfighting which in turn drives the doctrine.[11] In future, military conflicts may witness the obsolescence and refinements of existing conventional doctrines which would be necessary to conform with the political, social and economic compulsions at the strategic level and to keep abreast with technological developments at the operational and tactical levels. To understand 'what has changed that needs to be fixed', it would be in order to discuss three defining facets of warfare that have transformed the character of warfighting.

First, the emergence of the nebulous nature of wars shall obliterate the boundaries between political and military objectives at the strategic level. The Second Lebanon War in 2006 witnessed an intriguing air offensive undertaken by IsAF and the operation ended up being one of the most inconclusive performances by the Israeli Defence Force (IDF) in their accomplished history and culminated without a clear military victory on Israel's part.[12] The war showcased that military actions are futile in case political objectives are not met and unlike in the past, victory will not be measured by land annexed, aircraft lost and soldiers killed. The wars of future would therefore witness the conventional military sequential campaign planning process being replaced by a multitude of simultaneous applications of military and non-military operations by disparate agencies in space and time. A campaign of such intent and intensity is likely to blur the traditional boundaries between the three levels of warfare and hence success or failure of tactical actions, including operations by helicopters, can enforce ramifications at the strategic level.

Second, the emergence of new methods of warfare would witness the harnessing of pioneering technologies and the evolution of revolutionary concepts and doctrines. Andrew Marshall, former Director of the Office of Net Assessments has stated that a major change in the nature of warfare would be brought about by the innovative application of new technologies combined with dramatic changes in military doctrinal concepts, a concoction which would fundamentally alter the character and conduct of military operations.[13] The drone attack by the US that eliminated General Qassem Soleimani in January 2020 demonstrated that in future, expertise in surveillance and precision in attack would take centre stage. The IDF demonstrated the effective employment of Artificial Intelligence (AI) against the Hamas during Operation 'Guardian of the Walls' in 2021 wherein AI and supercomputing were extensively employed at the operational and tactical levels.[14] History is replete with examples wherein doctrines were modified to either exploit or counter technological developments which subsequently sparked changes in warfighting.

Lastly, the rising influence of Information warfare and perception management would compel the decision-makers to prevent their own casualties and hence suppress the desire to commit men and equipment into the combat zone. The wide publicity garnered and subsequent public outrage after the loss of two helicopters and military personnel in the unsuccessful operation in Mogadishu forced the Clinton Administration to withdraw from Somalia[15] which validates the theory that a failed tactical action can produce cascading effects at the operational and strategic levels. The question that emerges is whether the military planners would risk pushing a slow-moving aircraft, with soldiers on board, into an uncertain threat-infested region? Or will they be tempted to employ other safer means which are capable of producing similar results while shielding their own forces from the hazards of the battlefield. Substantiating this thought process is the emphasis being laid by defence forces on the development of Unmanned Aerial Vehicles (UAVs), ballistic missiles, loitering munitions, disruptive technology and capabilities for cyber-attacks. The feasibility of drones performing some of the traditional roles of helicopters in future cannot be negated. Despite their limited load-carrying capacity and the absence of a pilot with instinctive skills, drones have the advantage of engaging or observing targets from stand-off ranges, in degraded visual conditions and with the desired accuracy. Drones are thus being heralded heralding them as contenders for Battlefield Air Strikes (BAS)/Battlefield

Air Interdiction (BAI) missions or as reconnaissance posts in a contested battlefield. In future conflicts, emphasis would be towards a holistic assessment to interpret the 'desired effects' that need to be produced at the tactical and operational level, and not the means, to achieve the stated objectives. While doing so, if helicopter operations emerge as an effective and potent option, the same shall and would be employed.

Helicopter Operations in Future Conflicts

Helicopters were conceived and designed for military operations to capitalise on the capabilities of versatility, mobility, agility and most importantly, the flexibility to meet operational requirements when responding to fast-changing situations. A contested battlefield is a congregation of ground weapon systems, manned and unmanned airborne elements, encrypted communication systems and a well-informed command-and-control structure. The ability of the helicopter to transgress such a volatile and formidable environment and thereafter be expected to emerge with a high assurance of success is the predicament that would challenge the conduct of helicopter operations. The compulsion to employ these aircraft in such a scenario would surface from answers to three questions. What is it that the commanders want the helicopters to accomplish that other military platforms cannot, given the restriction of force, space and time? Second, what are the enemy capabilities that are likely to thwart these helicopters from accomplishing the desired tasks? Third, subsequent to weighing the desired outcomes against the consequences of failure, is it worth accepting the risk?

Gen MM Naravane (Retd) wrote that the Russia-Ukraine war has brought to the fore the urgent need to re-assess warfighting doctrines and techniques since the armed forces are accused of training for and fighting as they did in the last war. As per him, it is an accusation which is unjust because it is near impossible to predict the character of future wars, a problem which has been exacerbated by the rapid pace of technological change and the inability of doctrines to keep pace with this change.[16] The Suppression of Enemy Air Defence (SEAD) missions flown by the AH-64 during Operation Desert Storm to destroy the radar facilities has been upheld as an example of the deep strike capability of the AH that conformed to the doctrinal definition of deep strike in terms of the ranges covered.[17] A decade later, the same helicopters witnessed one of the darkest episodes in the history of AH operations during the unsuccessful strike on the Iraqi Republican Guard Medina Division, better known as the 'Karbala Raid', during Operation Iraqi Freedom. Out of the 32 aircraft which were sent for a deep strike to destroy the armour and artillery of the Iraqi Division, 31 returned damaged and one was downed in enemy territory without any decisive engagement of planned targets.[18] The Iraqis adjusted their tactics and prepared defences to counter the deep strike capability while the AH crew, underestimating the threat from small-arms fire, flew into these defences using tactics, techniques and procedures inappropriate to the combat environment.[19] This mission put a question mark on the efficacy of helicopters to carry out deep strike missions and highlighted the need to constantly review the employment philosophy and tactics based on the capabilities acquired by the adversary. The doctrinal concept of helicopter operations in future battlefields and the subsequent strategies for their employment would emerge from the endangerment of the capabilities for which these machines were designed. Needless to say, in a contested battle space, the helicopters will not be able to ingress into enemy territory with impunity since their fundamental capability, to surprise the opponent, would become increasingly compromised because of the available battlefield transparency to the adversary.

At the tactical level, within the so what defined geographical battlespace, the number of aircraft and projectiles belonging to the own forces and the adversary are increasing exponentially, both in terms of quality and quantity. Notwithstanding, the helicopter will be one of the most important assets at the disposal of the field commander for swift movement and high mobility of ground forces within the theatre of operations. The Joint Doctrine of the UK defines air manoeuvre as the movement of forces through the medium of air to positions of advantage from which force can be applied or threatened.[20] The doctrine elucidates that air manoeuvre forces utilise the core attributes of air power and the agility of helicopters allows ground forces to move quickly between tactical actions providing them more opportunities. That said, the ongoing conflict in Ukraine has exposed the limitations of employing helicopters for conducting air manoeuvres in contested airspace. In the opening hours of the invasion, the elite Russian VDV airborne troops tried to capture the Hostomel airbase near Kyiv with an air assault operation. Dozens of transport helicopters, escorted by KA-52 AHs, ferried an assault force of paratroopers to the Ukrainian airfield. However, the air assault was ultimately a failure as Russia failed to undertake further helicopter missions to reinforce its airhead as the Ukrainians counter-attacked with artillery and shoulder-fired anti-aircraft missiles.[21] One of the primary reasons for the failure was the fact that Russians were trying to emulate similar operations which had been successfully accomplished by the US and other West European militaries, where the helicopters generally flew under the umbrella of air superiority and into a region with restrained threat from the ground elements.[22] Defence and aerospace analyst Sash Tusa argues that the technological advances in sensors and anti-aircraft weapons on display in Ukraine is an indicator of the fact that air assault and helicopter combat missions in general will become less viable.[23] In future, while large-scale insertion of troops is likely to be questioned, the feasibility of Special Ops by a suitable team of helicopters to address a time-sensitive target is an option likely to be exercised. These operations, in all probability, will be under the cover of darkness and protected by a robust and reliable Anti-Access Area Denial (A2AD) system.

In the ongoing Ukraine conflict, various reports indicate that by November 2022, at least 25 KA-52 Russian helicopters had been shot down by Ukrainian MANPADS and other guided weapons while engaging targets.[24] The Russians were succumbing to the perils of flying the helicopters which had limited technological capabilities combined with inappropriate employment philosophies and outdated tactics. To elaborate on the point, a KA-52 fires a beam rider Vikhyr missile which entails the crew to hover a few hundred feet off the ground and lase the target, as far as six miles away, before firing the missile.[25] For the next crucial seconds, the helicopter has to be stationary and the crew have to continue lasing the target till the missile impact and it was this extended exposure to Ukrainian MANPADS that proved to be the nemesis for these hapless aircraft and crew.[26] Additionally, the fact that most of these operations were carried out during day time assisted the ground forces in target acquisition and engagement. The Ukrainians also benefitted from the fact that the Russian AHs failed to release flares when engaged by MANPADS and the lack of armour plating, especially in the engine compartment, made the KA-52 vulnerable to even small weapons fire.[27] Therefore, analysing the capabilities offered by the helicopters and evaluating the threat environment would provide a solution to the desired modifications in employment techniques and changes in tactics.

Helicopter Operations in TBA

To undertake a mission in a congested TBA, the helicopter will require total integration with other airborne and ground elements involved in the operation. This can be achieved by integration with the Operational Data Link (ODL) architecture, advanced cockpit designs and computer-based mission management systems which would allow the crew to accurately and instantaneously process battlefield information. One such concept which is likely to gain recognition in future is the Manned Unmanned Teaming (MUM-T) concept wherein UAV/UCAVs are employed in conjunction with AHs. The United States Army Aviation Centre (USAACE) defines MUM-T as 'the synchronised employment of soldiers, manned and unmanned air and ground vehicles, robotics and sensors to achieve enhanced situational understanding, greater lethality and improved survivability'.[28] The capability of the helicopter crew, to assume control of the UAV or its payload, and to autonomously manage the imagery required to accomplish the given mission would ensure enhanced Situational Awareness (SA) in the fog of war. The United States Army employs this technology with the AH-64 and MQ-1C Grey Eagle or RQ-7 Shadow Unmanned Aerial System (UAS).[29] Apart from providing real-time intelligence, this handshake stands in good stead for the accurate engagement of targets with minimum effort at maximum standoff ranges. For the utility helicopters, MUM-T offers the opportunity for battlefield reconnaissance minutes before the helicopter reaches the Landing Zone (LZ)/Insertion Zone (IZ). The One System Remote Video Terminal (OSRVT) is a system which can provide real-time information from a UAV to the crew and ground forces aboard a

UH-60 Blackhawk or CH-47 Chinook with the real-time video of the LZ/IZ,15 to 20 minutes prior to arrival.[30]

This novel concept of operations allows combat helicopters to be employed as a weapon platform capable of fulfilling strategic roles. The IDF has adopted this role for the AHs as part of their on-going conflict with terrorists and Palestinian groups in the Palestinian Territories and Lebanon.[31] The IsAF began pairing their AH-64 with UAVs which empowered the package for autonomous management of reconnaissance, target acquisition, precision attack and battle damage assessment. The UAV provided a stealth reconnaissance and guidance platform that could locate and identify the target, making the AH strike appear nearly instantaneous. On August 19, 2003, a Palestinian suicide bomber killed 19 civilians in Jerusalem and following the attack, the Israelis launched five missions of the AH-64 to eliminate ten Hamas militants. The final attack culminated with a UAV identifying a van transporting Abdullah Akel, Commander of the Hamas units in the Gaza strip, along with one of the leaders identified as having helped plan the bombing. A pair of AH-64 navigated the difficult urban terrain and engaged the van with five missiles which eliminated all intended targets.[32]

In a congested airspace, different airspace management procedures, complicated command chains and disjointed planning procedures are likely to create hurdles in air operations, especially when the operations are joint in nature. There would be a requirement for clearly designated agencies for direct and procedural control over the diverse actions being performed by various military elements.[33] The lack of secure communication is a detrimental influence which evokes the element of doubt in the minds of the aircrew and other operators in the air and on the ground. This incriminating belief amongst the participants on the battlefield forces them to refrain from sharing critical information which has been one of the contributory factors for disastrous helicopter missions, including incidents of fratricide. On the other hand, Operation Neptune Spear revealed that secrecy and secure communication would be the key ingredients for success during a mission involving diverse airborne and ground forces. The entire air effort used for the operation, including the four helicopters, operated in an impregnable airspace management and coordination system under the aegis of an E-2C Hawkeye providing the data link and communication relay while the E-6 Mercury executed the role of an airborne command post.[34] A reliable and secure communication network will ensure that airborne platforms, various sensors and weapon systems are adroitly networked for seamless sharing of information which would enhance real-time battlefield domain awareness[35] and an arrangement of such order would stand in good stead for safe and productive conduct of helicopter operations.

The air activity in the TBA is extremely compressed as both friendly and enemy aircraft are transiting airspace infested with long and medium-range artillery and a variety of missiles. For helicopters, even an unguided RPG-7 can be extremely dangerous at distances of tens to hundreds of yards, a reality which is in consonance with the famous adage 'at close quarters a sword is just as lethal as an assault rifle'.[36] To ensure that the helicopters are able to detect weapon systems of the adversary in time and execute timely evasive actions, the helicopters will have to be equipped with high fidelity terrain following radars, electronic Identify Friend or Foe (IFF), Radar Warning Receiver (RWR), Laser Warning Receiver (LWR) and Missile Approach Warning System (MAWS) with automated dispensing capabilities. The employment of dark flares which emit in the IR spectrum and are virtually invisible to the naked eye by night[37] would emerge as an operational necessity during night operations.

Future Helicopter Design

The helicopter design will need consistent transformation to match the operational requirements and mitigate the probable threats. They will have to fly faster to evade detection while modern avionics systems and night vision devices would enable operations in adverse weather conditions and during night. Incorporating stealth features would delay detection while a robust airframe would enhance the crash-worthiness capabilities thereby providing a fillip to the survivability quotient. According to 'The U.S. Army in Multi-Domain Operations: 2028', the likely changes to fight future conflicts would necessitate the inclusion of helicopters that are capable to operate in a highly contested operational environment, which cannot be easily isolated from the rest of the forces.[38] The next generation of helicopters will therefore need to be faster, more manoeuvrable, more lethal and technologically advanced, including the ability to team with autonomous aircraft.[39] In a recent talk on the future of helicopter design, Major General Walter Rugen, director of the Future Vertical Lift (FVL) cross-functional team of the US Army stated that the ability to fly low and fast would be one of the primary design considerations for future helicopters. The General highlighted that one tenet of modern warfare that has come into focus is the need for helicopters to remain outside the engagement zone of enemy weapon systems citing examples of the Nagorno-Karabakh War between Armenia and Azerbaijan in 2020 and the ongoing fighting in Ukraine.[40] The FVL programme is working towards the production of the Future Long Range Assault Aircraft (FLRAA) and Future Attack Reconnaissance Aircraft (FARA) which, apart from stealth design and modern avionics, incorporates hybrid composite structures to provide more dynamic crash conditions along with greater agility.[41]

Helicopter Operations: Indian Context

In the Indian context, synchronisation of helicopter operations with the progress of the ongoing battle on the ground in a contested battlespace would be surrounded by discrete caveats entailing serious understanding of the operational requirements, evolving technology and mitigating measures. The amorphous nature of future wars and capabilities acquired by the adversaries would entail IAF to equip itself with state-of-the-art helicopters coupled with procedures and tactics for the execution of integrated operations with various stakeholders on the battlefield. The induction of AH-64 E, CH-47 and the recent indigenous Light Combat Helicopter (LCH) into the IAF fraternity is an acknowledgement of helicopters being visualised as a force multiplier and the patronage helicopter operations are likely to secure in future. The LCH, apart from being equipped with a potent self-protection suite is designed for low visual, aural, radar and infrared detection.[42] HAL is designing and developing the Light Utility Helicopter (LUH) which has a service ceiling of 6,500 m and is capable of carrying payloads of up to 500 kg. The helicopter is expected to perform diverse missions including transportation of cargo and troops, surveillance and medical evacuation.[43]

The future conflicts in the subcontinent may be confined to limited wars restricted over a defined geographical space, as was seen during the Kargil conflict. In such situations, calculated and calibrated employment of the helicopter by a prudent Commander can increase and sustain the tempo of operations by shifting forces within the theatre, providing immediate logistical support or kinetic engagement of targets of value. An important aspect is the fact that a considerable proportion of such operations will be at high altitudes where the dynamics of warfare and employment of air power attain a different and difficult pedestal. Apart from the reduced performance by the aero-engines and aerodynamic constraints on the airframe, mountainous terrain increases the exposure of a flying platform to air defence weapons due to the reduced vertical proximity between the shooter on a ridgeline and the aircraft flying in the valley. Additionally, the helicopters are forced to follow a predictable flight path in such topography thereby transferring the 'surprise element' capability to the opponent. The Soviet Union lost hundreds of helicopters to camouflaged Mujahedeen guerrillas armed with anti-aircraft guns and missiles during their ten years of combat in the mountains of Afghanistan. It is claimed that the primary reason for the Soviet withdrawal from Afghanistan was the Stinger missile which enforced cessation of helicopter operations and compelled them to fight on foot.[44] Helicopters can play an important role in the alleviation of terrain friction and sustenance of battlefield potential in mountainous terrain but such operations would necessitate the formulation of progressive employment techniques, requisite training for the crew and procuring technology to defeat or create windows of opportunity against a potent air defence system.

Military Efficiency denotes the capacity to produce a certain desired result from an action with minimum expenditure or depletion of resources while Military Effectiveness is the process by which armed forces convert resources into fighting power and can be defined as the combat potential or effective war fighting capability that a military is able to generate from the available resources.[45] Helicopter operations, when executed with proactive planning and professional ingenuity, can assume a defining role in ensuring that military actions on the battlefield are conducted efficiently and effectively.

Conclusion

Colin S. Gray elucidated that the character of war is always changing and this pace of change, augmented by technology-driven RMA, ensures that war is waged in a noticeably different manner.[46] However, despite the changing character of warfare, military conflicts in future are likely to be driven by the same factors that have historically provoked wars and during such military campaigns, principles of war like maintenance of aim, concentration of force, economy of effort, surprise and flexibility will remain all pervasive. These time-tested and battle-proven principles would ensure that the role of helicopters will remain undiminished and they would continue to be exploited as vehicles of vertical envelopment in orchestrating changes in the battlefield.

Conventionally, helicopters have been players in the tactical battlefield as they lacked the prowess to corroborate the proverbial tenets of 'reach' and 'speed', capabilities which air power theory has consistently and passionately endorsed. But the helicopter's potency to take to the skies and remain there without a supportive aviation ecosystem has been its greatest strength. In due course of time, some of the roles of helicopters like delivery of fire power, reconnaissance and airborne control could get side-stepped to more technologically advanced and expendable systems but as long as warfare hinges on the 'boots on the ground' concept, helicopters shall continue to retain their primacy in the battlefield of tomorrow and none of the technological advancements is likely to evict them from their traditional roles. They would continue to be the proverbial 'worker ants' of the battlefield, laying the ground for the victors to claim their victory and the heroes to achieve their heroics. However, to accomplish the mission in a congested, contested and chaotic battlefield of the future would necessitate a review of doctrinal precepts, impetus on development programmes for improving the design features, the evolution of novel employment philosophies, innovative tactics and corresponding training methodology.

Notes

1. William S Lind, "A Brief overview of Fourth Generation Warfare", Military Society of Marine Corps University, January 1993, p. 1.

2. Kathleen H. Hicks, "Russia in the Gray Zone", Centre for Strategic and International Studies, July 25, 2019, at https://www.csis.org/analysis/russia-gray-zone.

3. P.A. Gautron, "Beyond Karbala: the US Army's approach to Apache Doctrine", Canadian Forces College, JCSP 39, p. 7, at htttps://www.cfc.forces.gc.ca /259/290/299/286/gautron.pdf.

4. Etienne de Durand, "Helicopter Warfare: The Future of Air Mobility and Rotary Wing Combat", IFRI Laboratoire de Recherche sur la Defence, Bruxelles, January 2012, p. 9, at https://www.ifri.org/en/publications/etudes-de-lifri/focus-strategique/helicopter-warfare-future-airmobility-and-rotary-wing.

5. M. J. Hirschberg, *"The American Helicopter, An Overview of Helicopter Developments in America 1908- 1999"*, Ross & Perry, 2002, p. 22.

6. Ioan Mischie, "Helicopters in Combat: Methods for Helicopter use in Special Operation", Review of the Air Force Academy, Bucharest, No.1 (36)/2018, at https://www.afahc.ro/ro/revista/2018_1/1-IoanMISCHIE.pdf.

7. Herbert P. Lepore, "The Coming of Age: The Role of the Helicopter in the Vietnam War", Army History, U.S. Army Centre of Military History, Winter 1994, No. 29, p 30, at https://www.jstor.org/stable/26304086?seq=1#metadata_info_tab_contents.

8. E. Durand, "Helicopter Warfare—The Future of Air Mobility and Rotary Wing Combat", IFRI Laboratoire de Recherche sur la Defence, Bruxelles, 2012, p. 15, at https://www.ifri.org/en/publications/etudes-de-lifri/focus-strategique/helicopter-warfare-future-airmobility-and-rotary-wing.

9. Laura Lambert, "Operation Eagle Claw", *Encyclopedia Britannica*, January 13, 2023, at https://www.britannica.com/event/Operation-Eagle-Claw.

10. Carl von Clausewitz, *On War*, ed. and trans. Michael Howard and Peter Paret, (Princeton, NJ: Princeton University Press, 1984), p. 75.

11. Joseph A. Gattuso Jr., "Warfare Theory", *Naval War College Review*, Autumn 1996, Vol. 49, p. 113, at https://www.jstor.org/stable/44638720.

12. Benjamin S. Lambeth, *Air Operations in Israel's War Against Hezbollah: Learning from Lebanon and Getting It Right in Gaza* (Santa Monica: Rand Corporation, 2011), p. xviii, at http://www.rand.org.

13. V K Kapoor, "Future Wars in India", SP's Land Forces, Issue: October-November 2012, at https://www.spslandforces.com/story/?id=226.

14. SC Tyagi, "Future Wars: Artificial Intelligence, Drones and Cyber Weapons", *Financial Express,* July 8, 2021, at https://www.financialexpress.com/defence/future-wars-artificial-intelligence-drones-and-cyber-weapons/2286333/.

15. Douglas Delaney, "Cutting, Running, or Otherwise? The US Decision to Withdraw from Somalia", *Small Wars and Insurgencies*, Volume 15, Issue 3, 2004, p. 29.

16. MM Naravane, "Drones are Changing Warfare Faster than War Doctrines Change", *Times of India*, October 27, 2022.

17. P.A. Gautron, n. 3.

18. Gregory Fontenot, E.J. Degen and David W. Tohn, "Army Attack Aviation: The 11th Attack Helicopter Regiment's Deep Strike in Karbala", in Jack T Ken (ed.), *Deep*

Maneuver Historical Case Studies of Maneuver in Large-Scale Combat Operations, Army University Press, 2018, p. 157, at https://apps.dtic.mil/sti/pdfs/AD1120410.pdf.

19. Ibid., p. 158.
20. Joint Doctrine Note 1/16, "Air Manoeuvre", Development, Concepts and Doctrine Centre, Ministry of Defence UK, September 2016, Chapter 1, Section 2, p. 5, at www.gov.uk/mod/dcdc.
21. Stavros Atlamazoglou, "The Fighting in Ukraine Shows the Vulnerability of One of Modern Militaries' Most Important Weapons", *Business Insider*, Military and Defence, June 22, 2022, at https://www.businessinsider.com/fighting-in-ukraine-shows-growing-vulnerability-of-helicopters-2022-6?IR=T.
22. Ibid.
23. Sash Tusa, "The Future of Air Assault", Aviation Week Network, Podcast (00:22:10—00:26:45), at https://aviationweek.com/defense-space/podcast-future-air-assault.
24. Sakshi Tiwari, "Russia's 'Most Advanced' Attack Helicopter that wreaked havoc on Ukraine falls to the West", *The Eurasian Times*, December 29, 2022, at https://eurasiantimes.com/russias-most-advanced-attack-helicopter-that-wreaked-havoc-on-ukraine/.
25. David Axe, "Ukraine has Shot Down a Quarter of Russia's Best Attack Helicopters", *Aerospace and Defence, Forbes*, October 26 2022, at https://www.forbes.com/sites/davidaxe/2022/10/26/ukraine-has-shot-down-a-quarter-of-russias-best-attack-helicopters/?sh=2b6d2d531879.
26. Ibid.
27. Sakshi Tiwari, "Russian Ka-52 Alligator Flown by Elite Military Unit Shot Down", *The Eurasian Times*, December 5, 2022, at https://eurasiantimes.com/ukraines-air-defense-brigade-shoots-down-a-russian-ka-52-alligato/.
28. Livio Rossetti, "Manned-Unmanned Teaming: A Great Opportunity or Mission Overload?", Joint Air Power Competence Centre, Journal Edition January 29, 2020, at https://www.japcc.org/articles/manned-unmanned-teaming/.
29. Valerie Insinna, "Army's Helicopter-drone Teams to get Capability Boost in 2019", Defence News, October 9, 2017, at https://www.defensenews.com/digital-show-dailies/ausa/2017/10/09/armys-helicopter-drone-teams-to-get-capability-boost-in-2019.
30. Thomas von Eschenbach, "Unmanned Aircraft Systems - Manned-Unmanned Teaming", *Army Aviation Magazine*, at armyaviationmagazine.com/index.php/archive/not-so-current/589-unmanned-aircraft-systems-manned-unmanned-t.
31. Benjamin Armstrong, "Precision Approaches: Leadership Targeting and the Helicopter as a Strategic Strike Asset in Small Wars", Defense & Security Analysis, November 10, 2009, at https://doi.org/10.1080/14751790903201414.
32. Ibid., p. 278
33. Anil Chopra, "Managing a Congested Airspace over the Future Battle Area", *Indian Defence Review*, Issue Vol. 36.4, Oct-Dec 2021, January 9, 2022, at http://www.

indiandefencereview.com/news/managing-a-congested-airspace-over-the-future-battle-area/.

34. Ajay Lele, "Operation Neptune Spear and Role of Technology", *Journal of Defence Studies*, Vol. 5, No. 4, October 2011, p. 128.
35. Harvijay Singh, "Tactical Battle Area: Under the Digital Shield", *Defence Strategy*, Vol. 13, Issue 6, January 20, p. 31, at https://www.defstrat.com/magazine_articles/tactical-battle-area-under-the-digital-shield/.
36. Carlo Kopp, "Are Helicopters Vulnerable?", Australian Aviation, March 2005, p. 61, at http://ausair power.net.
37. Elbit Systems - Land Survivability and Protection "'*SPARCS-Flares™' - Spectral IR Decoys*", at https://elbitsystems.com/media/SPARC36-Flare-1.pdf.
38. Lockheed Martin, "Helicopters of the Future: Technologies that lets Pilots Focus on the Fight", May 2019, at https://www.lockheedmartin.com/en-us/news/features/2019-features/helicopters-of-the-future-technology-that-lets-pilots-focus-on-the-fight.html.
39. Ibid.
40. Ryan Finnerty, "Low and Fast Matter': Future Vertical Lift Top General reflects on Six Months of Ukraine War", Flight Global Article, August 22, 2022, at https://www.flightglobal.com/helicopters/low-and-fast-matter-future-vertical-lift-top-general-reflects-on-six-months-of-ukraine-war/149994.article.
41. Frank Colucci, "FVL: Protected Across Domains", Vertiflite, Mar/Apr 2022, p. 28, at https://vtol.org/files/dmfile/fvl_v_marapr-2022.pdf.
42. Sayan Majumdar, "The HAL Rotary Wing Lightweights", *Vayu Aerospace and Defence Review*, Vol. IV, 2021, p. 52.
43. Ibid.
44. Franz-Stefan Gady, "Afghanistan and The Stinger Myth: What Actually Forced the Soviets to Withdraw from Afghanistan in 1989?", *The Diplomat*, July 1, 2015, at https://thediplomat.com/2015/07/afghanistan-and-the-stinger-myth/.
45. US Air Force Doctrine, Volume 3, Chapter 2.
46. Colin S. Gray, *Strategy for Chaos: Revolutions in Military Affairs and The Evidence of History*, University of Reading (Frank Cass Publishers, Crown House, 47 Chase Side, Southgate, London, 2005), p. 39.

11. From an Air Force to An Aerospace Force

T H Anand Rao

The space domain has become as vital for national security and the economy as the land, sea and air domains. India, like all major space-faring nations, opposes the use of space as a warfighting domain. India continues its diplomatic efforts in favour of the efforts towards safety, security, and sustainability of space operations. India is committed to retaining the character of space as a global common and strives towards a peaceful utilisation of outer space in accordance with the UN-mandated regulations and treaties.

Military utilisation of space for deriving the benefits of space services and applications is a globally accepted practice. Satellites with their various applications—strategic reconnaissance, communication, navigation, early warning, weather prediction, etc.—have become a necessary component of all our strategic functions. Therefore, the armed forces are taking major steps in the field of space applications, in line with our national security strategy.

In doing so, the armed forces, which have the primary responsibility to defend the territorial integrity of the nation on land, sea, and air, have to ensure the modernisation and continuity of our capabilities in space. These capabilities will be in consonance with India's national security requirements. The armed forces need to elaborate on the steps necessary to achieve an optimal level of utilisation of space resources in their doctrinal strategies.

The Indian Air Force (IAF) has the primary responsibility towards Air Defence (AD). In addition to integrating the use of satellite services and applications into its overall strategy, which is a common goal for all three services, the IAF also needs to integrate Space Defence strategies with AD, to ensure a seamless transition between air and space mediums for all physical platforms transiting between the mediums, including the tracking of space-bound objects and earth-bound objects as well as for missile defence requirements.

The IAF has taken a conscious decision to expand its reach beyond the airspace into the realm of space to transform itself into an Aerospace Force, which is a clear statement of intent in the newly released "Doctrine of the Indian Air Force (IAP 2000-2022)".[1] This entails a broad spectrum of activities for capability enhancement in the space domain as well as ensuring contiguity in operations between the domains. Merging Air and Space systems will provide a comprehensive view of the Aerospace domain and will facilitate resource decisions based on capabilities that produce the desired military effects regardless of which domain the platform operates in. Hence, the IAF's outlook must be to integrate air and space capabilities to have a common picture of the aerospace medium. Integrating operations in the near space and sub-orbital region with airspace would be a good starting point.

Rising Threats, Emerging Challenges, Growing Concerns

Space is experiencing a revolutionary transformation. More space systems are being built today than ever before in support of myriads of applications, both commercial and military, with a major role being played by the private industry. The possibilities offered by space services and applications for being networked and informationised are infinite, limited only by imagination and innovation.

Satellites and satellite services have become a prerequisite for effective military operations. This has been seen in all major military conflicts since the Gulf War of 1991. The dependence on space is increasing resulting in a situation where future wars cannot be executed without the help of space assets. This dependence on space services is also a vulnerability which has made satellites targets of anti-satellite (ASAT) weapons. So, we have a situation where—on the one hand space is a matter of survival for military operations be it land, sea or air—and on the other hand these assets in space providing services are also targets for attacks. This factor has resulted in the warfighting domain shifting space wards. Effectively, space—which the military saw as a high ground—has now become a warfighting domain in itself.

The rise of China as an ASAT-capable nation in an arena dominated by the two major space powers—the US and Russia—has led to a different kind of space race: the race for space dominance. In the absence of stringent laws prohibiting weapons in space, more countries are joining the fray to ensure their freedom of access to space. Another remarkable development is seen in the demonstration of proximity operations in space like the inspection or refuelling of satellites, which is a dual-use technology having covert ASAT utility. US, Russia and China have been actively pursuing this capability for many years. France has also stepped into the arena and has outlined military space projects which include swarms of nano-satellites that would patrol a few kilometres around French satellites, ground-based laser systems to dazzle snooping satellites, and even kinetic weapons on board satellites.[2] Space is no longer a sanctuary where space-faring nations can operate with impunity. Despite global interest in avoiding militarisation and weaponisation of the space domain, the major space powers including China—a potential adversary for India—have identified the use of space for gaining a military advantage and are actively fielding systems to protect their own space infrastructure as well as deny the use of space by adversaries in a conflict. Against this backdrop, space security by military means becomes relevant for nations to freely exploit space for various purposes, civil and military.

In our neighbourhood, China is leveraging its space infrastructure to transition into a truly informationised and intelligentised force. Its space capabilities form the backbone of its Anti-Access Area Denial strategy (A2AD), with a high level of integration between the space control centres and military battle management systems to enable an integrated battle management concept. This allows a seamless information flow of the space services for undertaking military operations. China's exploitation of satellite services for the armed forces is perhaps the most intricate, resilient and ubiquitous providing it an edge in any military conflict.

In this area of space operations, China has developed multiple options for space launch systems including space launch from the sea which gives it the capability of responsive launch.[3] This gives China the ability to replace lost satellites as well as the tactical flexibility for space surveillance. From its imagery capabilities to its Beidou navigation system and a wide range of communication satellites, China has transitioned from *fighting local wars under modern, high-tech conditions, to orchestrating and engaging in wars under informationised conditions.*[4]

Threats to Space Assets

Satellites and other space systems are technologically complex systems and are vulnerable to a variety of threats. These threats include natural as well as deliberate acts. Protection against natural phenomena can be mitigated to a certain extent through SSA including space weather. Deliberate acts would include the use of all types of ASAT weapons, DEWs, co-orbital satellites, electronic jamming and cyber-attacks. The vulnerability extends to ground control stations and the networks and datalinks which link these ground stations to the satellites. While the vulnerability of ground systems is being addressed in many ways, particularly cyber security measures, the vulnerability of the space segment has emerged as a major challenge in the aftermath of China's ASAT test of 2007. Threats to the space segment now extend beyond Direct Ascent KE ASAT weapons to other ASAT techniques. The prominent emerging threat to space assets is through the use of proximity operations which has fundamentally changed the space security strategies of space powers. Also, the war in Ukraine has brought to prominence the vulnerability of commercial space systems to cyber and electronic attacks.

Role of the Armed Forces in the Space Domain

Outer space has always been regarded as the ultimate high ground since the beginning of the space age. The importance of space to the armed forces and other security organisations is indisputable. It affords an operational advantage against potential adversaries through the variety of space services and applications that can be exploited.

Over the last two decades, the world has witnessed a noticeable rise in the use of space assets for critical defence requirements. Space orbits have now become a core instrument of surveillance for many militaries across the globe. With rapid developments in military technology, satellites have become an integral part of operations and strategy building for the armed forces. Space will continue to be critical for military use in the coming years. Space surveillance capabilities will increase in importance as the observation systems in space improve in quality, quantity and variety giving a near-continuous surveillance potential. Position, Navigation and Timing (PNT) is emerging as a core requirement for precision weapon delivery for avoiding collateral damage. Communications applications will see increasing demand as aircraft—civil and military—would need even more detailed information with their continuously improving sensor suites while delivering weapons, cargo, passengers, and payloads over long distances. This information has to be processed in real-time as the situation changes rapidly. Also, with the increasing use of unmanned systems, data relay through space platforms will become a critical factor for longer ranges of these aerial systems. Operational circumstances will change quickly over time necessitating the use of space services for better battlefield transparency through space services and applications. In effect, the use of space services offers information dominance for the armed forces. For an Air Force, some key operational elements where space affords information dominance are:

- C4ISR—Shortens the decision cycle
- Navigation—Enables precision targeting
- Weather forecast—Gives mission go/no-go decision
- Battle Damage Assessment—Assessment of mission success
- Real-Time Targeting—enabled by space C4ISR
- UAV/AWACS operations—Increased operational range through data relay
- Strategic Communications—facilitates Command & Control beyond borders and in inaccessible terrain
- Data services for Network Centric Capabilities

Potential adversaries understand the reliance on space services by modern armed forces and equip themselves to exploit the vulnerability of satellites and degrade a nation's access to space in times of conflict. A wide range of counter-space capabilities can be employed as discussed earlier to intercept and exploit satellite links or threaten and potentially destroy space systems. These counter-space capabilities have effectively shifted the warfighting domain space wards, making space an operational domain. Space and cyber have now been recognised as operational domains. Space is now the fifth operational domain and no longer just a high ground.

A growing concern is the pace at which space powers are aligning with the acceptance of space as an operational and warfighting domain. The US declared space as a warfighting domain and formed a *Space Force* in December 2019, to counter the increasingly contested nature of the space domain and the resultant threat to their space assets which are critical infrastructure for their military.[5] To protect its satellites, France too revealed an ambitious space weapons programme that would allow it to make the transition from space surveillance to the active protection of its satellites.[6] North Atlantic Treaty Organistion (NATO) alliance declared space to be an operational domain.[7] Recently, the US has also affirmed to extend its security guarantees in space to its treaty allies like Japan in order to protect Japanese satellites as China and Russia have ramped up military activity in Japan's neighbourhood.[8] All these developments are stark pointers to the changing nature of the space domain where the security of space assets and uninterrupted space services are not guaranteed.

Against this backdrop, it is essential to understand the need for the involvement of armed forces in space; to decipher their role in space. The military has two critical reasons to be in space, which are mentioned below:

- **Securing Function**. Space services for civil as well as military users will be disrupted by adversaries through counter-space activities during times of conflict. Continuity of uninterrupted space services entails securing national space assets and ensuring freedom of operations in space. This involves defensive and offensive actions in space which need to be orchestrated by a military force. Hence the primary role of the armed forces in space is to protect the interests of a nation in space by securing national space assets in the space domain. This is the military means of achieving space security.

- **Enabling Function.** Space services like space-based surveillance, navigation, communication, weather forecasting, etc., enable all operational functions of the armed forces in an emerging land/sea/air battle environment. The armed forces gain an advantage of Information Dominance through space services and applications. Hence the enabling function of space services is the primary utility of space for the armed forces.

Figure 11.1: Military Role in Space

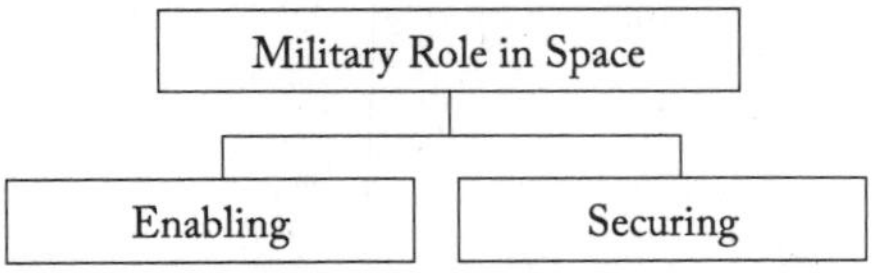

Source: Author's own creation.

The Air and Space Continuum Argument

Space has no limits and extends to infinity, but it is the lower margins of space which face contentious issues. The primary reason for overlapping jurisdictions between the *Air* and *Space* mediums is the absence of a clear defining boundary between the mediums with legal backing, and global acceptance, which can be implemented through regulations.

While there are varying schools of thought on how the space domain is to be viewed for military exploitation, the IAF is of the firm belief that 'Air' and 'Space' are a seamless continuum.[9] The absence of a clear defining line between air and space manifests into an overlap in air and space operations in the near-space region. While the operating principles may be different in each medium due to the distinctive physical properties of the domains, the strategies for the utilisation of military assets remain the same. Viewing the two domains as a seamless continuum by the Air Force helps in ensuring continuity in command and control and operational contiguity for military operations overlapping both domains. The primary reasons in support of this understanding are:

- The similarities between operations in airspace and space.
- The proximity of the space domain to airspace and the need to maintain the contiguity of operations.

- The vast expertise available to Air Force personnel in airspace management, which fits in well with the future requirements of space traffic management.
- Airspace is a medium of transition for all objects destined to space and on return from space. This requires traffic de-confliction as well as identification of traffic entering sovereign airspace which is best done by the custodian of air space.
- Missile defence being an extension of AD, the surveillance and engagement ranges extend into outer space. Also, mid-course and boost phase engagement of incoming missiles would happen in the space domain. Hence, effective command and control of these systems demand close coordination between the air and space elements of the armed forces. This would also require a common air and space situation picture to include at least the sub-orbital region.

The IAF has the primary responsibility towards AD. In addition to integrating the use of satellite services and applications into its overall strategy, which is a common goal for all three services, the IAF also needs to integrate space defence strategies with AD, to ensure a seamless transition between air and space mediums for all physical platforms transiting between the mediums, including the tracking of space-bound objects and earth-bound objects as well as for missile defence requirements.

Merging air and space would imply the integration of systems, strategies, and organisational verticals to facilitate decision-making while providing a comprehensive view of the aerospace domain. To achieve this, the preliminary requirement for the IAF would be to achieve capability enhancement in multiple verticals of space applications while gaining a foothold in critical space operations. This evolution can only be fast-tracked by bringing synergy amongst all stakeholders.

Desired Capabilities of an Aerospace Force in the Space Domain

An aerospace force should be capable of shouldering the responsibility of ensuring continued access to space systems for both civilian requirements and military operations. Space defence will hence have to be a critical capability. Space defence while being an exclusive military activity, has overlapping requirements with other space operations which could be civil or military. The capability to undertake space operations which include all physical aspects of military activities in space will be the key differentiator between an aerospace force and other services of the armed forces. The Air Force, being closest to the operational medium of space, thus needs to equip itself to provide the full spectrum of capabilities in the aerospace domain.

The reasons for the armed forces to be in space have been explained earlier as the enabling role and the securing role. When the difference between these two translates into a statement of capability for an aerospace force, without undermining the salience of air operations, it needs to be addressed as two distinct verticals for understanding as given below:

Figure 11.2: Functions of an Aerospace Force in Space

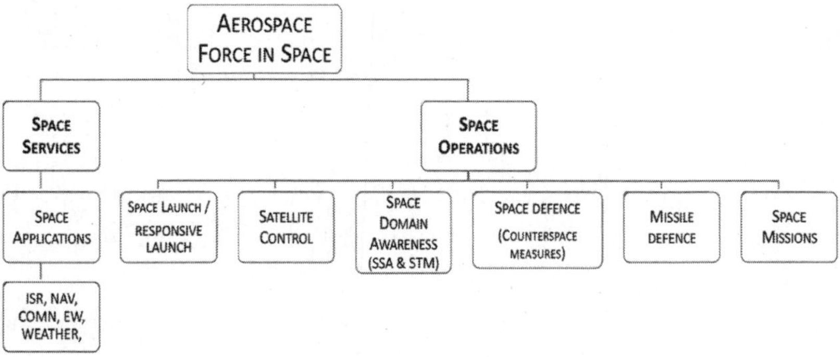

Source: Author's own creation.

The difference between space services and space operations could well mean the difference between being an Air Force and an Aerospace Force. This would also fall in place when we consider that all three services of the armed forces and other security organisations also use the same space services in equal measure. While the two categories of space utilisation help in understanding how an aerospace force would be different from other forces, an aerospace force will have space capabilities which rest on four pillars of strength as mentioned below:

- Space Services and Applications (Space Force Enhancement)
- Space Situational Awareness or Space Domain Awareness

- Space Operations
- Counter-space measures for space defence

Figure 11.3: Aerospace Force at a Glance

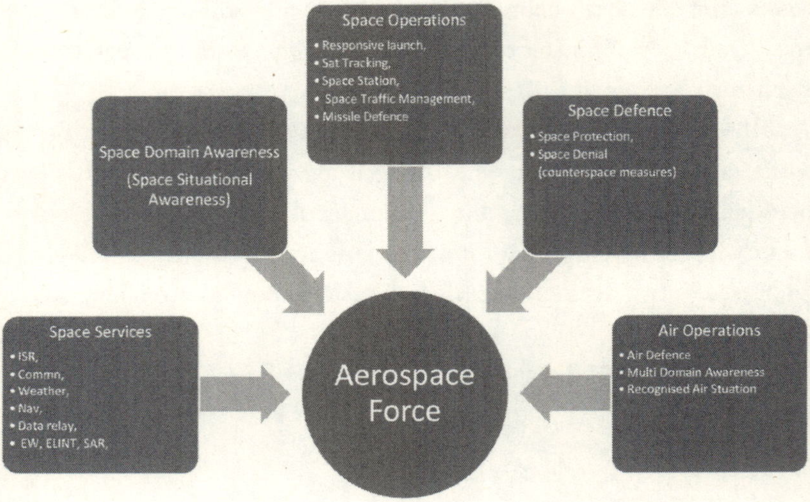

Source: Author's own creation.

Each of these activities is interlinked with the other activities in space. For example, SSA would form the foundation and backbone for the conduct of all space activities. The use of space services is a continuous activity in peacetime as well as wartime. The utilisation of these services would increase over the years necessitating many more satellites to be launched. With significant military space assets in orbit, the need for satellite tracking and control, SSA and space defence measures would increase manifold to an extent which would make it difficult for a civilian agency to manage. The role of space defence would be required to be undertaken by the aerospace force only if they control the military satellites and have the required level of SSA. Therefore, operational efficiency necessitates that command and control of space operations need to be vested with a single organisation or force. This organisation needs to be in control of the air domain too to ensure the contiguity of operations in overlapping domains as brought out earlier.

Space Services and Applications

Space services and associated applications form an essential part of any modern Air Force that can complement many of its operations as a major force enabler as well as force enhancer. Armed forces across the world use satellites for Communication, ISR functions, early warning, navigation, weather, and allied services. A modern Air Force needs to integrate its operations with space services and adapt to the near real-time decision process to avoid an information overload and be able to exploit the full potential of air power. The assets required for such an Air Force are a fleet of satellites in diverse orbits equipped with payloads that meet specific applications. Evidently, one needs to have the means to launch the satellites and manage them in orbit, as well as handle the data gathered from these satellites. This would entail dedicated ground infrastructure for receiving and processing satellite signals and ensuring the availability of processed data at the user end.

Communications

Seamless communication networks and real-time airspace and battlespace awareness are vital in operations. Satellite Communications (SATCOM) will have to meet the challenge of the IAF's need for greater connectivity with larger bandwidths. An integrated SATCOM system needs to deliver unparalleled options for mission success. While delivering on performance, the system needs to have the resilience necessary to address a 21st-century contested space domain. Such a system should possess the following characteristics:

- Accommodate disruptions and loss and still deliver effects.
- Optimise usage of RF spectrum allowing proactive management of SATCOM resources, capable of responding to changing operational environments and adversary actions.
- Deliver and fuse real-time information to support decision-makers.
- Provide cyber resiliency by managing the operational risk, and keeping mission platforms operational.
- Be capable of absorbing innovative capabilities, commercial and military, that make the communication systems more flexible, agile and resilient.

IAF needs dedicated and secure communication links for networking with their assets on the ground and in the air. This purpose is served partly by the GSAT-7A and other shared satellites, which serves the present-day communication requirements of the IAF. Future communication requirements for voice and datalinks need greater penetration into the space segment. A constellation of small satellites in LEO should complement the available communication satellites in GEO with secure, encrypted and assured communication. While on the one hand, larger satellites in GEO are preferable to meet communication requirements with a lesser number of satellites, on the other hand, small satellite mega-constellations in LEO are also an economical option providing resilience. Both these options need to co-exist in satellite communications. Orbital and spectrum congestion is also on the rise. The solution appears to be in improved satellite technology which will enable lower physical separation as well as lower separation in allotted frequencies between satellites. Optimisation of the allotted spectrum also needs to be explored. Further, to cater for high data transfer rates, High Throughput Satellites (HTS) will be required.

Innovative RF communications techniques are essential to meeting projected future mission requirements. These techniques must cater for higher bandwidths, high transfer rates and diverse frequency spectrums. Spectral congestion in the RF spectrum has necessitated a shift towards 'optical communications' and 'quantum communications'. These emerging technologies can enable streaming high-definition imagery and secure data communications over interplanetary distances. The data transfer rates achieved can be much faster than RF links.

Space-Based Surveillance (SBS)

SBS has a vital role in military functioning. Intelligence, surveillance and reconnaissance (ISR) play a critical role in the conduct of military operations. Despite the benefits of airborne ISR systems, they are just one element in the full spectrum of intelligence collection. Present generation ISR assets provide more data than the previous generation systems. However, there is a massive challenge of information overload when intelligence inputs arrive from multiple sources. Hence, the focus should be on fused intelligence that can be readily used for operations without overburdening the users with data. ISR capabilities should be such that they can provide access to the most difficult targets with operational flexibility, responsiveness, interoperability, and greater precision.

Satellite Imagery for ISR. Imagery through satellites is a vital component of the ISR matrix, which supports many important missions. This imagery gives decision-makers a more complete picture of the area of operations. To be useful for ISR applications, satellite imagery should have adequate spatial and spectral resolution. India's earth observation satellites provide military-grade imagery but may not be adequate in all conditions to cater for emerging military requirements. Satellite revisit time is critical and this can be reduced by having a constellation of earth observation satellites in LEO for near-continuous observations.

Electronic Intelligence (ELINT). ELINT through space resources has proven to be of much use in gathering the electronic intelligence of an adversary. This would also complement the signal intelligence collected through aerial resources with the advantage of having vast ground coverage. Space-based ELINT capability is critical for real-time alerts, and detection in mountainous terrain and the vast Indian Ocean Region (IOR). China has demonstrated a near continuous electronic surveillance capability over their perceived hotspots with their Yaogan constellation of satellites. India requires a similar constellation of satellites for ELINT.

Positioning, Navigation and Timing (PNT)

Space-based navigation is another critical requirement for air operations. GPS and GLONASS systems have been providing positioning, navigation and timing services for nearly three decades, and their accuracies have been improving over the years. EU's Galileo and China's Beidou are also developing highly accurate global PNT systems. However, concerns about the availability of precise signals during periods of conflict, data ownership, need for autonomy and redundancy, have resulted in the development of India's own space-based navigation system called IRNSS or NavIC. Having an indigenous satellite navigation system helps in boosting military capabilities across the spectrum of operations, from basic navigation to high-precision munition delivery. However, the development of only a navigation system is not enough, it needs to be integrated with the equipment and munitions used by the forces. A variety of receivers are being developed by the private sector for providing information and application services based on this system. NavIC systems for the IAF will have to be manufactured to the specifications laid down for various equipment. Besides the induction of user equipment, IAF will have to strive for better accuracy of NavIC signals and increase the coverage area to have a global footprint.

Early Warning

An aerospace force needs satellites equipped with IR sensors to detect the thermal signature caused by a missile launch. This is an important capability to get an early warning of a missile launch for alerting the missile defence and AD systems. Multiple satellites will be required to give global all-round coverage. This alone may not be sufficient to detect advanced missile technologies like hypersonic missiles. The key to countering more advanced missile threats, will be in ensuring that satellites are integrated with sensors that can detect a launch and sensors that can track the missile.

Space Layer for Missile Defence

Space-based sensor concepts for missile defence have been employed since many years. To intercept a missile in its mid-course phase requires the capability to detect its launch, track its flight, and then discriminate the warhead from any decoys and countermeasures. Satellites in space with sensors for the detection and tracking of missiles will add another layer to the existing missile defence mechanism. An aerospace force will have to upgrade and integrate all the available sensors and intercept systems to achieve a gap-free missile defence system.

Ground Support Infrastructure

The ground-based infrastructure or the ground segment is the critical link for successful space operations. The support functions of the ground segment are; control of satellites, health monitoring, tracking to determine their present and future positions, collecting the satellite's mission data, analysing the data and distributing these data to users. A key component of the infrastructure is the ground station and its networks. As new technologies are developed for complex space missions, ground systems must be able to support these developments.[10]

Desired Capabilities

A summary of the desired capabilities in space systems is given below:

Space Application Type	**Threshold Capability Desired**	**Global Developments**
Communication	• Global Coverage • Multiple frequencies • High bandwidth • Secure Communication • Electronic Protection Measures	• In Orbit Servicing • High Throughput • Bandwidth > 100 Gbps + • Optical communication • Quantum Communication • LEO constellations
Earth Observation / Imagery	• Sensors—EO / SAR / IR/ Multispectral/ Hyperspectral • Sub metric Resolution • Low revisit time (near continuous coverage over area of interest) • High repetivity • Launch on demand • Small sats in readiness for launch on demand	• Resolution < 0.1 m • Revisit < 3-4 hrs • Global repetivity < 1 hr • Choice of multiple sensors • LEO Constellations
Weather Observation	• Multiple sensor & bandwidth • Frequent updates	• Near real-time updates in satellite picture
Navigation (IRNSS)	• Multi-band receivers for military eqpt, aircraft and ships with countermeasures against spoofing. • Global Coverage • Position accuracy < 1 m • Spare satellites for replacing losses • Secure restricted signal for military	• Global Coverage • Position accuracy < 10 cm • Interoperability with GNSS

Missile Defence	• Early warning of missile launch • Space layer for detection and tracking	• Space-based IR sensors and missile tracking. Exo-atmospheric / Mid-course intercept
Data Relay Satellites	• For global operations	• Multiple TDRS for uninterrupted coverage
ELINT	• Near continuous coverage of IOR and neighbouring countries • Accuracy of localising transmissions to within 5 km^2	• China's Yaogan 30 Elint constellation can localise transmission to a 25 km^2 area by triangulation • Yaogan 30 can slew other ISR satellite sensors to suspected area • Global coverage 35° N-35° S
SSA	• Radars—more MOTRs geographically dispersed in India as well as friendly nations • Optical telescopes of the Indian Astronomical Society of India to be integrated • Space-based sensors to monitor GEO belt • SSA sharing agreements with other space agencies • Regional SSA and STM centres operated by the Aerospace Force	• Ground and space-based sensors of the Space Surveillance Network. Major gaps exist in present SSA coverage
Ground Segment	• Geographically distributed receiver and satellite control stations integrated with Armed Forces Operations and mission control centres	• Full user integration exists between the space ground segment and military ops centres

Space Situational Awareness (SSA)

The population of satellites in orbit is set to grow exponentially in the coming years, triggered by the use of new small satellite constellations as against large single satellites. Lower orbits in particular are becoming increasingly dense with satellites and debris resulting in anthropogenic hazards, and placing satellite operations at risk from collisions. Besides space debris and orbital crowding due to mega constellations, the other major reason for this is the uncertainty of what is happening in space. This is also accentuated by the covert military activities in the orbital region. Therefore, preventing collisions, space surveillance and managing space traffic is going to be a challenge. SSA and Space Traffic Management (STM) are therefore the most challenging activity today in outer space and will remain relevant in the coming years. This is particularly so for nations that are dependent on space surveillance networks of other states' space agencies. These space surveillance networks give selective visibility for open source users as well as for those organisations having an SSA sharing agreement, albeit, with higher accuracy. Indigenous SSA is therefore crucial to ensuring space security.

SSA is the pillar of strength for an aerospace force, which is a foundational requirement for all other space activities. Further, it enables all the facets of space defence operations. A gap-free surveillance would require sensors on the ground as well as in space. SSA can be considered as the primary requirement for any kind of operational capability in space. Therefore, SSA for an aerospace force should meet some distinct needs as given below:

- Position information of own satellites and spacecraft as well as objects in their vicinity.
- Assessment of the threats that adversary space systems can pose to our satellites and spacecraft, and to our ground infrastructure.
- Capability to Geo-locate radio frequency interference (RFI) threats and Directed Energy Weapons (DEW) sources as well as adversaries' ELINT usage.
- Provide accurate inputs for proximity analysis and collision avoidance measures.
- Sharing of space object information with other organisations and space agencies.
- Provide the necessary information network for Space Traffic Management (STM).

Sensors for SSA have an inherent overlap with air defence radars and the missile defence network. The success of any SSA system is only possible through the integration of inputs from all sensors in a common air and space situation picture. This will enable a smooth transition between AD weapon systems and missile defence systems for a shortened OODA loop resulting in a successful engagement. Even in a passive space posture, SSA will give an early warning for defensive actions. An aerospace force needs to recognise the challenges of SSA and work towards getting the bigger picture—which is vital to be in a position of advantage.

Space Traffic Management

Space Traffic Management (STM) is a new concept gaining momentum and is under deliberations with the UN-monitored committees. STM is fundamentally different from SSA. While one aims to make objects in space visible, catalogue them, and predict behaviour, the other aims to prevent collisions through regulations and active control. Both are complementary to each other and essential activities in space. STM would involve a mechanism of widespread international SSA data sharing to build an operational structure of space traffic controllers, responsible for coordinating space-bound and Earth-bound traffic, allotment of orbital slots and coordination of collision avoidance measures. This would involve a more comprehensive and internationally integrated system of space surveillance than exists today. It would be virtually impossible to be done from a single ops control centre. It would require geographically dispersed regional control centres where inputs from regional sensors can be fed and screened for a conjunction analysis.

STM will soon become a reality. There are significant technological, legal, organisational and manpower issues to be resolved. This is an opportunity which India should not miss. An aerospace force would be ideally positioned to take on the responsibility of the operations part of STM based on its experience in airspace management. However, this is likely to involve the functioning of regional STM centres in coordination with a global STM organisation. Secrecy of military missions in space can only be ensured if the control of such activities at a national level is vested with an aerospace force.

Space Operations

The exploitation of space for military applications requires a joint services approach due to the commonality of requirements and the limited nature of resources available. Military space operations on the other hand would require a professional service-specific approach due to the nature of the task and core competency available in each of the services—in this case, the Air Force. Some of the core competencies that need to be considered by a service of the armed forces for military space operations are:

- Contribution towards SSA for comprehensive space surveillance and tracking through the integration of radar surveillance observations.
- Adaptability to the future scenario of STM as a part of any regional STM organisation which would be akin to airspace management in the IAF.
- Space weather prediction as an extension of atmospheric weather predictions.
- Counter-space defences and operations of certain ASAT weapons capabilities.
- Responsive Launch/Launch on Demand capability for ISR and ELINT using small satellites.
- High-altitude drones and balloons for ISR, ELINT, space observation and airspace observation from near space.
- Ballistic missile defence, which will extend into space for mid-course and boost phase interception.
- Keeping a trained pool of astronauts for undertaking human spaceflight for manning of space stations.

Technological developments in the space sector have opened up many possibilities for the exploitation of space by the armed forces. The areas of space operations that need to be adopted by an aerospace force as a threshold capability are given in subsequent paragraphs.

Launch Capability

Launch capabilities are infrastructure intensive and need to be maintained and operated by the designated space agency. However, the critical requirement for an aerospace force would be the capability for 'launch on demand' or 'responsive launch'. This is an essential requirement for the reconstitution of the space resources and redundancy of the space segment. It also gives tactical leverage for 'on-demand' imagery requirements. An aerospace force will have to maintain and operate mobile small satellite launch systems, which could place mini/microsatellites in VLEO with less reaction time. These could be vehicle mounted for mobility or could be co-located in existing IAF infrastructure.

Space Cargo & Logistics

Space transportation is being envisioned as a novel concept which would entail passengers and logistics being space lifted from one place to another on the Earth. This will be made possible with fully re-usable rockets becoming a reality. Space lift is akin to airlift, the difference being in the mode of transport. A rocket with load and passenger carrying capacity could be launched, orbited, and made to land at a destination across the globe in a matter of a few minutes. Space lifts could be particularly useful for the strategic transportation of military equipment and personnel.

Near Space Operations

The expanding space domain has diminished the demarcation between airspace and outer space. At the closer orbital ranges, satellites are being positioned for Very Low Earth Orbits (VLEO) and as Pseudo satellites. Balloons and high-altitude drones are also being used for exploiting the near-space region. The ambiguity between airspace and near space is even more predominant with the proliferation of aerial platforms in the near space region which could be in an adversaries airspace, yet would not be violating the sovereignty of the adversaries airspace. It could be operating in the region of ambiguity—near space—where detection and targeting capabilities are still to mature. This domain is well within the operating jurisdiction of an aerospace force, and the IAF must develop capabilities to operate in the near space region for ISR, communication, real-time data links and radar tracking of aircraft.

Human Space Flight

The exhaustive training imparted to Air Force pilots equips them with some of the same skills and similar resilience as astronauts, which makes them ideal candidates for spaceflight. The requirement for astronauts will only increase over the years. Although civilians have also been in space as astronauts, the core competency remains that of the Air Force. An aerospace force will thus have to be in a position to shoulder this responsibility and take it forward and meet the nation's future needs. This will require streamlining of human resource requirements, training standards, and establishing training centres, while working in coordination with the space agency undertaking space exploration.

Counter-space Measures

Space defence strategies which form the basis of counter-space techniques to be adopted, essentially involve protecting space infrastructure and space-based assets from disruption or damage by an adversary or any other agency knowingly or otherwise. It comprises three major components; space protection, space denial and space situational awareness. While space protection involves securing own space assets from disruption/damage, space denial means denying an enemy access to its space resources during the conflict. The strategy for space defence can either be defensive (protecting its own space assets) or offensive (degrading/destroying the enemy's space assets). Space situational awareness would be a prerequisite for any space operation or mission, more so, for space defence. While space dominance is an overwhelming superiority in space and offers unrestricted freedom of operations in space, space defence through space protection and limited space denial measures will be limited in scope and would be a more practical approach for an emerging aerospace force.

Space protection, space denial and space situational awareness are hence the primary requirements towards space security through military means which can be adopted by an aerospace force and need a doctrinal approach for planning, training and execution.

An Aerospace force will have to define the scope of space operations and adopt the required mix of counter-space techniques based on the threat perception, space security strategy for the armed forces and organisational requirements including inter-organisational dependencies. When employing space denial techniques for active defence, the options range from Directed Energy Weapons (DEW) and proximity operations to cyber-attacks and interference in the radio spectrum. These ASAT techniques will provide options for a hard kill as well as a soft kill with varying effects and attributability. An appropriate ASAT counter space measure needs to be selected based on the threat level, desired impact, and cost-effectiveness. Command and control of offensive and defensive ASAT weapons will have to be with an aerospace force in any future scenario in the absence of a dedicated space force. This will ensure better coordination of air and space missions in conflict.

Air Operations

Air defence operations are enhanced with the integration of space assets. Space-based systems provide crucial capabilities for situational awareness, early warning, communication, and surveillance, creating a more robust defence network. With advanced imaging and radar systems, satellites detect and track airborne threats, including aircraft, missiles and UAVs, over vast areas. These systems continuously monitor airspace, identifying potential threats before they enter the sovereign territory. Space assets enable Battle Management and Command and Control by integrating with wider defence networks. This integration improves decision-making and enhances operational effectiveness. However, space-based assets alone are not a complete defence system. They work in conjunction with ground-based radars, aircraft, surface-to-air missiles, and command and control infrastructure, creating a multi-layered defence network. Air operations benefit from enhanced situational awareness, early warning, threat identification, and the integration of data sources. This provides a refined and recognised air situation picture, including aircraft identification, location, and status. Integrating data and intelligence from space-based assets with ground, air, maritime, and cyber systems enhances multi-domain awareness. Decision-makers thus gain a comprehensive understanding of the operational environment, identify threats, and make informed decisions for operational superiority.

Conclusion

The primary objective of the IAF is to ensure the defence of national air space, air and space domain and contribute to the defence of national territory, maritime areas, and other relevant domains.[11] Space being considered a continuum to the air domain, IAF is ideally positioned to take on the responsibility of being an 'Aerospace Force'. It would be unwise to believe, that the IAF's capabilities which prevailed in the past, will be adequate to deal with threats and conflicts of the future, particularly in the space domain. Air and space are now critical to the Information cycle, which is pivotal to military strategies. It is inevitable that air superiority and space superiority will eventually merge making 'Aerospace' as an integrated whole. This will make an Aerospace power as the force that can respond within hours with great accuracy and focus.

IAF, the most versatile force that the nation possesses, has assumed a larger role in the conduct of military affairs. It will be used, one way or another, when the nation is confronted with a crisis on its borders or beyond. Employment of air and space assets in an integrated and coordinated manner will be critical to the outcome of any military operation.

The dimensions of military space are still expanding. Vast improvements still lie ahead in space applications, space weapons and the capabilities of space vehicles. The dividing lines between air power and space power will continue to blur. In the integrated arena of aerospace, air power and space power share common operational characteristics and freedom from the geographic constraints of the Earth's surface. The inherent features of aerospace allow the IAF to act with effectiveness and flexibility. It is with this consciousness that the IAF needs to evolve a strategy for dealing with its role in space which encompasses the enabling and securing functions. The mission of the IAF should be to advocate and pursue the command of the aerospace medium and its operations in it.

The IAF needs to undergo essential changes to embed space services and space operations into its operational philosophy to transform itself into an aerospace force. The success of this new approach rests on the effectiveness of the aerospace strategy of the IAF. The aerospace strategy must consider the critical role played by space operations in differentiating between an air force and an aerospace force.

Notes

1. "Doctrine of the Indian Air Force (IAP 2000-2022)", at https://indianairforce.nic.in/wp-content/uploads/2023/01/2MB.pdf. Accessed on February 20, 2023.
2. Eric Berger, "To Protect its Satellites, France Outlines Ambitious Space-weapons Program", *arstechnica*, July 26, 2019, at https://arstechnica.com/science/2019/07/france-says-it-will-create-its-own-space-based-weapons-program/, accessed on March 1, 2023.
3. Andrew Jones, "China Launches 14 Satellites with New Solid Rocket from Mobile Sea Platform", *Space News*, December 9, 2022, at https://spacenews.com/china-launches-14-satellites-with-new-solid-rocket-from-mobile-sea-platform/#:~:text=The%20Jielong%2D3%20was%20China's,mission%20highlights%20two%20separate%20developments, accessed on February 28, 2022.
4. Dean Cheng, "China's Military Role in Space", at https://www.airuniversity.af.edu/Portals/10/SSQ/documents/Volume-06_Issue-1/Cheng.pdf, accessed on March 1, 2023.
5. "Trump: 'Space is the world's newest war-fighting domain'", BBC News, December 21, 2019, at https://www.bbc.com/news/av/world-us-canada-50875940, accessed on March 4, 2023.
6. Eric Berger, n. 1.
7. Alexandra Stickings, "Space as an Operational Domain: What Next for NATO?", RUSI Newsbrief, October 15, 2020, at https://rusi.org/explore-our-research/publications/rusi-newsbrief/space-operational-domain-what-next-nato, accessed on March 4, 2023.
8. Rieko Miki, "Japan, U.S. extend security treaty into space to protect satellites", January 12, 2023, *Nikkei Asia*, at https://asia.nikkei.com/Politics/International-relations/Japan-U.S.-extend-security-treaty-into-space-to-protect-satellites, accessed on January 23, 2023.
9. Doctrine of the IAF, n. 1.
10. Mission Assurance, *a.i.solutions*, https://ai-solutions.com/mission-assurance/, accessed on March 5, 2023.
11. Doctrine of the IAF, n. 1.

Index